The Sociology of Consumption

The Sociology of Consumption

A Global Approach

Joel Stillerman

polity

First published in 2015 by Polity Press
Reprinted 2016 (twice)

Polity Press
65 Bridge Street
Cambridge CB2 1UR, UK

Polity Press
350 Main Street
Malden, MA 02148, USA

ISBN-13: 978-0-7456-6127-8
ISBN-13: 978-0-7456-6128-5 (pb)

A catalogue record for this book is available from the British Library.

Library of Congress Cataloging-in-Publication Data

Stillerman, Joel (Sociologist)
    The sociology of consumption : a global approach / Joel Stillerman.
        pages cm
    Includes bibliographical references and index.
    ISBN 978-0-7456-6127-8 (hardback : alk. paper) -- ISBN 978-0-7456-6128-5 (pbk. : alk. paper) 1. Consumption (Economics)--Social aspects. 2. Consumer behavior. I. Title.
    HC79.C6.S755 2015
    306.3--dc23
                                                                                    2014038635

Typeset in 10.5/12 Plantin by
Servis Filmsetting Limited, Stockport, Cheshire
Printed and bound in the United Kingdom by Clays Ltd, St Ives PLC

For further information on Polity, visit our website:
politybooks.com

Contents

Acknowledgments

Several individuals were important to the completion of this book. First, I would like to thank Emma Longstaff at Polity for inviting me to write this book and for her support and guidance as it moved from an initial idea to a manuscript. Jonathan Skerrett, Lauren Mulholland, and Elen Griffiths helped me move the manuscript toward completion. Clare Ansell and Helen Gray provided expert support with copy-editing and production. Tomás Ariztia, Omar Lizardo (who identified himself as one of Polity's external reviewers), and two anonymous reviewers provided invaluable comments and criticisms that allowed me to make significant improvements on the initial proposal and manuscript. Kristy Marchard, Samantha Schires, and Katherine Parr provided me with extremely helpful research assistance as I developed the manuscript. Prior to writing this book, several journal and book editors published my work on consumption in Chile. I would like to thank Don Slater, George Ritzer, Anthony Orum, Javier Auyero, Alfonso Morales, John Cross, Dan Cook, Gay Seidman, Kent Sandstrom, Anna Pertierra, and John Sinclair for providing me with a venue for my scholarship and helping me to sharpen my thinking on this topic. Finally, my daughters, Micaela and Gabriella, and my wife, Leyla, have been enormously patient and supportive throughout this process. We can all breathe a sigh of relief now that "Daddy's book" is done.

1

Introduction

Pop singer Beyoncé Knowles was the headline act during the Super Bowl 2013 half-time show. This event illustrates several dimensions of contemporary consumption explored in this book. The Super Bowl has the largest audience of any televised program in the United States, fans engage in many rituals while viewing the game, and Super Bowl advertisements set industry trends for the upcoming year. The game tells us something about contemporary American culture, our habits of consuming food and media, and what many of us think is important, since millions of us tune in. It also illustrates group identities and their expression, as fans wear their favorite team's jerseys and build replicas of the football stadium with sandwiches and potato chips. Additionally, men and women have different viewing habits and watch with different levels of attention. Finally, the Super Bowl is one of the few rituals (shared, meaningful activities) in which a large cross-section of Americans participate.

In 2013, advertisers paid approximately $4 million dollars per 30-second spot with the hopes that their humorous or eye-catching ads would secure brand loyalty among the diverse age, gender, income, and ethnic/racial groups that view this event (Konrad 2013). The ads reflect and influence our ideas and behaviors in relation to work, leisure, money, gender, sex, race, and everyday life.

The half-time show often features established performers that commercial sponsors (Pepsi this year) hope will appeal to a broad range of viewers and persuade them to increase their purchases of the sponsor's product. This year, Beyoncé had a small problem, as she had been caught "lip-syncing" "The Star-Spangled Banner" during President Barack Obama's inauguration into his second term just weeks before (Moody 2013). Hence, many journalists, bloggers, and observers believed Beyoncé had to give a superb performance in order to "rescue" her career. Like other half-time shows, Beyoncé's performance included a massive light show and highly stylized dancing with female performers sporting sexually provocative clothing.

Apart from the usual ingredients, the Beyoncé show made some interesting implicit comments about gender and race. The fact that the band is all female visibly contrasts with women's traditional roles in pop music as singers rather than instrumentalists in a male-dominated profession (Milestone and Meyer 2012). Further, Beyoncé is part of a long tradition of music and dance cultivated within the black community. At the same time, being an entertainer is one of the few occupations relegated to African Americans by a dominant white majority (Jones 1963; Dyer 2009).

This event contains many of the ingredients of our complex and dynamic consumer society. Nonetheless, it is only a small piece of the puzzle. This once-a-year, turbo-charged spectacle has little to do with our daily consumption. To study consumption is to address its spectacular forms, like the Super Bowl or purchases of luxury goods, as well as its mundane, everyday forms – eating, grocery shopping, buying clothing, and visiting the gas station. Further, the Super Bowl is meaningful primarily for Americans, though it may be viewed in other countries. To what extent does the "larger than life," "bigger is always better" model of consumption symbolized by the Super Bowl reflect the consumer behavior of most Americans, and how is it similar to or different from consumption in other countries?

This book seeks to understand the fast-changing world of consumption – the desire for, purchase, use, display, sharing, exchange, and disposal of products and services. Other general works offer valuable insights on this phenomenon, and I will build on their ideas throughout this book (see Slater 1997; Lury 2011; Lee 2000; Schor and Holt 2000; Sassatelli 2007; Smart 2010). However, this book is different from these works in three important ways. This book focuses on global consumption, consumption and inequality, and consumer citizenship.

General discussions focus on consumers in the United States and Europe; but today, some of the most important areas of expansion of consumption are outside the Global North (the U.S. and Europe) in the regions we now call the Global South (Parker 2009). These are non-European societies, many of which were colonized by European powers or financially dependent on the U.S., but whose wealth has expanded in recent decades. The economically most important of these countries are the so-called BRICs (Brazil, Russia, India, and China), though these changes are present in many countries throughout the world. Having studied consumption in the South American country of Chile since the late 1990s, I am acutely aware of how models of consumption exported from the Global North affect countries of the Global South, but also how countries in the Global South have distinct patterns of consumption that reflect their different histories, cultures, and societies. Since Europe and the U.S. only represent a small percentage of the world's population, an analysis of consumption must take into account patterns in the Global South.

However, this book will also explore cross-national and cross-regional variations in consumption and its meanings that call for finer distinctions than the broad division between "North" and "South," take into account the difficulty of classifying some countries as belonging to the North or South (like South Korea, a former colony that developed rapidly in recent decades and is now considered a wealthy country), and examine the mutual influences and exchanges of consumer styles across countries and regions. Some examples of these exchanges include the popularity of Japanese cartoons among teens in many countries or the emergence of "crossover" celebrities like Shakira. This Colombian singer has become a global superstar, having appeared on the U.S. reality television show *The Voice* and performed the theme songs for World Cup soccer championships in South Africa and Brazil.

Additionally, many scholars argue that since the 1970s, we have been experiencing the phenomenon known as globalization – intensified economic, social, cultural, and political contact across national and regional borders. In reality, globalization is a very old phenomenon, dating back at least to the Asian empires of the Middle Ages (Abu-Lughod 1991). However, the process of contact and influence across borders has accelerated and intensified over recent decades due to changes in technology, market competition, the organization of capitalist firms, public policies, and international migration (Harvey 1990).

Therefore, we need to understand not only how consumption varies across countries, but also how the diffusion of consumer goods and lifestyles across borders affects receiving societies. One obvious example of this pattern is the spread of U.S. pop music and media companies. In Latin America, U.S. media channels and Hollywood films have made major inroads in domestic music and film markets in recent years (García Canclini 2001). However, the main source of visual entertainment around the world is national broadcast television. Indeed, soap operas (*telenovelas*), news, and variety programs produced in the region are more popular than foreign programs (Straubhaar 2007: 7). We need to look at variations in consumption across the world, as well as the mutual influences of consumption patterns between countries.

Another distinctive feature of this book is its focus on inequality. Many discussions of consumption implicitly assume that all consumers are white, middle class, and residents of the Global North. However, this assumption ignores how social inequalities based on class, race, gender, sexuality, and age differentiate consumers (Zukin 2004; Bourdieu 1984; Gill 2009); how individuals use consumption as a way to signal their difference from consumers with different backgrounds (Schor 1998); and how ideas about inequality inform consumer choices and consumption-based identities (Milestone and Meyer 2012; Crockett 2008; Goldman and Papson 2000). Hence, consumption reflects an individual's social position (e.g., their gender or race), but individuals also use consumption as a way to achieve social status in relation to other groups.

Scholars have examined how consumption interacts with class differences (Bourdieu 1984), and many researchers acknowledge that consumption has often been conceived as a feminine activity (Milestone and Meyer 2012). However, scholars have paid less attention to race, sexuality, and age as bases of differentiation between consumers. Yet we need to look carefully at these differences to avoid the mistake of assuming that most individuals buy and use products and services in roughly the same way, or that all individuals have the same capacity to access valued goods and experiences.

Finally, this book differs from general accounts of consumption through its focus on consumer citizenship. We often think of consumption as promoting political apathy or as a politically neutral activity (Adorno and Horkheimer 2000). This perspective overlooks the fact that governments promote and manage consumption by subsidizing (artificially reducing the price of) "essential" goods (gasoline and corn are two obvious examples in the U.S.), providing tax incentives to citizens for the purchase of certain goods (allowing homeowners to deduct mortgage interest from their taxes, hence promoting homeownership), and setting the rules for managing the money and credit supply that may promote purchases and/or specific industries (Zukin 2004; Cohen 2003; Manning 2000). These government policies are part of an implicit bargain between elected officials and citizens – the government will make specific goods available in exchange for political support (or at least compliance).

When governments cannot fulfill their part of the bargain (e.g., when gas prices spike or when there are shortages of essential goods), citizens blame individual officials or the government as a whole. For example, it is widely believed that U.S. President Jimmy Carter (1976–80) did not win re-election in part because of price inflation linked to the 1979 increase in the cost of gasoline. (In fact, oil producers based mainly in the Middle East had generated the gas price increase by reducing fuel supplies; President Carter had little to no influence on oil prices.) Similarly, many scholars argue that the Soviet Union and its satellite states collapsed in 1989–91 in part because of consumer goods shortages (and the visible example of consumer plenty in Western Europe) (Chirot 1990). Citizens thus expect their rulers to promote and safeguard a socially acceptable level of consumption.

Consumption is also a medium through which citizens demand respect for their rights and those of other groups. In the early 1900s, trade unions promoted boycotts of companies with anti-union policies to pressure them to negotiate. In a better-known example, during the 1950s and 1960s, African American college students staged "sit-ins" at Woolworths lunch counters to demand their rights to consume alongside their white counterparts. This tactic was one of many that helped crush Jim Crow, the legal segregation system of the U.S. South. Similarly, during the 1970s under the leadership of Mexican-American activist Cesar Chavez, the United Farm Workers Union promoted grape boycotts to pressure California landowners to recognize the union (Gabriel and Lang 2006; Cohen 2003; McAdam 1982; Morris 1981).

In the contemporary era of globalization, the arena of citizenship has expanded so that individuals around the world may mobilize and/or consume in ways they hope satisfy their ethical and political goals. One type of activism is an extension of the traditional boycott extended to the international arena. For example, during the 1980s, college students pushed their universities to divest (to withdraw their investments) from South Africa, which at the time was considered the most racist government in the world. The divestment campaign was a major factor leading to the fall of the apartheid regime (Gabriel and Lang 2006).

More recently, members of United Students Against Sweatshops (USAS) have attempted to gain greater control over the conditions under which athletic apparel for their universities' sports teams is produced. Growing awareness that global brands like Nike and Reebok subcontract production of their clothes to "sweatshops" (employing women and children under hazardous conditions), in

Asia and Latin America, led students to pressure their universities to review their licensing contracts (whereby universities receive funds from companies in exchange for exclusive use of their goods for sports teams). Students created organizations to review the working conditions in factories contracted to fill their universities' orders (Klein 2010).

A third arena of consumer citizenship is what many scholars call "ethical consumption." Here, individuals seek to purchase goods that have been produced under ethical conditions or in ways that are not damaging to the environment. Increasing awareness of the prevalence of sweatshops, poor wages for food producers (like coffee-bean pickers), and the environmental damage caused by industrial food production have led an important segment of consumers to purchase ethically certified and environmentally friendly products. Their choices have led large producers and retailers to stock environmentally friendly lines of goods in addition to their traditional brands and products (Micheletti 2003; Barnett et al. 2011).

Ethical consumption may also involve purchasing specific goods whose producers donate a portion of their proceeds to a charity. This can range from companies that develop agreements with charities (like the Susan Komen campaign for breast cancer research), as well as full-scale events devoted to charitable causes, like the "Brand Aid" concerts. Scholars question the effectiveness of ethical consumption in that it may be a poor substitute for volunteer work or political activism directed toward achieving the charitable goals promoted by the companies involved, it has not led to major governmental or inter-governmental legal regulation, and it may also bolster the image of companies engaged in unethical activities toward employees or the environment (Jaffee 2012; Smart 2010).

Understanding Consumption: An Initial Overview

Before outlining how I explore each of these issues in the text, I will first briefly note some of the key ways scholars have understood consumption. While the use of objects to satisfy biological needs and to construct meaningful lives is a cultural universal (Sassatelli 2007; Douglas and Isherwood 1996; Lury 2011), this book focuses on modern consumption, which is largely (though not exclusively) based on the purchase of goods and services on the market.

In addition to the acquisition of goods through market exchange, modern consumption occurs in societies where individuals and groups shape their identities in relation to goods. As we explore in chapter 2, scholars disagree about when such a society emerged. Traditionally, economic historians focused on the Industrial Revolution in eighteenth-century England as ushering in the modern era. However, recent scholarship challenges this view, arguing that a consumer or commercial revolution coincided with and may have precipitated the Industrial Revolution (McKendrick et al. 1982). Others suggest that there were precedents for the eighteenth-century consumer boom in the Middle Ages (Sombart 1967), the European Renaissance (Mukerji 1983), sixteenth-century England (McCracken 1988), and seventeenth-century Holland (De Vries 1975, 1993).

Many of our ideas regarding modern consumption began in the eighteenth and nineteenth centuries with economists' efforts to define the new identity of the "consumer." Classical economics argued that consumers are rational actors seeking the best price for a given product. According to this view, the combined actions of consumers ultimately determine the prices of goods, and hence shape and discipline markets. However, this view ignores the fact that desire rather than calculation motivates much of consumption, gift-giving does not necessarily satisfy personal needs or desires, and advertisers often influence consumers' choices. The view of the consumer as an isolated, rational individual ignores the fact that non-rational motives and social influences shape consumption (Slater 1997; Smart 2010; Campbell 2005; Sassatelli 2007). Further, Trentmann (2006a) suggests that the British began to view themselves as consumers in the nineteenth century primarily due to political struggles, the law, and warfare. Consumer identities emerged differently elsewhere: in Germany, individuals were politically mobilized as members of interest or class groups like "workers" or "women" rather than as individual consumers. In sum, modern consumption did not necessarily coincide with people's identification of themselves as consumers, a process that varied across time and space.

Karl Marx (1967) disagreed with classical economists who argued that supply and demand shaped modern economies. He argued that employers' exploitation of workers in *production* generated profits, in contrast to economists' view that profits resulted from *market exchange*. He contended that while we assume that a good's price reflects its value in relation to other goods, this assumption is mistaken because it ignores the labor needed to produce that product and the fact that business owners earn profits by paying workers less than the value of the goods they produce. Marx called this confusion *commodity fetishism*, which he understood as a type of superstition.

He argued that this superstition hides the true source of profits in employers' exploitation of workers.

Marx (1978a) developed the related concept of ideology or the dominant "worldview" present in a given society. He argued that during every historical era, the dominant class develops a worldview that justifies its rule to the rest of society. In the contemporary United States, one example of ideology is the American Dream – the idea that any hard-working individual can become wealthy. Following Marx, the idea that each individual has an equal opportunity to become wealthy makes capitalism seem like a just system, while hiding the fact that the wealthy minority control the resources, connections, and political influence that maintain their dominance and make "rags to riches" upward mobility unlikely for most individuals.

Additionally, Marx (1978b) argues that production and consumption are mutually dependent. Production is also a form of consumption: factories use raw materials and machinery wears out, and workers use up their energy but also develop their skills at work. Similarly, consumption is also a form of production: consumers satisfy their biological needs and produce their identities through consumption. Moreover, producers provide consumers with specific goods that shape and at times create their needs, like the contemporary need for a cellular phone, which was not perceived as a "need" a few decades ago. However, a product only exists as such if it is used. The consumer makes it a product by using it: a dress takes the form of a product only after a person wears it. Finally, when individuals consume a product, they generate demand for additional production.

These three ideas are important to later criticisms of consumer society, particularly the idea that advertisers can convince consumers that a particular car, article of clothing, or lipstick will magically transform its owner (Jhally 1990; Haug 1986). Further, commodity fetishism hides the "dirty little secret" of capitalism: we see the attractive Nike athletic shoe but are unaware of the deplorable conditions under which children in a Vietnamese sweatshop work to produce it (Klein 2010; Smart 2010).

Several authors argue that production shapes consumption and that the advertising and entertainment industry persuade consumers that products will enhance their lives in ways that transcend their physical properties. Adorno and Horkheimer (2000) argue that producers and advertisers create false needs for new goods or services and manipulate consumers into buying these goods. Products provide individuals with momentary but ultimately unsatisfying pleasures, leading them to accept their exploitation under capitalism: consumption becomes an ideological system.

Further, commercial culture erodes individuals' interest in high culture, and hence leads to a declining audience for genuine artistic expression. Slater (1997) dates this concern back to the early modern era when members of the nobility feared they would lose their monopoly over luxury goods and hence criticized the decline of culture resulting from the majority of the population gaining access to luxury goods (for related arguments, see Galbraith 2000; Haug 1986; Smart 2010). Baudrillard (1996, 2000) takes this argument further, contending that modern advertising takes control of modern culture so that there is no way for individuals to see beyond the frontier of advertising and media.

Another critical perspective on consumption draws on the work of Max Weber (1958), who argued that ideas and subjective attitudes encouraged the rise of modern capitalism. This view contrasts with Marx's emphasis on property ownership and employers' extraction of profits from workers. Weber argued that the religious Reformation in Europe ushered in new ideas and habits that indirectly influenced the rise of capitalism. Specifically, the Calvinist doctrine that urged believers to work hard in a calling and save money rather than enjoying worldly goods had the effect of encouraging individuals to work, invest their savings, and evaluate their actions through rational analysis, all values necessary for operating a modern business. He argued that even after Calvinist and other Protestant doctrines lost influence, the ascetic values promoted by Calvinism remained. In his related work on bureaucracy (1946a), he argued that modern businesses and governments were much more efficient than family firms because of their hierarchy, division of labor, and clear rules. Like the Calvinist worldview, modern organizations encourage rational, efficient action, but also discourage emotional and creative expression, making them cold and heartless.

These two ideas have importantly influenced analyses of modern consumption. Campbell (2005) models his book after Weber's *Protestant Ethic*, but he departs from Weber's notion that modern businessmen lived ascetic lives and consumed little. Rather, he posits that a romantic ethic developed from several breakaway Calvinist sects in Great Britain. These sects rejected the idea of predestination and argued that individuals could display their redemption in God's eyes through both "conduct and character." Expression of character could come through emotional displays of pity and empathy with others. The sects promoted emotional expression and suggested that pleasure could be gained through experiencing emotion. Later, in the eighteenth century, middle-class and aristocratic women became avid consumers of gothic and Romantic novels and poetry, building their identities through art appreciation and imaginative pleasure-seeking, or modern hedonism. Thus, Campbell argues that orthodox Calvinism promoted ascetic conduct in business affairs and the breakaway sects encouraged hedonistic pleasure-seeking in consumption. Through this argument, Campbell seeks to explain the enormous rise in consumption that began in eighteenth-century England.

Other scholars trace the rise of consumption further back in history. Sombart (1967) argues that the growth of luxury consumption dating back to the Middle Ages spurred on modern capitalism. He points to celebrations in the ecclesiastical courts, and the increasing role of courtesans (mistresses of noble or wealthy men) in secular courts of the Renaissance as spurring on hedonistic consumption, which, in turn, stimulated demand for luxury goods. Mukerji (1983) suggests that the growth of painting, printmaking, map-making, science, and fashion in the Renaissance and early modern Europe spurred on industrialization: consumption, rather than ideas or religious values, spurred on the rise of capitalism. Finally, De Vries (1975, 1993) focuses on peasants (small farmers) to explain the rise of modern con-sumption and capitalism. He finds that beginning in the seventeenth century in localities of the Netherlands, Britain, and France, peasant families began to use women's and children's labor to produce more food for sale, which allowed them to purchase goods, in contrast to their traditional pattern of maximizing free time. He describes this as the "industrious revolution" rather than the "industrial revolu-tion," suggesting that peasants' hard work directed toward consump-tion created more demand for industrial goods and hence reflected changing cultural attitudes toward consumption, which stimulated industry. We explore each of these ideas in chapter 2.

Analysts of contemporary consumption underscore the importance of both rational calculation and pleasure-seeking for understanding modern consumption, drawing upon or criticizing Weber's analysis of the Protestant ethic. Bell (1976) argues that contemporary capi-talism is contradictory in that it encourages asceticism at work and hedonistic instant gratification in consumption, values supported by access to credit and the ideas of the 1960s counterculture. Illouz (1997) develops these ideas in her analysis of romantic love in the U.S., arguing that courtship and romance have been linked to consumption since the beginning of the twentieth century, but contemporary women's magazines encourage readers to perceive the process of identifying a soulmate and maintaining a marriage as an exercise of rational study and calculation. Hence, dating and affairs are linked to hedonistic consumption, while committed relationships and marriage are described as requiring the same skills of rationality and self-control as those used in the workplace.

Two recent works follow Weber's (1946a) analysis of bureaucracy. George Ritzer's (2008) concept of "McDonaldization" explores how McDonald's and many large companies have perfected the key elements of bureaucracy Weber identified, delivering standardized, inexpensive products that are extremely popular, but that crowd out more unique, higher-quality products and services from the market.

In contrast, Holt (2004) and Holt and Cameron (2010) argue that consumers often rebel against the "soul-crushing" character of modern bureaucratic workplaces, companies' periodic tendencies to shed employees in the name of "efficiency," and firms' production of standardized products as well as promotion of conformist lifestyles (like the white, middle-class suburban ideal of the 1950s). Consumers resist these processes by forming subcultures whose members rebel against bureaucratic values. "Hillbillies," "outlaw bikers," "hippies," "bohemian artists," "slackers," "dirtbags," "foodies," and blue-collar workers rejected bureaucratic work, standardized products, and conformist lifestyles. Companies often appeal to these groups (many of which are mainly comprised of white males) with messages that affirm their values while promoting the products to broader populations. Brands like Jack Daniel's, Mountain Dew, Budweiser, Volkswagen, and Patagonia have successfully used an anti-bureaucratic cultural message (even though many of these companies are in fact large bureaucracies) to tap into consumers' frustrations and anxieties and to affirm their attitudes and practices.

Additionally, Holt and Cameron (2010) suggest that large consumer-product companies have become "brand bureaucracies." Their adoption of "sciency marketing" that relies on extensive statistical research sidesteps the innovative and creative market research and advertising needed to appeal to contemporary consumers. Hence, in an interesting twist on Weber, they suggest that bureaucracies' tendency to stifle creativity actually makes them *less* effective businesses than small, upstart innovators, like Ben and Jerry's ice cream, whose unique origins and eclectic approach to product development and marketing make them more grounded in consumer subcultures and more able to generate "breakthrough" ideas that build customer loyalty. In some exceptional cases, "rebels" within large firms adopt similarly effective strategies of "cultural creativity" in advertising, as in the Levi's 501 jeans campaign in Europe. These two works suggest that bureaucracies are efficient machines that can satisfy many consumers, but that also have worrisome shortcomings that may limit the creative and unique aspects of consumption.

Weber (1946b) also developed the concept of status, or social honor. He argued that the upper class of a society attempts to maintain a monopoly over access to luxury goods in order to maintain its image of superiority to other groups. Contemporary examples might include Italian sports cars, vacations to islands unknown to most of the population, or attendance at elite private schools. Once others in the population gain access to these goods (or cheaper imitations), the upper class begins to consume new products to maintain its sense and image of superiority.

Simmel (1957) developed a similar argument in his analysis of fashion. He contended that fashion expresses modern individuals' desire for personal self-expression and to be part of a group. The wealthy tend to be at the cutting edge of fashion, while lower-income people often imitate them, leading the wealthy to move on to another trend. Wealthy individuals pursue fashion to be part of a group but also, as noted above, to exclude outsiders. Further, subordinate groups, like women, may adopt fashion as a "mask," allowing them to fit into society without having to share their individual opinions and thus "stand out" in a crowd. Hence, in addition to being a principle of social exclusion (as in Weber's understanding), fashion also expresses modern individuals' psychological desires to experiment with new goods as well as the contrasting effort to blend in with a crowd. Simmel's essay has been summarized as the "trickle-down theory" of consumption. McCracken (1988) modified this idea to understand how professional women seek to appropriate male symbols of power through workplace fashions. His ideas have widespread influence in the field (Slater 1997; Sassatelli 2007).

Status remains an important concept for understanding how consumption can contribute to the creation and maintenance (or *reproduction*) of social inequalities based on social honor rather than money alone. Thorstein Veblen's (1979) idea of the *leisure class* parallels Weber's notion of status. For Veblen, the upper class of society marks its superiority by opulent displays of wealth through consumption, while members of other social classes seek to imitate the upper class in order to gain greater social status. Further, Pierre Bourdieu's concepts of *economic* (money) and *cultural capital* (education, taste) draw on Weber's concept of status and Marx's understanding of the antagonistic relationship between employers and workers. For Bourdieu, both wealth and education can be used through consumption to assert or claim status. Consider feasting on a portion of *filet mignon* (a symbol of wealth) vs. attending a gourmet cooking class (reflecting education and taste) as two ways individuals might assert status through consumption. We develop these ideas in chapter 4.

While these critiques of modern consumption focus on the power of producers, advertisers, and status in shaping consumption, several perspectives focus on consumers' active role in crafting meanings through consumption. One perspective refers to the *relational* character of consumption. This view originates in anthropological studies of gift-giving, rituals, and kinship. Douglas and Isherwood (1996) argue that individuals use consumption to create, sustain, and repair personal relationships. Consumption also becomes meaningful through rituals such as birthdays, graduations, weddings, and funerals. These consumption rituals allow individuals to mark the passage of time, move on to the next stage in the life course, and to recognize themselves as part of meaningful social groups (family, friends).

Daniel Miller (1998, 2012) and Viviana Zelizer (1989, 2005a, 2005b) further develop this perspective by examining how mothers seek to satisfy the needs and desires of family members through shopping, and how family members distribute money and expenses based on distinct family roles. This view is an important counterpoint to works focused on advertising or status in that it shows that important aspects and arenas of consumption are not simply a reflection of advertising messages or self-centered efforts to seek social honor. Rather, consumers are often motivated by a sense of social obligation toward others, and goods often connect individuals through shared rituals rather than separating them through status competition.

Daniel Miller (1987, 2005) has developed a broader but similar perspective known as the material culture approach. This perspective seeks to understand how individuals reinterpret and recontextualize mass-produced goods to shape their individual identities or to cement their connections to valued social groups. Miller uses the term "objectification" to describe the process through which human beings create objects that appear separate from themselves and then reappropriate those objects to use them as a source of identity and meaning. One example of these practices is seen when working-class families decorate the inside of their public-housing apartments (which all look the same from the outside) with a wide range of goods to place their personal stamp on these dwellings (compare McCracken's 2005 concept of "homeyness" whereby individuals seek to create a feeling of warmth in their home via its design and decoration with personal photos and handmade goods). For Miller, we create a meaningful personal world via consumption.

Colin Campbell's (2005) argument on hedonistic consumption described above challenges the ideas that status competition or advertisers drive consumption. He argues that the Romantic movement in early nineteenth-century Europe linked pleasure and authenticity with consumption. He contends that in modern consumption, individuals engage in an insatiable search for novelty through new goods as a way to satisfy their desires and to construct authentic selves. Economists' view that individuals rationally rank their desires in relation to their available resources ignores desire's centrality as a motivation for consumption (Slater 1997). Campbell's view focuses on irrational desires that classical economists have ignored (compare Illouz 2009). Campbell's argument has influenced research in marketing where scholars argue that, today, individuals seek meaningful experiences rather than specific goods, and this desire for authentic experiences is based on emotions (Addis and Holbrook 2001; Arnould and Price 1993; Jantzen and Fitchett 2012).

Cultural studies researchers also criticize the argument that advertising and status drive consumption. Some scholars examine how members of youth subcultures like hippies or punks develop unique consumption-based lifestyles to rebel against the dominant culture (Hebdige 1979, 2000; Milestone and Meyer 2012). Marketing scholars working within the paradigm of "consumer culture theory" (Arnould and Thompson 2005) extend this focus to a wide range of class, gender, regional, and lifestyle-based subcultures (e.g., Belk et al. 1988; Cova et al. 2007; Holt 2004; Holt and Cameron 2010; Kates 2002; Kozinets 2001, 2002; Thornton 1996). This work demonstrates that some social groups may reject advertisers' messages as well as social pressures demanding they consume in specific ways to increase their social status. Additionally, advertisers may draw on subcultural styles to promote branded goods to "hardcore" members and mainstream consumers.

Other scholars build directly or indirectly on the ideas of Michel de Certeau (1984), who argued that individuals appropriate objects in unique ways that are not prescribed by advertisers. These unique uses of goods represent a subtle form of resistance to the cultural dominance of producers and advertisers. In this context, several scholars argue that consumption is an arena of self-expression and autonomy for women that they have been denied in the labor market or political sphere. Women may gain pleasure through shopping for themselves or satisfying family members' needs (Fiske 2000; Nava 1997; Bowlby 2001; Miller 1998).

Practice theory is a recent and distinctive approach to consumption. Scholars in this tradition challenge the idea that individuals choose to purchase or use a product based on their personal calculations or desires. Rather, they argue that consumption emerges from everyday routines, behaviors, and attitudes as they intersect with an expanding array of products. These scholars focus less on a person's desires than their capacities to use a product, their understanding of the rules involving its use, and their level of involvement in its use. We could thus differentiate typical drivers from amateur/professional race-car drivers and "low-rider" enthusiasts, regarding their knowledge, skills, and commitment to driving (Warde 2005). They also understand choice as involving a physical (or embodied) reaction to a good or service that reflects an individual's prior experiences, relationships, and networks, rather than based on "information processing" or "conscious desire" (Allen 2002). Finally, these scholars suggest that practices draw on beliefs and attitudes that interface with the use of complementary products with specific capacities (like cooking in a kitchen with a variety of appliances or using a computer, fax machine, and printer). Hence, products are part of meaningful, routine practices, but these products' physical and technical features limit and shape how people use them (Ingram et al. 2007). Practice theory shifts our attention from desires, status, and meaning to consider how products fit into our everyday routines and how those routines shape our identities.

An obvious example of how this works is the smartphone. The rise of cellphones as well as Internet-based chat applications has changed both our forms of written communication and our expectations about public behavior. Cellphones allow individuals to be linked to two places at one time (where they are physically present in one place while in connection with the person on the other phone in a different location), raising new questions about acceptable behaviors in each place, and the relationship between individuals' physical and virtual presence. Additionally, Rojek (2011) suggests that the shuffle functions on iPods and other digital music players have changed our relationship to specific songs and musicians because the object sets the play list rather than the listener, and the song played is taken out of the context of the CD of which it is a part. Further, individuals may listen alone rather than in groups because of the personalized nature of the device. Hence, the practice of listening to music changes with the evolution of technology.

A final approach, which is linked to practice theory, examines the actual work of marketers and advertisers, as well as how their practices and interpretations affect consumers and consumption. While there is a long tradition of research examining advertising messages, only recently have scholars examined what marketers actually do, and how these practices affect consumers. Many scholars in this area are influenced by actor-network theory (ANT), which emerged from the field of science and technology studies (STS). ANT scholars argue that people and things operate in an interactive web with unpredictable consequences (Latour 2005). The scholars argue that objects and ideas affect people just as people affect objects. They develop this idea using the term "market devices," which refer to objects, technologies, and ideas that help market actors to calculate prices and act efficiently. However, these devices are "performative" in that these calculations and efficiencies also shape the actions and perceptions of producers, advertisers, and consumers (Muniesa et al. 2007; McFall 2009). For example, advertisers use the results of a marketing survey to develop a campaign. However, this "device" only gives a partial description of actual consumers, and hence it may subtly affect how advertising "creatives" view consumers and the campaign they produce. In this sense, this "market device" has "agency" insofar as it shapes the advertising process (Ariztia 2013).

Scholars have drawn on these ideas to look at the ambiguous image of marketing as existing between economy and culture (Slater 2011); how marketers sought to build an image of competence to legitimate their role in universities and the marketplace (Cochoy 1998); how independent grocers used several technological innovations (like self-service shopping and shopping carts) to attract shoppers, which also changed employees' relations with customers (Cochoy 2011); how current marketing practice enlists consumers to provide their free labor to promote products (Foster 2011); and how department store credit-card risk analysts use statistical data to identify and recruit very poor consumers into the credit system as a source of profits (in spite of the high rate of default), as well as a means to promote credit cards to other consumers (Ossandon 2013). Like practice theory, these studies shift our attention to consumers' complex interactions with marketers and products, and the subtle ways objects, texts, and ideas affect marketers and consumers.

Like other authors (Lury 2011; Sassatelli 2007), this book questions the idea that a single theory can explain all or most of consumer behavior. Rather, to understand contemporary consumption, we must integrate several theoretical perspectives, each of which illuminates a different dimension of this complex social phenomenon. Therefore, this book will draw on the different approaches outlined above, while emphasizing relational, material culture, and status-based analyses of consumption.

Since this book focuses on consumption in a global context, it enters into the debate regarding whether consumption is becoming more standardized or more diversified in the era of globalization. Some authors argue that the rising power of transnational corporations based in the West is leading to the increasing standardization of consumption along American lines around the world (Ritzer 2003; Smart 2010). In contrast, others argue that individuals and groups in specific countries incorporate global products and images into their distinctive local and national cultural contexts, either combining them with local products and practices, rejecting them, or reinterpreting them in local terms (Caldwell 2002; O'Dougherty 2002; Straubhaar 2007; Miller 1997, 2012). This book follows the latter authors, arguing that to understand consumption in any geographic and cultural setting, it is necessary to carefully examine how individuals and groups use and understand local and imported goods.

Chapter Summaries

I develop each of the themes noted above in the following chapters. Chapter 2 examines the rise of modern retail and credit from the mid-nineteenth century until World War II. While modern consumption first emerged in the period between the Middle Ages and the sixteenth century, our current patterns of consumption date back to the industrial era when factory production began in Europe and the U.S. and department stores sprung up in mid-century Paris (Slater 1997; Sassatelli 2007; McKendrick et al. 1982; Williams 1982). The chapter examines the rise of department, discount, and grocery stores; how these retail innovations changed women's access to public areas; and the emergence of credit, advertising, and branding as key ingredients of the first phase of modern consumption from 1870–1930. The chapter continues by examining the rise of the supermarket and shopping mall in the postwar era, how malls changed the nature of shopping, and variations in mall habitats across the world.

Chapter 3 focuses on changes in retail, marketing, and technology since the 1970s. Most scholars argue that the youth counterculture of the 1960s played a crucial role in the shift from the standardized, mass consumption of the postwar era to the customized, lifestyle consumption of today. These changes are evident in the diversity of consumer lifestyles present today as well as the niche marketing strategies adopted by producers and advertisers. We contrast arguments that see contemporary consumption as increasingly individualistic with others that emphasize consumers' participation in subcultures and "tribes." The advance of the Internet and wireless communications has similarly influenced consumption. Consumers have now become producers through social media sites like YouTube. We have instantaneous access to information about product quality, and we may inadvertently do free labor for companies and advertisers by recommending products to friends on websites like Facebook and Myspace. Illegal downloads and file sharing as well as new technologies for making music have transformed the music industry. This chapter considers the implications of each of these phenomena for the nature of contemporary consumption and the degree to which their global reach has produced a "global" consumer culture with largely similar features.

Chapter 4 explores how consumption reflects inequalities based on social class and status, and how these inequalities may be reproduced across generations. We consider some of the classic arguments about class and status competition by Marx, Weber, Veblen, Simmel, and Bourdieu, and examine some arguments regarding whether or not class-based consumption differences have begun to change or erode in recent decades. We also explore the extent to which these patterns of class and status differences vary across countries within Europe, the U.S., and the Global South, where scholars have recently conducted similar analyses of class and consumption. Additionally, this chapter considers how poverty affects consumption and, finally, explores how class differences take shape in the retail and housing markets.

Chapter 5 examines how gender and race figure in consumption. With the rise of modern consumption, shopping was considered a feminine activity, and yet we have not fully considered how men's and women's consumption differ and how gender ideas shape advertising, product design, and consumer desires and attitudes. This chapter considers two contrasting viewpoints on gender and consumption – that advertising reinforces gender inequality and that consumption is an arena through which women have gained a degree of liberation. We further consider how lifestyle consumption has broadened the range of identities that men can adopt. Finally, we consider debates regarding acceptable forms of consumption for men and women in predominantly Muslim societies.

Race is an even less commonly studied category in the study of consumption. While sociologists have written extensively about racial inequalities in the job, housing, and education areas, there has been little consideration of how racial groups consume differently and how racial ideas affect consumption. We consider how racial prejudices have affected the consumption opportunities of African Americans, Hispanics, and Asian Americans; as well as how black, Latino, and Asian performers, athletes, and musicians have become "crossover" successes with white audiences. Additionally, we consider how consumption may play a role in the development and evolution of racial identities. We also explore consumption in other racially stratified societies in the Global South. Finally, we examine how some authors have used the concept of intersectionality to examine how class, race, gender, sexuality, and age simultaneously differentiate consumers and shape individual consumption choices.

Chapter 6 focuses on consumption across the life course. We examine how adults consume on behalf of children and what this tells us about our views of childhood. Next, we examine how consumption is an important vehicle of socialization and self-expression for children. We continue by exploring youth consumers as early adopters of new technologies, members of subcultures, and as perceived threats to adults. We continue exploring how consumption figures in the now extended period between adolescence and marriage, committed relationships, and parenting, known as emerging adulthood. Next, we explore the role of consumption in weddings, and how parents choose their children's schools and educational enrichment activities. Finally, we consider the growing population of elderly persons and the extent to which advertisers and marketers view them as a consumer market.

Chapter 7 looks at consumers as citizens. We often think of consumption as opposed to citizenship, but, in fact, the two go hand in hand. First, governments seek to promote consumption to secure citizens' support. From the 1930s to the 1970s, this took the form of providing citizens with services (education, subsidized housing, healthcare) as part of their membership in national communities. Further, some governments encouraged citizens to mobilize politically as consumers to secure their rights. Since the 1970s, governments have attempted to privatize services and broaden consumers' access to imported goods as a way to reduce the prices of goods and hence build political support. Further, consumption and citizenship are linked in the different ways citizens have used consumption (or the refusal to consume) as a way to achieve political objectives. Boycotts and sit-ins are crucial tactics consumers have used to expand their own rights or those of others.

Chapter 8 focuses on consumer citizenship in the contemporary era. With the decline of the welfare state and the rise of globalization, individuals have begun to conceive of their citizenship rights in a global context. Numerous campaigns have attempted to pressure companies to act more ethically through boycotts, culture jamming, and certification of ethically produced goods. Further, consumers seek to achieve their objectives by purchasing goods that are healthy or fulfill their moral goals. We consider the motivations behind this global consumer activism as well as the extent to which activist consumers have achieved their goals.

Chapter 9 reviews the key arguments in the book and considers their implications for understanding consumption and the broader social contexts in which it happens. How do consumption and inequality go together? How does consumption vary across different locations in the world? How are consumers simultaneously citizens? We consider the extent to which we have answered these questions and how our answers provide insight into the dynamic and ever-changing world of consumption.

2

Marketing and Retail from the Modern Period until the Postwar Era of Mass Consumption

Introduction

When we think about shopping today, this might involve checking online for sales, driving to the local mall, and then making a purchase. We might learn of specific products or sales on the Internet, on billboards, in television advertisements, or through friends. Shopping could also involve a trip to the local big-box supermarket, browsing at boutiques in a shopping district, a long car drive to an "outlet mall" to purchase brand-name goods at a discount, or the purchase of "unique" goods while on vacation. As noted in the introduction, we might even find a particular brand appealing after seeing a clever ad while watching the Super Bowl.

This diverse and complex retail and advertising landscape did not always exist as it does today; nor is our experience of shopping in the U.S. the same as others' experiences in the wealthy societies of Europe, Asia, or the Global South. In this chapter, we explore the origins of our retail environment in early modern Europe, its rapid expansion in the industrial era in the U.S. and Europe, its consolidation after World War II, and the distinct ways that shopping developed within and beyond the Global North. Simultaneously, we will examine the development of advertising, marketing, and branding. Taking this historical and international journey will help the reader see that today's retail world is not "natural"; rather, it is the product of different stages of economic and technological development. Furthermore, the mid-twentieth-century model of "standardized" retail in the U.S. and to some extent in other parts of the Global North is distinct from the locally based and uneven development of retail and advertising in the Global South. Hence, we will explore what globalization and localization have meant for advertising and shopping until the 1970s.

Human beings have participated in the exchange or sale of goods for a few thousand years. We can trace shopping back to the bazaars and trading hubs of the Middle East and North Africa. Indeed, in many cities in these regions, the bazaar still plays a central role in the retail sector and in local culture, even though modern department stores and shopping malls coexist with this traditional sector (Dokmeci et al. 2006). A visit to a bazaar or public market is different from our typical experience of shopping. Customers need to bargain with traders, relying on their wit and performance skills to gain an advantage or assess a vendor's honesty. Shopping at a bazaar or similar market is a much more sociable experience than shopping at the mall because vendors attempt to make the shopper feel that they are trustworthy through expressions of enthusiasm, if not affection (Zukin 2004; Lehtonen and Mäenpää 1997).

Other important shopping sites include the ancient Greek *agora*, or public square, which provided space for both retail sales and political activity. In contrast, many researchers today bemoan the fact that mall owners or managers discourage or forbid political expression inside shopping centers (Cohen 2003; Staeheli and Mitchell 2006). In the Middle Ages, regional festival markets hosted food and crafts sales as well as public performances. Similarly, carnival, signaling the beginning of Lent, was an important opportunity for the poor to momentarily feel that they had power over the rich. Today, carnival still is an important and popular event as evident in the globally renowned Mardi Gras festival in New Orleans, Louisiana, and carnivals in Rio de Janeiro (and other Brazilian cities), Trinidad and Tobago (British West Indies), and Oruro, Bolivia (Gotham 2007). While these carnivals have become major profit-making ventures designed to lure tourists, they retain their religious and traditional meanings for many local participants and the quality of "turning the world upside down," as evident in the beautiful costumes, music, dancing, and sexual permissiveness at many of the events.

The Origins of Modern Consumption

This brief description of traditional retail venues shows that throughout recorded human history, shopping was an important activity with rich meanings and social importance due to its political or religious dimensions. Modern retail takes a different turn with its shift in focus to the satisfaction of individual desires. As elaborated below, Sombart (1967) dates modern consumption back to the twelfth century, when papal courts sponsored ostentatious celebrations. Mukerji (1983) focuses on the increasing production and purchase of paintings, prints, and illustrated books during the Renaissance of the fifteenth and sixteenth centuries. Others date modern retail back to the sixteenth century during the "Age of Discovery" when European monarchies colonized the Americas, Africa, and Asia. Although some scholars argue that new forms of consumption were restricted to wealthy traders, nobles, and royalty, we begin to see an important shift in the role of shopping and consumption among those groups. These existing and emerging elites began to consume many imported "luxuries" such as spices, silks, tea, coffee, sugar, and chocolate.

The importance of this new pattern was twofold. First, slaves and peasants produced these goods and hence this consumption solidified the unequal relationship between Europe and the rest of the world that continues until today, while involving elites of the Global South in luxury consumption based on European innovation. Second, luxury consumption was important for its social meaning. No longer was consumption tied to subsistence or specific religious ceremonies; rather, consumption was part of the creation of an *individual* identity, a phenomenon still present in many parts of the world (Slater 1997; Sassatelli 2007; Lury 2011; McKendrick et al. 1982; Mintz 1985; Bauer 2001).

Today scholars reject previous studies that argued that modern consumption was the result of industrialization. As noted in the introduction, Marx and Weber offered distinct explanations for the rise of industrial capitalism in the nineteenth century. While Marx focused on the growth of capitalist property in factories, banks, and land based on its forcible seizure from peasants and craftsmen, Weber emphasized the changing mindset of businessmen emanating from religious ideas. Yet both of these views use the rise of *manufacturing* to explain the emergence of modern consumption. Nonetheless, critics suggest that a "commercial revolution" preceded or coincided with the Industrial Revolution, and that the former phenomenon was the spark creating modern consumer societies. However, as suggested in the introduction, these scholars disagree about *when* modern consumption became important as well as *how* and *why* consumption promoted modern capitalism.

I consider their perspectives chronologically. Sombart (1967) disputes Weber's view that capitalism rose alongside Protestantism in the sixteenth and seventeenth centuries. He looks back to the late Middle Ages, and finds evidence of luxury consumption in the religious courts of the Catholic Popes. Additionally, he argues that the Renaissance courts of Italian cities reflected changes in attitudes about romantic love. He suggests that during the Middle Ages, ideas about love shifted from an emphasis on religious obligation toward notions of beauty and pleasure. This change is evident in the increasing presence of courtesans (mistresses) accompanying kings, noblemen, and wealthy men. Sombart (1967) argues that these women's tastes for luxury and men's efforts to satisfy them to gain their romantic attention influenced consumption patterns throughout society, and created demand for goods produced by profit-oriented factories. Hence, the consumer tastes of the royalty, nobility, and wealthy stimulated demands for capitalistically produced goods, rather than Weber's view that businessmen's asceticism (focus on investment rather than consumption) promoted capitalist development. While Sombart's views are intriguing, his evidence is inconsistent, he uses a very broad definition of capitalism, and his argument jumps back and forth across long periods of time, raising questions about the plausibility of his analysis.

Mukerji (1983) focuses on the Middle Ages and Renaissance to examine modern *materialism* – a growing focus on exchange and consumption. Rather than examining religious ideas, she argues that changing patterns of production and exchange during the Renaissance created and reflected cultural shifts that fueled modern capitalism. Craftsmen and artists began to produce prints, books, and paintings with an eye to profit rather than maintaining the traditional view during the Middle Ages that excess wealth should be saved or shared among one's peers. The growing mass production of prints for sale to common people and creation of paintings for the wealthy and nobility helped shape modern class structures and stimulate modern consumer behaviors. Additionally, printed maps promoted long-distance navigation that brought luxury goods and precious metals to Europe, but people also used maps to decorate their homes. Finally, during the seventeenth century, the growing British demand for cotton calicoes made in India led British cotton producers to develop machines that allowed them to create modern factories and thereby respond to foreign competition. For Mukerji, the production and marketing of prints and cotton clothing stimulated modern production.

McCracken (1988) focuses on consumption in sixteenth-century England. He argues that Queen Elizabeth used hedonistic consumption as an instrument of rule. She threw elaborate parties and invited many among the nobility to attend. In an effort to gain the Queen's favor, these noblemen spent much of their resources to participate in these elaborate parties and to compete with one another in extravagance, making them more economically dependent on the Queen. Hence, they spent more time at the Royal Palace than in their home villages, and developed a form of consumption that departed from existing styles that emphasized inherited goods showing the "patina" or wear and tear of old age. This early modern shift foreshadowed the status competition that Veblen and Simmel later emphasized.

De Vries (1975, 1993) examines peasants (small farmers) in the seventeenth and eighteenth centuries. His research is interesting in that we often look to the behaviors of the wealthy and powerful as motors of economic change. Hence, rather than Weber's and Marx's focus on businessmen, or Sombart's focus on the nobility, De Vries identifies farmers as among the first modern consumers. He sees a similar shift in attitude that Mukerji noted. Farmers traditionally had worked only as much as necessary to survive and sought to maximize their free time. However, some farmers located near trading areas in the Netherlands, Britain, and France began to change their economic behavior. They worked harder and more family members worked (particularly women and children) with the goal of selling their products to purchase manufactured goods. He suggests that farmers, rather than businessmen or nobles, were the prototypical modern consumers, and their "industrious revolution" created the demand that helped spark the eighteenth-century Industrial Revolution.

McKendrick et al. (1982) focus on increasing purchases across social classes in Britain in the second half of the eighteenth century. They suggest that while these earlier examples were important precursors to modern consumption, they only affected a small segment of European societies. In contrast to these other authors, they argue that in the context of rising wages and population, innovations in marketing and advertising stimulated status competition and growing consumption among people from all walks of life in Britain. They argue that Josiah Wedgewood's efforts to gain royal, aristocratic, artistic, and diplomatic patronage for his ceramic goods, his use of exhibition halls and traveling salesmen, and his efforts to adapt decorations on pottery to appeal to different social classes and consumers in different countries led to massive purchases of his products. Further, George Packwood's innovations in newspaper advertising led to rising consumption of his shaving strops (a leather strip used to sharpen razors). Thus, the authors emphasize how innovative marketing, market research, and advertising techniques created markets for the goods produced in modern factories. The eighteenth century witnessed a commercial revolution that went hand in hand with the Industrial Revolution.

As suggested in the introduction, Campbell (2005) has vigorously criticized explanations of consumption that rely on status competition or advertisers' manipulation of customers. He, too, examines the commercial revolution of the eighteenth century, but he is unconvinced that status competition or advertising (which predated that century) can explain the qualitative shift in attitudes and behaviors linked to consumption. He returns to Weber's focus on religion. He asks: if Protestantism promoted asceticism, how could the businessmen that Weber analyzes also be hedonistic consumers, as McKendrick has documented for eighteenth-century England?

He answers this question through an analysis of changing religious attitudes among the middle classes during the seventeenth and eighteenth centuries in England. He finds that some British Calvinists began to question aspects of this sect's religious dogma, with important implications for modern consumption. He emphasizes the rising importance of emotion as a sign of religious faith among dissident Calvinists. Expressions of compassion for the poor and downtrodden were signs of faith, but, importantly, these dissident Calvinists began to find pleasure in emotional expression and experience. This was the key, for Campbell, to the rise of modern hedonism, which involves the imaginative longing for goods and experiences. He sees the beginning of this phenomenon in middle-class and aristocratic women's consumption of gothic and romantic novels in the eighteenth century, and in the nineteenth-century rise of the Romantic movement in poetry and fiction, which emphasized authentic, emotional experience as a sign of individual virtue. This Romantic ethic contrasted with the asceticism noted by Weber as well as the aristocratic ethics of heroism and pride. Hence, he suggests that modern consumption among the middle classes did *not* reflect their imitation of the nobility (as McKendrick suggests); rather, it reflected dissident Calvinists' religious values. Hence, the Protestant ethic and the Romantic ethic emerged from two branches of Calvinism, and they could coincide in the same person.

It is difficult to determine which of these diverse accounts best explains the rise of modern consumption and capitalism given the different time periods they cover, the distinct explanations they offer, and the different social groups they focus on. However, it is now clear that there were instances of modern consumption that preceded the eighteenth-century rise of industrial capitalism, and these consumption patterns contributed to the Industrial Revolution. Furthermore, these studies demonstrate that modern consumption resulted from shifting cultural attitudes and practices in different populations rather than people's simple reaction to the rising supply of goods or higher incomes.

While each of these accounts locates the origins of modern consumption in periods ranging from the Middle Ages to the eighteenth century, historian Frank Trentmann (2006b) suggests that they confuse the rise of market-based purchases with the appearance of "the consumer" as a widely recognized identity that individuals and groups adopted. He provides evidence that the concept of "consumer" was only adopted in the context of political struggles beginning in late nineteenth-century Britain over the collective rights of water users in relation to a monopoly industry. He further shows that use of the term "consumer" varied cross-nationally. At the turn of the twentieth century, British citizens and organizations spoke of consumer "rights" to access inexpensive goods through free trade; German activists were skeptical of the idea that "consumers" represented the nation; and, in China, the government asked "patriotic citizens" to buy nationally made rather than imported goods. Further, consumer activism varied across time and space, and was often stated as a matter of ethics and policy rather than market exchange. Trentmann cautions that we cannot assume that "the consumer" is a social identity that results automatically from participation in market exchange; rather, it is a political and moral category that has varied cross-nationally and reflects distinct national political traditions.

With this discussion in mind, we now turn to the rise of "mass consumption" in the nineteenth century. As employment shifted from farming to industrial wage labor for much of the population, and as industrial and transport technologies advanced, Europe and the U.S. experienced a massive expansion in the availability of factory-made goods. In an effort to make these goods more appealing to customers, several important changes occurred in the retail, financing, and advertising of consumption from approximately 1870 until 1930, which still have implications for much of the world.

Advertising and Branding

Before considering retail settings, we explore the beginnings of advertising and marketing, branding, and consumer credit. The changes in these fields coincided with the rise of modern retail, but it is useful to analytically separate them for clearer understanding. Advertising and marketing as large-scale phenomena originated in eighteenth-century British newspapers, though they became more widespread in the second half of the nineteenth century (McKendrick et al. 1982). With the rising supplies of goods and the growing population of industrial and farm workers earning wages and salaries, markets for these goods expanded. In the first half of the nineteenth century in the U.S. and in many parts of Europe, much of the population still lived on farms and produced most of their own finished goods as well as their own food. As large portions of the population moved into the money economy, they had to acquire these goods via the market. Furthermore, the growth of cities concentrated large populations with disposable incomes that could serve as markets for manufacturers (Strasser 1989; Leach 1993).

Brands first emerged as vehicles to assure customers of the quality and reliability of specific products, while providing manufacturers with opportunities for profit unavailable to unknown producers. Producers developed insignias and slogans to differentiate their own products from the competition (Lury 2011). McKendrick et al.'s (1982) case studies of Josiah Wedgewood and George Packwood in eighteenth-century Britain are important precursors to this process in the nineteenth century. Advertising rose in tandem with branding, as companies used newspapers, postcards, and other printed materials to promote specific products.

In the first half of the twentieth century, advertisers began to target specific segments of the population with a given product, product line, or brand. Until the 1960s, advertising directed messages to demographic groups such as men and women, adults and children, and different social classes. Since the 1960s, marketing has become much more precise as advertisers use vast databases to precisely target age or lifestyle groups, as we explore in the next chapter. As communications technologies developed, advertisers increasingly used the radio and later the television to target customers. Further, with the advance of survey research techniques beginning in the 1930s, researchers began to carefully study the buying attitudes and practices of various social groups by analyzing their radio listening habits, for example (Strasser 1989; Leach 1993; Williams 1982; Leiss et al. 2005; Schor 1998).

After World War II, advertising and marketing professionals began to dissect consumers, using more complex tools than dividing them into broad-based demographic groups. Most notably, these professionals began a gradual shift from promoting the physical properties of goods to associating products with positive emotional states or needs. Examples of this approach include telling mothers not only that a cereal is healthy but that it will make her child happy, or that a car does not simply function well, but that it gives its owner power, freedom, and makes him (car ads at that time were mostly directed toward men) sexually attractive (Zukin 2004; Lury 2011; Baudrillard 1996; Smart 2010; McCracken 2005; Leiss et al. 2005; Holt 2004; Holt and Cameron 2010).

In addition to associating goods with specific emotional needs or desires, advertisers and marketers began to classify consumers within specific psychological categories that were not reducible to demographic groups. This approach, known as psychographic market segmentation, might distinguish *traditionalists* from *adventurers* and identify a set of products and buying behaviors that the marketers believed fit with this grouping (Zukin 2004).

Since World War II, scholars have intensively debated the effects of marketing and advertising on consumers. From one influential perspective, which originates with German social theorists Theodor Adorno's and Max Horkheimer's (2000) essay on the "Culture Industry," advertising manipulates consumers into buying goods. For these authors, advertising and mass entertainment (radio, film, and popular music) are produced in a similar way as mass-produced automobiles or other manufactured products. Their idea was initially influenced by their brief stint working in the "studio system" in Hollywood after their exile from Germany to the U.S. in the 1930s (Davis 1990). In that era, the Hollywood studios pushed writers to constantly produce new films using standard formulas that were appealing to audiences. Based on this experience, their observations of other types of mass entertainment, and comparisons with Nazi propaganda, Adorno and Horkheimer viewed advertising and popular entertainment as standardized, artless, and manipulative. These products offered the general public cheap thrills that provided them with compensatory pleasures after a day at a dissatisfying job. Playing to consumers' emotional vulnerability, music, film, and advertising offered instant gratification without true satisfaction while helping them to tolerate unacceptable working conditions. In short, the culture industry is a form of mass manipulation that works to sell entertainment products while keeping the working masses happy, to discourage them from protesting poor wages and working conditions.

A long line of scholars has followed this basic idea, though with somewhat different foci. Thus, for example, economist John Kenneth

Galbraith (2000) argued that advertising played the same function of manipulation identified by Adorno and Horkheimer, but rather than seducing the masses into political apathy, it serves the function of convincing shoppers to buy new goods and hence to keep industry profitable. French social theorist Jean Baudrillard (1996, 2000) begins with a similar approach, arguing that advertising helps businesses solve the "realization problem," namely, how to sell the goods produced in order to keep businesses functioning and to reinvest sales revenue to make further profits. However, Baudrillard accords advertising a more central role in changing our culture. He argues that rather than focusing on the functional properties of goods (you need a dining-room table to eat dinner), advertising articulates their emotional or symbolic properties (you need a designer oak dining-room table to impress your family, co-workers, or romantic partner), thereby unleashing an endless process of consumption that has lost its connection to traditional forms of exchange (gifts, sharing) and only reflects a symbolic system that classifies goods into different categories. Further, products are no longer appealing for their individual properties; consumers only recognize them as part of a particular style, as in a living-room furniture set combined with specific colors of paint on the walls and other decorations. For Baudrillard, advertising has overtaken our culture and we are trapped in a world of symbols and the incessant need to consume.

More recent analyses focus on how the design of products, packaging, and advertising promotes the association between a product and emotional or sexual images (Haug 1986; Zukin 2004; Smart 2010), or examines how contemporary societies are increasingly organized around consumption rather than work (Lury 2011; Slater 1997). Hence, in order to be accepted by one's peers, it becomes necessary to consume at a certain level; otherwise individuals face rejection as "flawed" consumers (Bauman 2007).

Other scholars have criticized the manipulation thesis. Anthropologist Mary Douglas and economist Baron Isherwood (1996) developed one influential view. They argue that goods are a "communication system," and that most of our consumption is "ritualistic" – we consume to remain connected to others and to stay involved in the "information system." The goal of consumption is to maintain connections with family, friends, and others with whom we seek to develop ties. This view of consumption focuses on family dinners, weddings, funerals, and celebrations. These rituals allow individuals to find their place in the family or group, and to mark off stages in the life cycle. The authors suggest that the wealthiest group try to monopolize information about their consumption habits and tastes and retain an exclusive social circle for marriage and the exchange of information about employment. The wealthy discuss these crucial issues at consumption rituals. The middle class seek to gain access to these exclusive consumption circles because they know they can only gain power (jobs, prestige) by being part of these groups. The working class and poor, in contrast, try to keep consumption at equivalent levels in their group to maintain the network of support they need in the workplace and at home. Consumption is intimately tied to group membership.

In a distinct approach, Colin Campbell (2005) rejects the manipulation thesis for two reasons. First, he argues that this thesis distinguishes needs from desires, but there is no easy way to know what "basic" needs are because needs are always culturally defined in all societies. Second, he argues that advertising can persuade consumers to make purchases if it promotes images that are already appealing to the population. Hence, rather than manipulating consumers, advertisers use images that are appealing to consumers in order to convince them to make a purchase.

Another approach takes issue with the idea that individuals passively receive advertisements without critically evaluating them. Slater (1997) challenges the idea that consumers are "cultural dopes or dupes." He contends that individuals purchase products and services in response to their individual or cultural needs and dispositions, not merely because advertisers promoted a specific product to them. De Certeau (1984) and Fiske (2000) take a more assertive stance in this direction. De Certeau argued that producers and advertisers largely shape the landscape of goods and images available to consumers through what he calls "strategies," but consumers interpret and use these goods in their own ways through "tactics." The latter might entail using work materials to make products for one's own use or making a tribute video on YouTube. In his view, the consumers' unique interpretations and uses of goods are subtle forms of resistance to producers and advertisers. Miller (1987) offers a complementary argument noted in the introduction that individuals and groups appropriate goods and recontextualize their meanings, based on how they fit into their lives as well as the creative qualities they attach to these goods.

In a similar vein, scholars such as Fiske (2000), Nava (1997), and Rappaport (2001) emphasize the liberating aspects of consumption, especially for women. They argue that shopping and consumption, as domains that were not coded as "masculine" in the modern era, became the domain of women, and women gained status, satisfaction, and a degree of freedom by becoming skillful consumers.

Recent scholarship has moved beyond the debate regarding whether individuals are "active" or "passive" in relation to advertising. Leiss et al. (2005) argue that advertisers study society, recycle existing beliefs and practices, and broadcast those ideas back to society. They suggest that the importance of advertising lies not in whether or not it succeeds in selling particular goods; rather, it is significant because it has become integrated into our culture and affects how we view ourselves (compare Slater 2011).

Holt (2004) and Holt and Cameron (2010) similarly argue that successful advertising draws on existing beliefs and practices and reconfigures them in a way that resolves the psychological needs of specific groups of consumers. They contrast standard marketing practice that attaches specific physical or emotional qualities to a product based on statistical research to what they call "cultural strategy," whereby advertising "creatives" identify subcultures (groups whose consumption behaviors and beliefs set them apart from the mainstream) and utilize their lifestyles to construct campaigns that strike a "chord" with members of the subculture and a broader population affected by economic or cultural challenges. Hence, advertising recycles and reworks existing cultural practices in a manner that resolves psychological distress and uncertainty among specific social groups. Unlike Leiss et al. (2005), these authors assert that cultural strategy is indeed more effective at selling products. Both views, however, suggest that we understand advertising as the product of a dialogue between creative professionals and specific social groups.

Credit

Another major innovation in the early twentieth century was the development of consumer credit. Creditors needed to overcome religious and other traditional proscriptions against usury and the accumulation of debt. In reality, aristocrats had accumulated debts because of their free-spending practices in the early modern era (Sombart 1967; McCracken 1988), and the poor traditionally went into debt to storekeepers to purchase necessary goods (Strasser 1989), but during the nineteenth century, bourgeois attitudes discouraged the widespread accumulation of debt (Bell 1976; Williams 1982).

However, as wages rose after World War I, banks and retailers began extending credit to consumers in order to broaden the market for consumer durables, such as appliances and cars, beyond a small elite and develop an additional earning stream from interest payments. Today, it would be impossible to imagine a world of consumption without credit as so many of our expenses involve short- and long-term loans. Critics of consumer debt point out that it undermines consumers' capacity to save and that it may not be sustainable at the individual level should individuals face unemployment or illness. Authors further contend that traditional emphases on thrift and the transfer of property across generations have been undermined by consumers' long-term indebtedness. Nonetheless, even after major economic downturns, such as the mortgage meltdown of 2007–9, the growth of consumer debt continues unabated. Further, formal credit has recently expanded in countries of the Global South through creditors' use of sophisticated data analysis techniques to rate customers' credit worthiness (Bell 1976; Leach 1993; Manning 2000; Ossandon 2013; Baudrillard 1996; Smart 2010; Schor 1998).

However, patterns of credit use vary cross-nationally. As Garon (2006) argues, Japan had a long history, dating back to the seventeenth century, in which political leaders and later citizens' groups promoted thrift and saving. Until the late 1950s, popular attitudes and government initiatives discouraged excessive spending and encouraged saving. Although Japan was occupied by the U.S. after World War II, Japanese leaders looked to European countries' emphasis on austerity and savings in the early postwar era. It was not until the 1960s that the government encouraged citizens to purchase consumer durables, but, even then, they encouraged a balance between spending and saving, which led Japan to retain one of the highest savings rates in the world.

However, Japanese consumers did use installment payments throughout the twentieth century, though they only began to use revolving credit in the 1980s and most debt is paid in full on a monthly basis. After the 1970s, the Japanese savings rate declined, while its use of credit was higher than other wealthy countries. If we compare total purchases, credit use, and savings, the English-speaking countries (the U.S., U.K., and New Zealand) are the biggest spenders and lowest savers, while Japan's patterns of savings, spending, and debt are much more in line with the relatively austere patterns in continental Europe. Hence, Japan looks more like the "norm" in terms of savings and credit use than does the U.S. (Gordon 2006; Horioka 2006).

Branding and New Retail Channels

Historian Susan Strasser (1989) describes the complex process through which branded goods gained dominance in the U.S. marketplace after the Civil War. With the huge expansion of production made possible by advances in science and technology and their application to industry, large companies sought new outlets for selling this surplus of goods. Their main strategy was to build brands that could differentiate them from competitors and thus yield premium profits. The process of branding was aided by an 1890 court decision that allowed companies to patent trademarks and hence sue competitors for imitating their logos or products. This decision gave brand-name producers a decisive edge in the market and, through advertising, their products gained widespread recognition.

However, large brands confronted a distribution system in which local storeowners and regional wholesalers had considerable power based on their personal relationships with one another and with customers. Wholesalers often had their own suppliers for goods and sold these products to storeowners on credit. Hence, neither wholesaler nor retailer had an incentive to recommend specific brands. Furthermore, storeowners provided customers with credit and recommended products that offered them the highest profit margins. Brands, in contrast, sought to capture the lion's share of profits and hence offered local stores small margins.

Large companies used numerous strategies to compete with wholesalers and encourage storeowners to sell and recommend their products. Brands advertised their products, offered customers premiums ("special gifts") along with products or in exchange for trading stamps/company packages, offered storeowners bonuses, and decorated store windows with branded goods. Small storeowners were initially reluctant to promote branded goods, though these stores eventually had to adapt to competition from department stores, chain stores, and mail order catalogs, all of which offered lower prices as well as freedom from traditional haggling. However, the stores and wholesalers mobilized politically to block mail order sales and restrict chain store expansion, though they ultimately failed. Branded goods and larger retailers gained the lion's share of the market, as described in this chapter, but Strasser's analysis demonstrates traditional wholesalers' and retailers' powerful resistance to modern branding and retailing.

In addition to resistance from wholesalers and storeowners, large manufacturers needed to explain to customers how to use new goods and convince them to purchase branded goods they had produced on their own in previous generations. Hence, for example, Gillette had to convince men to purchase razors and shave themselves rather than go to the barbershop, and Kodak had to provide the contexts in which people might use a camera (like a vacation), since this was a new invention. Strasser (1989) argues that the introduction of new products in the late nineteenth and early twentieth centuries significantly influenced everyday routines as they became part of new habits and attitudes.

The Rise of the Department Store

The expansion of advertising, marketing, and consumer credit coincided with numerous innovations in the retail sector, as noted above. The first such change was the rise of the modern department store. Most historians argue that the Bon Marché, which opened in Paris in 1852, was the world's first department store, though this was followed by many others in France, England, the U.S., Australia, Canada, New Zealand, Argentina, Turkey, Japan, and China. In Paris, the department store coincided with another retail invention that impressed many observers at the time – arcades. The arcades were semi-enclosed pathways in Paris that included several individual shops. Writer Charles Baudelaire and social theorist Walter Benjamin marveled at the popularity of the arcades and how they captivated the imaginations of many upper-class Parisians. Both authors discuss a new social type, the *flâneur*, or wanderer – an upper-class gentleman who walks through the arcades, drawing on his imagination as he contemplates the goods behind glass. We can associate this image with the modern practice of "window shopping" and underscore these authors' observations that modern shopping is not simply the practice of buying products, but also involves imagining oneself as the owner of a product that one may not buy. Further, these authors link modern shopping with the rise of *individual* identities that are not strictly governed by tradition (membership in nuclear or extended families) or given social roles (such as gender, membership in a medieval estate). Both of these phenomena are still important elements of shopping (Slater 1997; Williams 1982; Leach 1993; Smart 2010; Guy 2012; Tokatli and Boyaci 1999).

The arcades prefigured more lasting retail changes. Large department stores grew alongside industrial production and urbanization. Indeed, the major department stores emerged initially in the larger cities of Europe and the U.S., following suit in Asia and parts of the Global South. As William Leach (1993) describes, U.S. department store owners imitated key elements of the medieval church to attract customers – "glass, color, and light." Early department stores also attempted to attract customers with live music performances, elaborate decorations, art showings, and restaurants (see also Williams 1982; Young 1999).

In her analysis of nineteenth-century consumption in France, historian Rosalind Williams (1982) sees department stores as part of a "consumer revolution." Before the French Revolution, the king, his court, and the nobility shaped fashion as a means of political rule. Courtly consumption, much as Sombart (1967) and McCracken (1988) argued, entailed the use of luxury goods and participation in ostentatious parties. After the French Revolution of 1789 ended royal authority, the aristocracy was no longer the chief source of political authority; nor did its members serve as fashion leaders. Furthermore, industry produced goods cheaply and in large quantities, making them accessible to businessmen and working people. Hence, Williams argues that France experienced the "democratization of luxury" whereby the general population sought to emulate the courtly model.

In her reading, world's fairs, department stores, photographs, films (in the early twentieth century), and promotional posters all communicated the idea that dreams of wealth, beauty, and sexual desirability could be achieved through consumption. In this context, four models of consumption emerged. The bourgeois (business owners) sought to imitate the aristocracy, but could not fully live as the nobility did because they lacked the resources to live a life of leisure or accumulate massive debts. The working class could purchase cheap imitations of the goods the bourgeois enjoyed, and they could also imagine they were wealthy by visiting stores or using credit via installment plans. These were the dominant modes of consumption.

Two models of consumption offered critiques of bourgeois and mass consumption. Dandies, or aristocratic men, criticized bourgeois conformism and sought to develop authentic individual lifestyles that rejected popularly used goods. Additionally, commercial artists created the decorative arts movement, designing goods and buildings that were useful to the general population but also beautiful, thereby bringing art to the masses. For Williams, none of these four models allowed consumers to avoid seeking identities through consumption.

Williams's account of the nineteenth-century class system in relation to department stores and other arenas of consumption contrasts with a large body of work focused on women's consumption. The first department stores played a significant role in women's increasing involvement in modern consumption. In the mid-nineteenth century, middle- and upper-class women in Europe and the U.S. were unlikely to venture outdoors without other male family members due to the prevailing view that women's presence in public implied their sexual freedom, which was shameful to themselves and their families. Department stores helped change these attitudes by offering unaccompanied women a "safe" environment, including female-only "rest areas" near bathrooms. Hence, several scholars argue that department stores facilitated the expansion of women's freedoms (women could not vote in most European countries and the U.S. until the late nineteenth and early twentieth centuries) (Rappaport 2001; Zukin 2004; Fiske 2000; Milestone and Meyer 2012).

Women's participation in consumer culture had important consequences. Women's involvement in modern shopping created a "moral panic" manifest in men's public statements in news editorials that women's presence in public was leading to moral decline in society. Indeed, some women were caught shoplifting at department stores, and they often claimed that the temptation to steal beautiful objects under glass was too great to resist. These concerns made their way into modern psychology, which classified shoplifting as a psychological "addiction" known as "kleptomania." Further, because upper-income women depended on their husbands for income (inheritance laws restricted women's access to family money), they could only shop alone if they used their husbands' credit. These purchases often led to legal disputes between husbands and storeowners, and the courts frequently ruled in favor of the stores, arguing that women were not legally responsible for their husbands' debts. In this regard, storeowners colluded with women against their husbands' wishes. Many of these concerns subsided over time as a greater percentage of women began to earn incomes and societal attitudes softened about women's presence in public (Leach 1993; Rappaport 2001).

However, one enduring effect of this period was the view of consumption as a female activity. We assume today that women "know how to shop" and "enjoy shopping," in part because we see women and consumption as fundamentally connected. This idea emerges from Enlightenment-era ideas about gender, associating men with rationality and production, and women with emotions and consumption. Implicit in this view is the idea that production is important and meaningful, while consumption is trivial, and consumption decisions are based on "whims" and "fancies." The idea of consumption as female, irrational, and trivial is still prevalent today. It should be obvious that women are not the only consumers, and that viewing consumption as trivial tends to trivialize women by association. Contemporary historians and cultural studies scholars have challenged these assumptions by arguing that shopping expanded women's freedoms and that women exercise a great deal of skill in making shopping decisions. We return to some of these issues in chapter 5 (Slater 1997; Miller 1998; Milestone and Meyer 2012; Zukin 2004).

Department stores were an important departure from street peddling and public markets in that they were enclosed, attempted to provide an image of order, and were owned by a single person or family rather than housing numerous independent vendors. These stores introduced the "one-price system" so that shoppers did not have to haggle with sales personnel, relied on low-cost labor, used a "high turnover" model in which employees quickly replaced depleted stocks with new goods, and used the division of stores into departments to monitor sales in each section. These innovations made the stores much more profitable than small, independent stores (Strasser 1989).

Another significant feature of department stores, until they were supplanted by shopping malls as the primary retail form for manufactured goods after World War II, was how each chain became identified with the city where it was located. Many of the "anchor" stores in downtown areas, such as Bloomingdale's and Macy's in New York and Marshall Field's in Chicago, became associated with the identities of these cities. Due to their location in the business and government centers of cities, the varied entertainment they offered, and their owners' active civic role, these stores came to wield an important influence on urban economic development, social issues, and major public events (such as the 1893 Columbian Exposition in Chicago and the annual Macy's Thanksgiving Day parade broadcast on television). Hence, department stores' economic growth depended on growing city populations and the increasing wealth of some, but they also affected the economic and cultural character of major cities, at least until World War II (Zukin 2004; Leach 1993).

As noted above, while we often associate department stores with Europe and the U.S., these stores also have an extensive history in different parts of East Asia and the Global South. Indeed, during the late nineteenth century in the European section of Istanbul, Turkey, the Bon Marché, British "high-street" clothing chains, and local department stores opened (Tokatli and Boyaci 1999). Shortly thereafter, local and multinational stores opened in China, Australia, New Zealand, Canada, Japan, China, Argentina, and Chile (Smart 2010; Guy 2012; Salcedo 2003; Young 1999). In many of these countries, the stores catered to a small economic elite, but, nonetheless, they had an important effect on the subsequent history of the retail sector.

Louise Young's (1999) analysis of department stores in Japan illustrates how stores varied cross-nationally. In Japan, department stores developed in the 1920s to cater to a growing middle class, in contrast to their appeal to a broad cross-section of the population in the U.S. (Leach 1993) and France (Williams 1982). New stores provided capital to construct new railway terminals, so that the stores could locate there and capture commuters in contrast to their free-standing location in the center of U.S. cities. Young describes the stores as "hybrid" forms in that they imported Western styles of shopping and recreational activity, but they did so in the context of local material and non-material culture. For example, the stores sold modern styles of kimonos, a traditional article of clothing for women. Japanese department stores borrowed elements from their Western counterparts and combined them with local cultural ideas and practices.

In another example, the three main department store chains in Chile are locally owned and were founded in the early twentieth century. These three chains still dominate the market, and U.S. (Sears, J.C. Penney) and Brazilian (Muricy) chains that attempted to enter the market failed. In Chile, the locally owned chains have become so successful since the 1980s that they have opened banks and travel agencies and set up shop in neighboring countries. Hence, it is crucial to examine the diverse forms of modern retail across national and regional contexts (Salcedo 2003).

Discount and Grocery Stores

Another significant change in the early twentieth-century U.S. was the rise of the discount store and the supermarket, both utilizing the new model of "self-service." Woolworths, Walgreen's, and other "five-and-dime" stores sought to take advantage of a mass market rather than the middle and upper classes that department stores targeted. By reducing the role of store personnel, they were able to decrease their operating costs and hence pass on savings to shoppers. Discount stores thus demand more effort from consumers, but also free them from sometimes unwanted entanglements with store personnel who may use "hard-sell" tactics to earn commissions.

These stores and larger supermarkets profoundly affected the retail landscape in the U.S. and Europe by reducing the market share of public markets (selling fresh food and produce), flea markets (selling manufactured new and used goods), and street peddlers that had previously supplied urban populations. This also meant that the intimate, personal, and sometimes complicated social interactions between vendors and customers faded away in much of Europe and the U.S. during the twentieth century (Strasser 1989; Zukin 2004; D'Andrea et al. 2004; Bowlby 2001; Lehtonen and Mäenpää 1997).

The process of establishing the self-service and "single-price" systems was complex, developed unevenly across societies, and involved considerable experimentation with different forms of store organization and technology. In his analysis of U.S. grocery stores from the 1930s to the 1950s, Cochoy (2011) describes the process of trial and error through which professionals writing in the *Progressive Grocer* journal sought to help small grocers modernize their stores. The professionals attempted to teach grocers how to expand their customer base and increase customers' purchases by redesigning stores. There was a gradual shift from the old model in which customers would line up at a counter and request goods, to the self-service model in which customers select goods on their own. Stores wanted to free customers' movement and increase their impulse purchases but also control theft. They used numerous technologies to free customers' movement and give them direct access to goods, such as shopping carts, shelving, and packaging. Conversely, they added technologies to reduce theft, since now goods were not "behind the counter." These included one-way turnstiles that allowed customers' in but controlled their exit, and the placement of cash registers by the door to allow employees to watch departing customers and prevent theft. Freeing customers' movement and access to goods while controlling their exits was ultimately highly profitable, and may have served as a prototype for large suburban supermarkets. Cochoy demonstrates that the physical layout of stores and goods can importantly influence the behavior of customers and store personnel. Bowlby (2001) brings this story up to date by exploring how stores developed computerized codes to monitor each customer's purchases through data analysis rather than individual human observation.

The relatively smooth introduction of self-service in the U.S. (though small, independent retailers battled unsuccessfully against catalog sellers and chain stores) contrasts with the experience in Britain. As Du Gay (2004) argues, British retailers attempted to adopt self-service after World War II but met with numerous challenges. First, government price policies meant that stores could not use the labor efficiencies promised with self-service to reduce prices and hence increase sales volume. Second, middle-class shoppers disliked self-service because they expected store personnel to take care of them. Hence, self-service was mainly used in bargain chains whose shoppers had little to lose by shopping at these stores. Third, many shoppers accustomed to being directed by store personnel to the goods they sought were disoriented by self-service. Hence, stores hired hostesses to direct customers, thereby diluting the model of self-service. Du Gay concludes that we cannot assume that technological changes like self-service are "inevitable" as they develop differently and to varying degrees in a wide range of societies. Self-service expanded much more rapidly in the U.S. and Sweden than in the U.K. because of specific government policies and customer attitudes in Britain.

Kjellberg's (2007) analysis of the Swedish wholesale food industry after World War II identifies similar challenges. In an effort to cut costs, a large wholesaler attempted to replace their salesmen – who traditionally filled orders at retail outlets – with order forms for retailers to complete, to cut the time and labor involved with securing orders for goods. When the wholesaler adopted the "new system," both the wholesalers' "contact men" and the retailers reverted to their old behaviors in spite of the new order forms. The British and Swedish cases reviewed here suggest that policies, consumer cultures, and the routines and technologies embedded in market transactions may short-circuit business managers' efforts to create more "rational" procedures that they believe will generate larger profits.

Today, discount retailing has become a massive and global phenomenon. Walmart is the largest private employer in the U.S. and the largest company in the world. Other large discounters such as Target, Costco, Tesco, and Aldi also have an important global presence. Scholars argue that Walmart has gained significant influence over manufacturers. Since Walmart is such a large distributor of manufactured products, they can pressure manufacturers to reduce their prices. Their policies increased the supply of inexpensive goods to consumers (especially in the U.S.) but also had catastrophic effects on the quality of work life for industrial workers. This is so because manufacturers often need to cut wages and benefits, lay off workers, or may even go bankrupt as a result of efforts to meet Walmart's low buying price (Zukin 2004; Smith 2004; Applebaum and Lichtenstein 2006).

Walmart increasingly uses international suppliers, especially in low-cost locations like China and Bangladesh. U.S. and European manufacturers cannot compete with firms from these countries because wages, benefits, and health-and-safety laws make production much more expensive in the Global North. On the other hand, the wages and health-and-safety violations in these low-cost locations have led to embarrassing scandals for companies like Walmart after activists demanded that these companies take responsibility for tragedies at their supplier factories (this occurred in 2012 and 2013 when major fires and building collapses in Bangladeshi clothing factories led to the deaths of hundreds of workers). Large companies are very concerned about maintaining a positive public image and hence scandals like these represent opportunities for activists to call for greater economic justice for their employees and the companies they do business with, as we explore in chapter 9 (Applebaum and Lichtenstein 2006; Hussein 2013).

Some also argue that Walmart specifically targets geographic areas with small independent stores for their new operations, in order to wipe out the competition and capture the market. Rather than locating solely in large metropolitan areas (cities and suburbs), Walmart often identifies a twenty-five or fifty-mile radius in rural areas that managers perceive are "underserved" before building new stores there. Critics accuse Walmart of "dumping" products on the market for less than their wholesale cost for a short time, until they have bankrupted the local "mom-and-pop" operations, and then raising prices (Smith 2004).

Finally, unions and workers' organizations have criticized Walmart's labor policies. They argue that Walmart discriminates against women (passing them up for promotions), offers employees inadequate health insurance (forcing them to use Medicaid, which drains public resources), pays employees the minimum wage unless they are in supervisory positions, limits job security through the use of temporary employment, and keeps unions out of the workplace. States have sued Walmart over its health insurance policy, a million women filed a class action suit against the company for gender discrimination (which the U.S. Supreme Court heard and dismissed), and as I write this chapter (during the summer of 2013), Walmart workers are on strike in several cities in the U.S. Hence, several groups have criticized its low-cost strategies. These criticisms echo those made at the beginning of the twentieth century in the U.S. by small retailers, political reformers, and labor activists against chain stores and supermarkets (Rosen 2006; Nguyen 2013; Berfield 2013; Strasser 1989, 2006).

Notwithstanding these criticisms, some authors and commentators commend companies like Walmart for keeping prices low and hence making many products available to low-income consumers. They also applaud the company's organizational and technological innovations. They argue that Walmart is able to keep products cheap because its databases allow the company to identify the least expensive suppliers and to only purchase products that consumers are buying in large numbers: it is the epitome of a lean, efficient corporation. Others suggest that Walmart is such a large retailer because many poor people have no other place to shop and hence the company has filled an important market niche. In this regard, Walmart has contributed to the "democratization of consumption" whereby low-income citizens gain access to popular appliances and comforts such as large-screen televisions, video-game consoles, or attractive clothing (Zukin 2004; Smith 2004).

Shopping Malls

Shopping malls, which are today fixtures in the Global North and increasingly in the Global South, originated in the U.S. after World War II. The mall's development reflected a major shift in U.S. federal government housing and transportation policies that jump-started the growth of the suburbs. While the first suburbs emerged in the early twentieth century, massive suburbanization began after World War II. The startling growth of single-family dwellings in the outskirts of cities resulted from banking policies begun during the 1930s. Because of the Great Depression following the 1929 stock-market crash, government officials looked for ways to reactivate the construction industry and to make home mortgages more widely available. Prior to the 1930s, banks only provided mortgages to the wealthy because they feared that those with lower incomes might default on loans. Those who did not qualify for mortgages had to save money and buy their homes outright.

In order to reduce banks' risks, the federal government first created a system of home-mortgage insurance through the Home Owners' Loan Corporation (HOLC). The HOLC and later the Federal Housing Authority (FHA) agreed to pay back loans to private banks in case of foreclosures. With federal support, banks began to lend money more widely. Further, after World War II, the GI Bill and the Veterans' Administration provided many veterans with guaranteed mortgages that did not require down-payments. The loan guarantees

and easy lending terms coincided with overcrowding and deteriora-
tion in cities. Thus, the 1950s witnessed a massive exodus to the
suburbs that has continued until today. However, until the 1970s,
banks used discriminatory practices to deny mortgages to members
of racial and ethnic minority groups. The rise of a massive suburban
population created a market for shopping malls (Dreier et al. 2004;
Satterthwaite 2001; Duany et al. 2010; Cohen 2003).

Furthermore, after the war, federal transportation policy shifted
from a focus on urban and inter-urban public transit (trains, trolleys,
and buses) to a massive highway building program. The Highway
Act of 1956 created a trust fund financed by gas taxes that under-
wrote the construction of the U.S. federal highway system. The law
reflected the influence of the "highway lobby" (the auto, tire, road
construction, and oil industries) on transit policy. The creation of
highways facilitated the design of automobile-accessible enclosed
shopping centers (Dreier et al. 2004; Satterthwaite 2001; Duany et
al. 2010; Cohen 2003).

Victor Gruen, the designer of some of the first shopping malls in
suburban New Jersey and New York, viewed them as the new "civic
centers" that would serve the same functions as the streets and parks
of urban downtowns. While malls attract large crowds, they are not
genuine public spaces. First, malls are privately owned, which means
that managers can restrict political speech much more than can city
authorities in parks. Malls' private ownership allows them to "screen"
customers and customer behavior, excluding individuals and groups
whom mall authorities believe deter the more affluent shoppers they
seek to attract. This screening is most evident in the exclusion of pan-
handling and curfews for teens, some of whom engage in horseplay
that other adult shoppers find annoying or offensive. Furthermore,
because most U.S.-based malls are primarily accessible via automo-
bile and located in suburbs that for several decades were closed to
members of minority groups, they indirectly exclude poor and minority residents (Cohen 2003; Staeheli and Mitchell 2006).

Sociologists have developed distinct interpretations of malls' significance as consumption sites and quasi-public settings. Some authors
emphasize malls' appealing designs, arguing that, much like the
Paris arcades Walter Benjamin described, these settings encourage
consumers to adopt a dreamlike attitude that allows them to imagine
themselves as owners of goods at the mall. In this regard, malls discourage social interaction among strangers. In a similar vein, authors
following the ideas of Jean Baudrillard argue that malls use recognizable and appealing symbols or *signs*, such as palm trees, carousels, or

brand-name logos, allowing them to seduce consumers into making purchases. Here, malls discourage consumers from exercising self-control (Gottdiener 1997; Goss 1999; Lehtonen and Mäenpää 1997).

Others focus on mall managers' surveillance of customers via security guards and cameras. Building on the discussions of malls as pseudo-public spaces noted above, these authors argue that mall managers exercise control over customers' behavior, and that consumers often internalize these controls. Controls can be direct, such as the use of security personnel; or indirect, through the design of hallways and stores that encourage visitors to walk by as many stores or products as possible, and the use of lighting and ambient music (much like department stores) to create a calm environment for consumers. This argument suggests that mall managers seek to minimize any spontaneous behaviors that might frighten or annoy shoppers, and to guide shoppers' behavior in a manner that encourages them to spend money (Staeheli and Mitchell 2006; Matthews et al. 2000).

A third perspective examines shoppers' attitudes and behaviors. These authors have a somewhat more positive view of the ways that mall visitors use these settings for their own purposes. Scholars note that two groups – teens and the elderly – use malls primarily as social settings rather than to spend money. While mall managers are not happy that large groups of people use these settings without spending money, they fear that directly confronting these groups might deter other shoppers. Further, others, following the work of Michel de Certeau (1984), note that visitors may chart out their own pathways in malls, which do not necessarily reflect owners' goals (Miller et al. 1998; Lewis 1989, 1990; Ortiz 1994). For example, Stillerman and Salcedo (2012) found that some mall visitors in Santiago, Chile, brought picnic lunches to the food court, teens rode skateboards in the mall, and other individuals who were not store employees sold small items to mall visitors. All of these activities are officially prohibited, but mall authorities turn a blind eye to them. These authors argue that visitors convert malls into meaningful spaces, or *places*, through their everyday actions of *appropriation* (they use the mall much as they would use a park or a subway car).

Many authors view the U.S. regional suburban mall, or "destination malls" (very large tourist-oriented malls such as the Mall of America or the West Edmonton mall), as prototypes for malls around the world (Gottdiener 1997; Goss 1999; Shields 1989). There is some truth to this perspective insofar as shopping centers build on ideas from the original malls in the U.S. as well as the technologies and management styles of successful American shopping centers. Similarly, many authors look at the global spread of U.S. and European retail formats (shopping malls, big-box supermarkets, and other large chains, as well as fast-food chains, for example) to argue that retail formats as well as consumer attitudes and behaviors are becoming more standardized around the world (Ritzer 2003; Smart 2010).

However, there are some significant differences between the retail landscapes in different nations and regions. Malls in the U.S. and Europe have distinct histories. Michelle Lowe (2000) argues that malls in the U.K. are much more integrated into their local urban environments than their U.S. counterparts. In the 1960s, British citizens rejected many proposals for new mall development because they wanted to avoid creating isolated malls that drained customers and resources from cities. Hence, malls have become town centers that are well integrated with other forms of retail and entertainment in regional cities, and are well connected to public transportation in large cities like London. Similarly, Lehtonen and Mäenpää (1997) contend that, traditionally, malls in Helsinki, Finland, were built in low-income suburbs with high rates of unemployment, but were highly successful. A newer mall built in the 1980s was well connected to downtown Helsinki via public transportation and included a variety of public services. These cases suggest that some European malls are less segregated from downtowns and poor populations than their U.S. counterparts.

Countries located in the Global South present a distinct scenario. There, supermarkets and malls still compete with public markets, street markets, and small independent markets for consumers. Hence, even in countries that are developing rapidly (like Turkey, Chile, or India), street markets, bazaars, and small local stores still sell a significant portion (and in some cases a majority) of all food and personal items, especially to their large poor populations. The experience of shopping in a street market is different from going to a grocery store or mall in that haggling may occur, informal credit is often available to those without debit or credit cards, vendors may develop a regular clientele with whom they have close personal ties, there is little surveillance via cameras or security guards, and there are fewer design features that channel consumer behavior – these markets are more spontaneous than supermarkets or malls (D'Andrea et al. 2004; Stillerman 2006, 2008, 2012; Stillerman and Salcedo 2012; Bromley 1998; Dokmeci et al. 2006).

The presence of street markets, street peddlers, flea markets, bazaars, and other forms of informal (untaxed) and semi-formal retail reflects shopping traditions, government policies (governments subsidized or supported street markets in some countries to provide the population with cheap food), and the absence of adequate employment, which forced poor residents to "invent" their own jobs. In the early 1970s, Keith Hart first coined the term "informal sector" to describe the large population of street vendors in Accra, Ghana. Later, researchers at the International Labor Organization (an arm of the United Nations), particularly Victor Tokman, studied informal retail occupations and small family-owned manufacturers. While this segment of economic activity forms the largest portion of the economy in many countries of the Global South, it is also present in wealthier nations in the guise of street peddlers, street musicians, and other small-scale occupations, especially in larger cities (Gilbert 1998; Portes 1994; Tanenbaum 1995; Belk et al. 1988; Sherry 1990a, 1990b).

In addition to diversifying the retail formats available to consumers, the large-scale presence of informal markets in many cities and towns of the Global South also affects the cultural landscape of shopping areas and the capacity of modern retailers (supermarkets, big-box stores, and malls) to screen shoppers as effectively as they do in the Global North. The presence of street markets reflects the persistence of shopping traditions with locally based cultural roots. Thus, shoppers may find bazaars, street markets, or traditional coffee houses "cheek-by-jowl" with malls or supermarkets, and the latter may seek to imitate these traditional formats in order to capture their regular clientele (Abaza 2001; Sandikci and Omeraki 2007).

Further, street vendors (when police allow them to do so) intentionally locate near the entrances of malls and supermarkets to tap into the large flow of customers. Additionally, shoppers may visit both traditional and modern retail areas and engage in comparison shopping between the two. This pattern of shopping is facilitated by the presence of public transit in many of the world's cities and the close proximity of malls and supermarkets to mixed-income residential areas (Anjaria 2008; Stillerman and Salcedo 2012).

Finally, religious traditions and debates affect the nature and clientele of malls. In Turkey, where a secular state dominated for much of the twentieth century but most of the population is Muslim, until recently, middle-class secular shoppers discouraged Muslim women wearing headscarves from entering malls (Gökarıksel 2012). In Dubai, developers have built "she-malls" for women only, so that Muslim women can remove their headscarves and feel comfortable. However, these malls have not been successful and secular women prefer Western-style malls (Baldauf 2008). Finally, Abaza (2001) found that teens in Cairo, Egypt, may go on dates at malls since they can remain anonymous and avoid the scrutiny of their religious parents. Hence, in specific political and religious contexts, mall managers and consumers may generate gender- and religious-based segregation.

What does this mean for the nature of shopping? First, the automobile-centered mall and supermarket we are accustomed to in the U.S. are much more accessible to pedestrians in many areas of Europe and the Global South, and hence the profile of shoppers is more diverse than in the U.S. Second, it is far more difficult for store authorities to control shopper behavior and screen customers in mixed-income settings in the Global South. Third, the retail environment in developing world cities and towns continues to be much more diverse than in the Global North, retaining important traditional features that give a different quality and experience to shopping, and provide a distinct employment setting for many vendors. Finally, malls respond to religious attitudes and conflicts in countries with large Muslim populations, while religious and secular consumers may self-segregate across different malls.

Conclusion

In this chapter, we have explored the rise of modern consumption in the Global North, and increasingly in the Global South. The early modern commercial revolution inaugurated the idea that *individuals* could engage in self-expression, seek pleasure, and develop unique identities via consumption. Large-scale trade, industrialization, and urbanization made modern manufactured goods available to the general population, beginning the process of the democratization of consumption that has continued in the Global North and to some degree in the Global South. However, the category of "consumer" resulted from country-specific political debates and conflicts and has varied across time and space.

The late nineteenth and early twentieth centuries witnessed major changes in advertising, branding, marketing, retail, and credit. Advertising and marketing began as means to inform consumers of the existence of a given product or firm. With the expansion of communications technologies and research on consumers, advertising and marketing became more sophisticated and successful means to persuade consumers to buy goods or services. Advertisers targeted groups of consumers with increasing precision, and manufacturers gained greater knowledge of their target markets.

Branding began in tandem with advertising and was initially designed to reassure customers of the quality of a given firm's products. By the end of World War II, branding became increasingly integrated with advertising and marketing and the brand's "message" focused more on the emotional states advertisers could associate with a given product. Consumer credit also became an increasingly important means to broaden the base of consumers who could afford a range of goods, though its forms varied cross-nationally.

While sales in the marketplace originated thousands of years ago, modern retail broke with traditional forms of sales in important ways. Unlike the street market, bazaar, or agora, which mixed commerce and politics, were largely open and public spaces, and involved intense haggling between sellers and buyers, the modern department store, supermarket, discount and grocery stores brought distinct features. Department stores sought to attract women through appealing designs, service, entertainment, and a sense of security in a society that still discouraged them from going out in public alone. Supermarkets and discount stores created inexpensive self-service formats that effectively competed against independent retailers, street hawkers, and public markets in the U.S. and to a lesser extent in Europe. The process of "creative destruction" is still evident today as retail giants like Walmart mow down their competition and pressure suppliers to reduce costs.

Finally, shopping malls emerged as an adjunct to growing suburbs in the U.S. Their automobile-centered designs and close surveillance of customers closed them off to significant portions of the population from outside the U.S. suburbs. Like other modern retail forms, malls are enclosed spaces with careful interior designs built to control the flow of customers, and are thus less open and spontaneous than traditional markets. The pattern was distinct in Europe, where shopping malls are better integrated into cities and better connected with urban public transit.

The story of retail development is distinct in poor and middle-income countries of the Global South. Unlike the Global North, street markets, flea markets, and itinerant vendors have retained an important share of the market even as Western-style retail has grown. The juxtaposition of traditional and modern retail in developing world cities creates a distinct shopping environment and a different social setting for modern retail spaces. Shoppers participate in diverse "genres" of shopping (Miller 1997), modern retailers compete against street and flea markets, and many modern retailers are more accessible to a broader cross-section of the population than in the U.S. suburbs. The greater accessibility of supermarkets and malls to pedestrians and those arriving via public transit mean that many malls in the Global South are less able to screen out and exclude lower-income customers than in the U.S. Hence, while modern retailers have "gone global," these stores and malls must adapt to the particularities of the local environment. We return to the phenomenon of globalization in the next chapter as part of a broader consideration of how advertising, marketing, branding, credit, and shopping have changed since the 1960s.

3

Market Fragmentation and Globalization

In 2013, more than a billion people purchased smartphones worldwide, setting an all-time record (International Data Corporation 2014). This means that approximately one in seven people in the world owns a smartphone (U.S. Census Bureau 2014). These devices allow individuals to surf the Internet; promote or "like" products on Facebook; tweet to their friends; share photos on Pinterest, Instagram, or tumblr; make purchases online; read restaurant reviews on sites like Yelp!; watch movies through free and subscriber sites such as Netflix or Hulu; listen to music; and engage in many other activities.

The experience of watching television has also changed in recent decades. Gone are the days of sitting with the family to watch a variety show, favorite sitcom, or sports game. Today, viewers subscribe to cable or satellite television, some own a digital video recorder that allows them to fast-forward through commercials or watch shows at convenient times, and others may consume all of their television content via the Internet or a DVD player, effectively opting out of television schedules. Music listening is highly individualized and fragmented, as much music is consumed in digital form, via a portable device, and alone. It is now less common than in the past for teenagers to sit with friends in a basement, bedroom, or living room to listen to records.

Each of these changes reflects the very rapid innovations in communications technologies in recent decades and their implications for the diversity of goods accessible to consumers, the complex means by which we learn about and purchase goods, the tendency of tastes and consumption to become more personalized, and the increasing isolation of some forms of consumption. This chapter considers these and other changes in a global context. Some of these technologies and consumption routines have "traveled" to the Global South, but consumers there have adopted them in distinctive ways, and the flows of goods and images often move across the traditional East–West and North–South divides through which we are accustomed to classifying the world.

Before considering recent changes in advertising, marketing, retail, credit, and consumer practices, we must first explore several explanations of these shifts. Different scholars argue that distinct changes in economic structure, cultural attitudes, and technology gave rise to a new model of consumption, though we view these perspectives as complementing one another rather than representing opposing viewpoints. Let us first consider changes among consumers and how they have "bubbled up" into marketing, product design, and retail, before analyzing large-scale structural changes in economy and technology.

The Emergence of Lifestyle-based Consumption

As noted in the previous chapter, several authors argue that post-World War II consumption was increasingly standardized across social groups in countries such as the U.S., France, Germany, and Japan. We can find illustrations of this view in the prototype of the American suburban subdivision with similar houses, a homogeneous white, middle-class population, and generally similar lifestyles. Other examples from popular culture might include well-known television shows from the 1950s like *Leave It to Beaver* or *Father Knows Best*, portraying the prototypical suburban white family engaging in middle-class consumer behavior. Further examples are well-known brands that dominated the market in the first two decades after the war, such as Kraft, Lucky Strike, and Chevrolet (Schor 1998; Cohen 2003; Haug 1986; Baudrillard 1996; Leiss et al. 2005; Holt 2004; Gordon 2006; Horioka 2006).

In recent decades, consumer lifestyles have diversified considerably, while the array of products and services on offer has changed in parallel fashion. In the U.S., since the early 1980s, an important segment of the middle classes has moved back from the suburbs to cities in search of an "authentic" experience or more "diversity" than might be found in the suburbs. It would be difficult to identify a single television show watched by diverse age, gender, class, and racial groups because of the sheer variety of television stations available, the rapid discontinuation of series, and the diverse types of shows on offer. Today, entire stations are dedicated to "foodies," "history buffs," sports fans, or "art film" aficionados, for example. Individuals can watch an entire series on DVD or online years after it ended. Finally, while brands and branding have increased in importance, it would be difficult to identify a single brand that one could associate with a given product line, like cheese, cigarettes, and cars, as in the examples above (Klein 2010; Jhally 1990; Holt and Cameron 2010; Lury 2011).

One explanation of these changes looks to the 1960s counterculture. Hippies and other members of the youth counterculture in the Global North challenged the styles and attitudes associated with standardized mass consumption of the postwar era. While their penchant for used, inexpensive, and craft goods might suggest that hippies had an anti-consumption ethic, this first impression is deceptive.

The youth counterculture developed a set of attitudes and practices that focused on individual self-expression, authenticity, nonconformism, and a rejection of standardization. While members of these movements framed this ethic as a criticism of conspicuous consumption and its focus on gaining social status, its main emphasis was on rejecting the older generation's conformity to social expectations.

Several authors suggest that the counterculture had the unanticipated effect of promoting a new model of product design, advertising, and consumption focused on the idea that consumption is our main means of self-expression. Ironically, the hippies' criticism of consumerism actually promoted a new and more intensified form of consumption. Manufacturers began to redesign their products and advertising messages to attract members of the counterculture, while some former hippies actually moved into the clothing, entertainment, and personal services industries. Recent work also finds that veterans of the British punk subculture moved into sports and music marketing (Holt 2004; Holt and Cameron 2010; Lash and Lury 2007; Cohen 2003; Klein 2010; Smart 2010).

The new focus on lifestyle and personal expression led to a distinct set of rationales for consumption, as well as the expansion of the range of products that could be tailored to lifestyle groups that were smaller than traditional demographic categories (like class and gender), but more numerous and hence more profitable. The fruits of this shift are evident in the rise of designer-label clothes, appliances, and furniture; the expanding range of specialty food products (gourmet coffee, craft breweries, wine tastings, restaurants led by celebrity chefs); the proliferation of lifestyle-related cable television channels and shows (the Food Network, the Travel Channel); and the intensification of branding (Zukin 2004; Milestone and Meyer 2012; Jhally 1990; Holt and Cameron 2010).

A second, related discussion focuses on changes in the class structure (which we explore in greater depth in the next chapter). Following the work of French sociologist Pierre Bourdieu, Mike Featherstone (2000) focuses his analysis on what he calls "cultural intermediaries." These individuals are members of a new segment of the middle classes working in occupations linked to the entertainment and personal care industries (e.g., television, music, advertising, fashion, interior decorating). Featherstone suggests that cultural intermediaries are important for two reasons. First, they tend to be early adopters of new fashions or lifestyles as they try out new ideas they may apply in their work setting. Further, because their work involves promoting specific lifestyles in order to sell goods or services, they have a significant influence on a broad swath of the population. He argues that these individuals adopted the ethic of self-expression through consumption, and their roles as individual trendsetters and as professionals who promote new lifestyles have contributed to what he calls the "aestheticization of everyday life." Here, he refers to the increasing role of self-care in the improvement of one's body and skills in order to gain social status and employability. Examples of this phenomenon include the widespread use of gymnasiums for workouts and relaxation (yoga), plastic surgery, the popularity of tanning salons, and enrollment in classes for self-improvement, such as cooking, dance, or languages (Sassatelli 2007; see also Maguire and Matthews 2012).

A third perspective draws on the concept of individualization. Sociologists Ulrich Beck, Scott Lash, Elizabeth Beck-Gernsheim, and Zygmunt Bauman have developed this influential idea. In their view, after World War II, universal access to higher education and social welfare benefits in Europe led to the erosion of traditional sources of identity provided by family, traditional authority, and work. Today, individuals are "free" from the chains of traditional external sources of identity, but this freedom comes at a price. Individuals are compelled to give meaning to their lives without the certainty that they are making the right choice that in the past had come from tradition. Individuals are forced to be reflexive, to examine their own lives and to determine which of the characteristics they inherited from parents or school they wish to retain, and which ones they want to discard. In this context, consumption may be a useful vehicle for constructing a life narrative that gives focus and meaning to individuals. Given that family, work, and tradition hold less sway than in the past, consumption can be a potent source of identity (Lury 2011; Lash and Lury 2007).

Postmodern analyses of consumption also focus on the increasing importance of individuals to contemporary consumption. Developing this perspective, Firat and Venkatesh (1995) argue that discussions in philosophy lead us to call into question widely accepted beliefs about "truth," the coherence of the individual self, and so-called "grand narratives" of progress dominant in Western cultures since the eighteenth-century Enlightenment. Drawing on the work of poststructuralist and postmodernist philosophers such as Foucault, Derrida, Lyotard, and Baudrillard, Firat and Venkatesh (1995) suggest that changes in Western cultures have led to the erosion of modernist ideas of progress, overly simplified binary distinctions like production and consumption, and the notion of the individual as a coherent and unified actor. They suggest that in contemporary societies consumption and production exist in a repeating cycle, retail sites and advertising have increasingly focused on producing images and symbols, and individuals seek identities through consumption.

These shifts have led to increasing specialization and customization of products, the creation of visually spectacular shopping environments, and the individual search for meaning and identity through consumption. Firat and Venkatesh (1995) argue that contemporary conditions are liberating for individuals to the extent that they can engage in consumption outside the sphere of the market, much like Miller's (1987) discussion of how consumers recontextualize goods. Their analysis is a description of contemporary consumption and a call to market researchers to study the creative ways individuals use and derive meaning from goods. While this perspective seems to reach similar conclusions to the work on individualization, the authors reach these conclusions via a distinct body of philosophical work. Cova et al. (2013) argue that postmodernism had an important effect on marketing practice and consumer culture theory during the 1990s. However, its incorporation into mainstream applied marketing and academic theory has led to its declining impact on the marketing discipline.

Scholars' focus on subcultures contrasts with discussions of individualization and postmodern consumption in that, for these scholars, consumption is tied to specific groups or communities rather than being solely a vehicle for individual self-expression. We can understand subcultures as groups that develop distinctive identities, rituals, and values via consumption, marking them as different from the broader society they inhabit. Early studies of subcultures focused primarily on working- and middle-class white British youths, who expressed opposition to the broader society through their consumption of specific music styles (reggae, rock and roll, and punk), distinctive dress, and shared values. In an early compilation of work on subcultures, Clarke et al. (2006) were interested in how working- and middle-class males developed resistant forms of self-expression in relation to their class background and the society as a whole. Hebdige (1979, 2000), a contributor to that early collection, developed seminal studies of British musical subcultures and groups linked to motor-scooter use. Hebdige is particularly interested in how members of subcultures appropriate and modify specific products – motor scooters, safety pins, clothing – as a way to create group identity and to reject dominant cultural values. We examine youth subcultures in chapter 6.

Subsequent research by scholars within the consumer culture theory paradigm departed from this initial focus on working-class males' group expressions through music, clothing, and biker gangs. Schouten and McAlexander's (1995) study of Harley Davidson riders focuses on riders' "macho" identities, patriotism, search for freedom through motorcycle riding, and the hierarchical nature of these groups. Regarding this latter point, the authors argue that new members of this group can only raise their status by showing increasing commitment to its values through consuming specific goods and engaging in consumption-based rituals.

While these authors studied what some might consider an "outsider" group (though their research subjects were not members of "outlaw" biker clubs), they depart from the early British research in two ways. First, they see membership in a subculture as "self-selecting." In other words, subcultures do not necessarily emerge from specific social classes; rather, membership is based on specific lifestyle choices by individuals who may come from different class backgrounds. Second, they diverge from the British authors' limitation of the subculture concept to "oppositional" groups. They suggest that mundane groups like gardeners qualify as subcultures as much as do illegal drug users, for example.

Kozinets' (2001) study of *Star Trek* fans moves even further away from the "deviant" or "outlaw" ethos identified in earlier studies, by rejecting the term "subculture" and replacing it with the more neutral "culture of consumption." While he focuses on the same phenomena as other studies – shared practices and meanings within a group – he rejects the idea that subcultures are necessarily oppositional. He finds that *Star Trek* fans are social misfits who attempt to combat loneliness through their strong attachment to the *Star Trek* series. These fans have an almost religious reverence for the series, but at the same time must develop techniques to downplay negative ideas about "trekkies" as addictive consumers who are obsessed with a fantasy story. Rather than the oppositional punks or Harley riders, trekkies are strongly influenced by the ideas developed by the creator of the series, as well as the stigma they endure – they are strongly shaped by the broader society and by the official imagery developed in the series.

Holt (2004) and Holt and Cameron (2010) move beyond the case-study focus of this earlier work to develop a broader theory of subcultural consumption based on a wide array of cases. They suggest that subcultures are rooted in specific class, regional, occupational, or lifestyle-based groups, such as ethnic groups, rural white men, or sports fans. These groups develop their distinctive forms of consumption-based identities in response to changes in the economy or political environment that generate tensions between their situation and their ability to achieve widely shared cultural ideals such as professional success. Like Kozinets, and in contrast to earlier studies, these authors see subcultures as functioning in a symbiotic relationship with mass-media products (such as film and music) and brands. As we detail below, subcultures do not exist in isolation; rather, journalists, film-makers, and advertisers use subcultural practices and identities as raw materials for the products they produce or promote. Hence, subcultures are intimately tied to dominant modes of consumption.

Cova et al. (2007) develop the related concept of "consumer tribes." They understand consumer tribes as groups who share identities and practices related to specific brands. Much like the work on postmodern consumption, these authors see individuals as being involved in diverse tribes – their identities are multiple and ambiguous. However, unlike the earlier postmodern work, research on tribes focuses on collective forms of consumption and identity rather than isolated individual consumers. Rejecting the domination/resistance dichotomy of earlier work on subcultures, these authors argue that consumer tribes are ambiguous in that their members may promote or undermine the brands they use. Rather than being resistant, consumer tribes are playful. They use the example of urban hipsters who made Pabst Blue Ribbon beer "cool" because its company did not actively promote it. The company became aware of its rising image and developed a low-profile advertising campaign that would not alienate its hipster fans. In contrast, they describe groups that boycott brands due to their labor practices, or others, like *Harry Potter* or *Star Trek* fans, who write new episodes of the books and films. These tribes are worrisome for companies because their "do-it-yourself" products wrest control of the brand's image away from the company or may tarnish its image through negative publicity. Hence, tribes are intimately but ambiguously intertwined with brands.

The research on subcultures and tribes serves as an important corrective to the work on individualization and postmodern consumption because it demonstrates that not all consumption emanates from individual choice. Rather, much like the material culture and relational traditions, this research reaffirms the claim that consumption occurs in social contexts and much of consumption is an integral part of meaningful social relationships rooted in families, friendship groups, and other communities in which individuals participate. While scholars focusing on the diversification of lifestyles are correct that consumer styles have multiplied in recent decades in contrast to the postwar standardization of products and styles in many countries, this fact should not lead us to imagine that group-based consumption identities have vanished. Rather, as students of contemporary subcultures and consumer tribes note, group-based consumption is not a direct or inevitable product of an individual's class position; rather, subcultures are rooted in a variety of groups, some subcultures or tribes may be weakly related to large-scale population groups (based in class, gender, or race, for example), and subcultures or tribes are constantly in flux.

Each of the above discussions focuses on how changes in social attitudes and group identities have influenced broader trends in the production, promotion, and consumption of goods and services since the 1960s. A different but complementary argument focuses on changes in production and government policy that led to a shift in the strategies of producers and consumers. Many of these arguments originate with the work of French economist Michel Aglietta. This author coined the terms "Fordism" and "post-Fordism" to describe two periods of production and consumption during the twentieth century. The term "Fordism" was first used by Italian Marxist thinker Antonio Gramsci. He wrote an influential essay that predicted that Henry Ford's model of factory management and labor relations would likely have broader global influences. Gramsci was interested in the possible effects of the introduction of American manufacturing techniques and social policy to Italy. Aglietta further develops some of these ideas in discussing the postwar U.S. and the period since the 1970s (Slater 1997; Harvey 1990; Smart 2010).

Aglietta is interested in Henry Ford's famous adoption of assembly-line production, as well as his creation of the "5-dollar day"

– a high wage for his workers – so that they could afford to buy his cars. Aglietta and others explored how the principles of the rational organization of production and the promotion of demand among workers were also developed at the national level in the Global North, beginning in the 1930s. After the Great Depression, many governments followed the ideas of British economist John Maynard Keynes, who called for a planned economy in which governments subsidized consumption to create demand for a surplus of goods. Beginning in the 1930s, but with greater force after World War II, many of these policies were formalized through the creation of social welfare measures (like social security or health coverage), greater government regulation of companies and banks, and national-level agreements between companies and labor unions that permitted growing wages and benefits for industrial workers and public employees. These government-level measures, along with a growing economy, permitted considerable expansion of consumption as well as its standardization across social classes. This standardization also reflected the assembly-line model of production, designed to produce large quantities of uniform goods, and the limited international competition resulting from the need of both Europe and Japan to rebuild after the war. Hence, according to this view, Fordism meant rising living standards for a wide spectrum of the population in the U.S. and later in Europe and Japan, and a fairly standardized package of goods consumed by a growing middle class (Schor 1998; Cohen 2003; Harvey 1990).

The Fordist model began to unravel in the 1970s. This resulted from economic woes tied to increasing oil prices, growing competition between producers in Europe, the U.S., and the Far East (Japan, Singapore, South Korea, and Hong Kong), and the decline of both the welfare state and union power. With growing competition, companies sought to differentiate their products from their counterparts through an increasing focus on style, product design, brand-name logos, and advertising. Further, the decline in government provision of many social services (such as housing, healthcare, and education) led to the commodification and branding of these services, imitating these processes in the sphere of production. Hence, in this view, national and global economic changes set the stage for lifestyle-oriented consumption (Harvey 1990; Smart 2010; Piore and Sabel 1984; Lash and Lury 2007).

Changes in transportation and communications technology also altered the production process and companies' internal organization. From the 1960s to the present, advances in shipping, air travel, and electronic communication (wireless, fax, email, Internet) made it easier for companies based in the Global North (the U.S., Europe, and Japan) to engage in the design and promotion of products and to subcontract or relocate the production to cheaper locations (as noted in chapter 2 with regard to Walmart). This allowed companies to reduce production costs while investing more intensively in market research, product design, branding, and marketing. Companies most famous for pursuing this strategy include Nike, Starbucks, Reebok, Adidas, and Ralph Lauren (Holt 2004; Holt and Cameron 2010; Lash and Lury 2007; Klein 2010; Smart 2010).

A related phenomenon tied to increasing international competition between companies is the shortened turnover time of products. This phenomenon reflects the pressure on companies to sell products and hence reap profits at a quicker pace in order to effectively compete. The acceleration of product turnover time has important implications for the design, production, and marketing of goods. Companies feel pressure to introduce new products or new versions of existing products on a regular basis. This is evident in the very brief clothing seasons, frequent updates of electronic equipment, and the proliferation of different styles of clothing and personal accessories. While companies feel compelled to invent, promote, and sell new or improved goods, individuals increasingly feel pressure to update their possessions and styles to remain attractive and current or to avoid social stigma. This process has negative implications for the environment, which we explore in chapter 8 (Harvey 1990; Smart 2010; Zukin 2004).

If we integrate the ideas of cultural change leading to the increasing importance of lifestyle with the rise of post-Fordism, we can begin to visualize how and why significant changes have occurred in consumption since the 1960s. Consumers create the demand for new products that permit their self-expression, while companies feel pressure to adapt to these demands and create new demand to remain competitive. The result is the intensification of consumption and the saturation of everyday life with marketing. Let us return to the focus areas of advertising, marketing, branding, credit, and retail to see the consequences of these complex changes.

Advertising and Marketing

Advertising and marketing have changed significantly during the period under study. While advertisers and marketers had already begun to explore consumers' emotions in the 1960s through the construction of psychographic market segments, more substantial changes have occurred since then. The first change has been the intensification of market research. Producers, retailers, and market researchers have carefully scrutinized individuals' buying habits. This research is carried out through traditional television-watching and radio surveys, but also via intensive analysis of credit- or debit-card transactions. This analysis has produced more precise market segments than the broad categories of income, gender, and age used during the 1930s–50s. Messages and promotions can be tailored by zip code (which is a good indicator of income and education); the content of email messages (as practiced by Google and other free Internet services); Internet searches and social media use; and lifestyle categories based on tastes such as gourmet food, tattoos, or skateboarding, which may bridge class, age, and gender categories (Schor 1998, 2004; Cohen 2003; Bowlby 2001; Leiss et al. 2005).

Further, companies use loyalty or reward programs to monitor the shopping behavior of micro-segments of consumers, steering specific promotions to a given individual or group or withdrawing promotions from others, based on their buying behavior. Hence, marketing operates within a feedback loop through which companies market their goods, observe consumers' shopping patterns, and then alter their messages and promotions based on these observations. The widespread use of data on consumer purchases as a way to tailor marketing messages raises questions about privacy (consumers often are not aware of how their personal data or shopping behaviors are used) and about whether or not these strategies subtly channel consumers' choices by offering or withdrawing specific rewards (Pridmore and Lyon 2011).

Advertisers and marketers have also used a variety of methods to get closer to customers. While market research traditionally used survey techniques, marketers have increasingly relied on qualitative methods like depth interviewing, participant observation, photographs of consumers, free-association exercises, and consumers' written diaries. The goal behind these methods is to gain a deeper understanding of consumers' attitudes, beliefs, feelings, and practices related to products, as a means to tailor product design and promotional messages to the consumers' mindsets.

Researchers also use these methods to identify new style "trends" among youth. This method is popularly known as "cool hunting." Companies buy this information so they can craft products and messages that appeal to young people, a major target of marketers, advertisers, and producers. Companies also employ young people to assist in product design based on what they and their friends perceive as cool. Additionally, marketers use word-of-mouth or "viral" advertising to rely on consumers' social networks in order to spread their message. Examples of viral marketing include the provision of free services, like Google or Hotmail, in which each email message is an advertisement for the company; or the attachment of a promotional line to all email messages, like: "sent from my iPhone." The readers of these messages are compelled to view the ads whether or not they want to (Schor 2004; Klein 2010; Holt 2004).

"Stealth marketing" is another strategy that focuses on getting close to consumers. This might involve smuggling a marketing message into a song or news broadcast so that it is "seamless" – it is difficult for the viewer/listener to distinguish the ad from the "real" content they are viewing/listening to – or using children as "secret agents" to test products with their friends without the latter being in on the secret (Schor 2004).

Juliet Schor (2004) raises several ethical concerns about market researchers' use of ethnographic methods or stealth advertising, especially with children. She points out that advertisers and market researchers are not held to the same ethical standards by their professional associations as are university-based researchers, and as a result there is no oversight regarding their use of children in research, their use of research subjects without their express written consent (in the case of stealth product testing), and the use of child labor for product design without adequate compensation given the potential economic value of their advice. Further, she worries that the employment of children to trick their friends into talking about particular products in an intimate setting without knowing that they are part of a research project will undermine trust among friends. Notwithstanding these concerns, in the U.S., there is little legal regulation of these activities or of advertising to children, as we explore in chapter 6.

These new modes of market research and product promotion have yielded new approaches in the development of television programs and television channels that find their counterpart in other arenas of consumption. The model of television that was developed after World War II in the U.S. (and that still exists to some degree in Canada, Europe, and other countries/regions with strong public ownership or regulation of television) is the broadcast model. Here, the government (in the case of the U.S., the Federal Communications Commission) licenses portions of the airwaves to specific channels, and, in their initial development, those channels produced many programs directed toward a broad cross-section of the population, even entire families. The model of television later shifted from producing programs that appeal to a wide range of people, to developing material (and shows) that increasingly target smaller segments of the population. To be fair, widely popular shows are still produced on broadcast and cable networks, such as *American Idol*, *Glee*, *Scandal*, and *Madmen*. However, the trend is toward narrowcasting – targeting a specific audience such as youth, older adults, or lifestyle groups that find a specific television format or topic appealing (Jhally 1990; Holt 2004; Holt and Cameron 2010; Schor 1998). Indeed, Cohen (2003) argues that early television had already begun narrowcasting by time segment, scheduling shows and advertisements directed toward children in the late afternoon, women during the day, and men during the evening. However, the targeting of television content and advertisements has become much more precise since the advent of cable television in the late 1970s.

Narrowcasting is evident in the music video channels (MTV, VH1, and BET), 24-hour news channels (Fox, CNN, and MSNBC), ESPN, the Food Channel, The Discovery Channel, the History Channel, and many others. The idea behind narrowcasting is that the watching public has become increasing fragmented in its tastes, and in order to sell products via ads (which pays for television) it is necessary to target a given demographic-lifestyle segment with specific content and advertisements. Thus, for example, the ads on MTV will target teenagers, those on the History Channel target older men, ads on BET target African American youth, and those on the Independent Film Channel focus on highly educated adults who view themselves as "alternative" consumers (Holt and Cameron 2010; Schor 1998; Jhally 1990; Lash and Lury 2007).

The customization of television has been further intensified through advances in information technology that have led to the increasing integration of the Internet, cellphones, and television. As the availability of streaming video on the Internet and the use of "smart" phones, tablet computers, and TVs with Internet access have grown, people have begun to access television and film through different devices, leading to the development of new vehicles for transmitting these media. Subscription services like Netflix, Hulu, and Amazon Prime allow individuals to view television series and movies on all of the above-noted devices at the time and place they desire rather than on a specific weekly schedule. Some of these services allow viewers to watch without commercials. Finally, subscriber services Netflix, Hulu, and Amazon Prime have now created their own series to compete with cable and broadcast providers, and some of these series like *Orange is the New Black* and *House of Cards* have become international hits. These phenomena have increased competition between the providers of different media formats and hence intensified the diversification of content, which we have already linked to the increasing importance of lifestyle to consumers.

Communications scholars Joseph Turow and Nora Draper (2012) raise serious concerns about the implications of current industry efforts to track the interests of consumers of online content and then use that data to further sales. They argue that contemporary data-mining techniques emerged in response to the fragmentation of television audiences that was reflected in cable broadcasting. Large international advertising agencies began to sell quantitative data about market segments to companies seeking to advertise their products. This first step intensified during the 1990s and 2000s as the Internet expanded and companies developed the capability to track individual Internet users' browsing habits with "cookies" and to then target advertising to those users. Subsequently, independent data-mining companies have begun to buy, sell, and combine information about users to help companies target advertisements and promotions to individual consumers.

These authors raise several concerns about these techniques. First, like Pridmore and Lyon (2011), they worry that companies will use customer data to customize the goods and messages they direct toward specific consumers, thus giving different individuals unequal access to information. Second, Turow (2010) further notes that many web users are unaware of how their private information is used and traded: companies may be observing their private habits to build promotional messages, while users may not wish to reveal these habits. Third, Turow and Draper (2012) worry that what they call "segment-making media" is overshadowing "society-making media." Here, they contrast the current tailored approach to advertising and promotion to the old broadcast model. In the current era, segmented marketing may lead individuals to communicate only with others similar to themselves and become less knowledgeable or tolerant of others who are different from them. The older model, while imperfect, encouraged viewers/consumers to consider society-wide problems. They call for a better balance between these two media forms.

A last arena of advertising that has experienced important changes in recent years is product placement within television shows and movies. In movies from the 1970s or earlier, brand-name goods are absent. Characters eat cereal from a generic box, drink brand-free beer, and smoke cigarettes from an indistinguishable pack. This changed with the deregulation of television advertising during the 1970s in the U.S. As a consequence, brands now saturate film and television as another source of "stealth" advertising. As documentary film-maker and media scholar Douglas Rushkoff (2004) explains, companies regularly meet with television and film producers before they begin a season or series to explore how their brand can be integrated into a narrative, or the media producers directly solicit corporate participation in their stories. Further, some brands have experimented with creating short stories focused on their company, as in the BMW "webisodes" featuring A-list actors and musicians. All of these phenomena speak to the intensification and diversification of market research and advertising today. These phenomena are also linked to the expansion of branding in recent decades, to which we now turn.

Branding

As discussed in chapter 2, branding began as a means to make a particular company's products recognizable and distinct from their competitors while assuring shoppers of the quality of goods produced under that label. For the first half of the twentieth century, branding largely focused on the functional qualities of goods, highlighting positive characteristics such as taste, healthiness, durability, and texture. In tandem with changes in culture, the economy, and the mass media, branding strategy began to shift in the 1970s. One important area of change was the incorporation of values and lifestyles from youth and oppositional cultures into brand images and advertisements. This is evident in the marketing of blue jeans, which were formerly standard attire for blue-collar workers and farmers and were subsequently adopted by hippies and musicians as a form of casual attire. The marketing of jeans as youthful and stylish, as well as their customization via their attachment to existing brands and designer labels (such as Calvin Klein, Lucky Brand, and Diesel), used their association with youth as a launching pad for expanding their market and reframing them as expensive, luxury items.

Images from the feminist movement also made their way into marketing, especially with the adaptation of the feminist slogan "You've come a long way, baby" as the official tag line of Virginia Slims cigarette commercials. Later, brands began to associate their products with the hip-hop subculture because they were popular among

African American (and later white) youth (as in the case of Tommy Hilfiger), African American sports icons, or as new brands created by individuals linked to the hip-hop music scene (like Fubu or Sean Jean). In each of these ways, brands attempted to extract the "coolness" from youth oppositional cultures and turn it into a profitable sales pitch (Klein 2010; Bordo 2000; Holt 2004; Holt and Cameron 2010; Leiss et al. 2005; Goldman and Papson 2000).

Brands have also attempted to construct an emotional message that builds on ideas of self-realization and fulfillment in contemporary cultures but also seeks to create new emotional experiences. Journalist Naomi Klein (2010) argues that "super-brands" like Nike, Starbucks, and Benetton have attempted to link their brands to the ideas and feelings of transcendence, community, and multiculturalism, respectively. One way brands seek to solidify these feelings is through celebrity endorsements that permit the shopper to imagine that s/he is like Michael Jordan, Tiger Woods, or David Beckham when s/he dons a pair of Nike athletic shoes; or, in the case of Starbucks, coffee buyers associate the brand with Bob Dylan, Herbie Hancock, and other musical artists who recorded CDs sold exclusively in Starbucks cafes. A third way brands seek to build an emotional experience for shoppers is through dedicated stores that sell branded items while also providing an exciting multimedia play environment. This is the case with Niketown, Swatch, and ESPN Zone stores. A final way brands seek to build a strong connection with consumers is by sponsoring sports or music events or clubs through which the brand becomes directly associated with the event in the minds of spectators (Zukin 2004; Smart 2010; Lash and Lury 2007; Kozinets et al. 2004; McCracken 2005).

With the enormous expansion of branding as a business strategy, many companies have built alliances through cross-promotion and market tie-ins. These strategies are evident, for example, in what sociologists Scott Lash and Celia Lury (2007) call the "thingification" of media. These authors contend that, today, the boundaries are blurring between the mass media and physical consumer products. They explore this idea through the production of licensed toys and souvenirs depicting characters from the *Toy Story* and *Wallace and Gromit* movies. They suggest that these toys, marketed by parent companies Disney and the British Broadcasting Corporation, are sold in stores or used to promote other products through the strategies noted above. For Americans, the example of "Happy Meals" at McDonald's (or their equivalent in other fast-food chains) is the most familiar: Disney and other animated movies use "free" licensed toys in fast-food meals as a way to promote their movies while the fast-food outlets use the toys as a hook to get children into the restaurant. The BBC used *Wallace and Gromit* collectibles to market branded foods and other goods. These toys help the movies "live on" after viewing, are the most profitable products associated with specific films, and also connect souvenir owners to the narrative and the brand.

Consumers have become weary of the marketing frenzy attached to brands. In many cases, viewers have become increasingly cynical about marketing gimmicks, and, as noted above, have used new media technologies (like streaming video and digital video recorders) to bypass commercials. In this context, brands have attempted to "connect" with cynical consumers through "anti-commercial" advertisements. This strange approach to marketing goes something like this. Brands create advertisements that make fun of commercials to tell consumers that they are smart and see through the manipulation in ads. In the end, however, the commercial still promotes the brand. Goldman and Papson (2000) call this practice "hailing." They argue that in the face of viewer cynicism, marketers "hail" or salute youth consumers' intelligence or oppositional attitudes in what appears as a critique of commercialism but is in fact a clever new vehicle for an advertisement.

Scholars disagree regarding the process through which brands connect with consumers. Anthropologist and applied marketing specialist Grant McCracken (1988) developed the influential "meaning transfer model" to understand this process. He argues that advertisers and designers identify meanings from the broader culture and transfer them to goods. They must identify meanings that make sense to consumers targeted by a specific good or brand. Additionally, fashion designers create new meanings by linking celebrities to new goods, as noted above. Journalists add to a good's meaning by serving as "gatekeepers" who may praise or criticize a new product. Then consumers transfer meanings from goods to themselves via rituals like grooming (selecting elegant clothes to attend a formal event), giving gifts they hope will influence the recipient, personalizing homes, and divestment (removing meanings from goods to be sold or donated or previously owned goods). In this way, consumers are the final "authors" of a brand's meaning. Hence, for McCracken, product design, promotion, and consumption are interconnected processes if and when the meanings that producers and advertisers attach to goods "fit" with consumers' understandings of the culture they inhabit, and if they provide consumers with meanings they seek to incorporate into their own identities.

Holt (2004) and Holt and Cameron (2010) provide a distinct model. They first differentiate "average" brands from "iconic" brands, with the latter gaining a long-term positive reputation and premium profits based on successful advertising. They contend that members of subcultures are actually the beginning of the process of meaning creation. In their reading, subcultures operate in "populist worlds" that are removed from centers of business and political power and their members engage in consumption because it offers them satisfaction, not because it provides any economic benefits. Subcultures exist for finite periods of time because they are often responses to economic and political changes. For example, hippies were a growing and visible subculture during the 1960s and 1970s, but are not a major influence on society today.

Successful advertisers draw upon existing subcultures to develop ads that reflect and speak to those subcultures while also appealing to a broader population. Hence, for example, during the 1990s, Mountain Dew depicted the "slacker" subculture of unemployed youth who rejected the values of professional success during a period when few attractive jobs were available for this age group. However, in addition to identifying a subculture, advertisers create new ideas that draw upon that subculture, like the series of commercials with "slackers" observing and rating the death-defying feats of extreme sports.

Holt (2004) and Holt and Cameron (2010) also argue, like Goldman and Papson (2000), that many successful brands develop "anti-ads" when political and social conditions make their ads no longer relevant. Hence the "Do the Dew" series followed earlier ads focused on rural white working-class men reacting against middle-class urban populations during the 1960s and 1970s. This conservative model was no longer appealing after the Civil Rights movement because of its association with racism, and hence was no longer appealing to audiences. "Anti-ads" often criticize earlier advertisements. For example, Budweiser offered serious ads appealing to the virtue of white working-class men during the 1980s, but later poked fun at those ads with spots featuring animated lizards, and the "Whassup" ads featuring African American men. Thus, sophisticated advertisers know how to make fun of the company sponsoring the ads in a way that appeals to new audiences. However, many advertisers fail over several years before they identify a formula that captivates audiences.

Holt (2004) and Holt and Cameron (2010) argue that corporate clients often stifle the creativity needed to construct "breakthrough" ads because they subscribe to what they call "mindshare" market-ing that focuses on a product's physical or emotional "benefits." However, they argue that many products in a category are essentially similar, so this strategy is doomed to failure. Rather, consumers seek identity myths that help them work through the challenges they face in everyday life via depictions of an entertaining fantasy world that draws on their values and experiences. Hence, in contrast to McCracken (1988), these authors suggest that consumers begin the process of meaning construction that advertisers then borrow and modify.

Holt and Cameron's (2010) harsh critique of the "brand bureau-cracy" through which corporations stifle creative and effective adver-tising serves as a bridge to recent analyses of the work of advertising professionals. This research complicates earlier discussions of adver-tising as either manipulative or a source of information or identity for consumers. Here, we learn of the complex and contradictory ways that advertising is achieved by professionals. Each of these scholars conducted research while working in advertising agencies or con-ducting market research, and they thus have an "insider's view" of the hidden world of marketing. Grandclément and Gaglio (2011) examine a common market research technique – the focus group. Examining two firms in France, they argue that while corporate exec-utives used focus groups as a way to "get close to real consumers," the conversations that occur in focus groups are heavily controlled by researchers to produce results that reproduce the corporate client's assumptions about their target market segment. In this regard, rather than being a reflection of social reality, the focus group is a product of the market research industry that serves to facilitate communica-tion and collaboration between market research firms and corporate clients.

Sunderland and Denny (2011), two anthropologists who work as applied market researchers, offer a tragicomic view of market research. They describe a study in which a large retailer asked them to examine shoppers who planned to host holiday parties. The coordination of the study suffered numerous mishaps, most notably because the corporate client could not or would not define the market segment they targeted and hence the researchers found it difficult to recruit research participants. In the end, the researchers produced a respectable pilot study, but their experience reveals that the idea that retailers or producers possess "scientific" information about consum-ers and can predict their every move is a fiction. Their account is an important antidote to Pridmore and Lyon's (2011) apocalyptic view of the use of "big data" to track consumers who participate in loyalty programs. It suggests that companies may aspire to "understand" consumers, but there are many pitfalls in this process.

Two studies of advertising in India offer similar lessons in a distinct cultural context. Mazzarella's (2003) study of advertising agencies in Bombay argues that advertisers in India sell their knowledge of Indian culture to multinational corporations who seek to penetrate that country's enormous market but have little understanding of India's distinct and diverse cultures. Local advertisers thus have a vested interest in making India seem different from the West so that Western companies will purchase their services. Cayla and Peñaloza (2011) have a different view. They describe how Indian advertising agencies seek to help international corporations sell new products to Indian consumers, much like Strasser's (1989) account of the rise of marketing in the U.S. at the beginning of the twentieth century. In their account, these advertisers try to convince Indian consumers to begin new practices like eating cold cereal, baking cupcakes or using laundry detergent. These efforts conflict with local consumption traditions. Unlike Mazzarella (2003), the authors find that these upper-middle-class advertising professionals have little understanding of the middle-class people they seek to persuade to buy products. In their reading, these professionals hope to work in the U.K., Canada, or the U.S. some day and have little identification with the Indian consumers to whom they seek to sell modern lifestyles. While these two studies interpret these materials differently, they both point to the challenge of selling goods produced in a distinct cultural context to consumers who have little experience with these goods and who may have little interest in adapting their lifestyles to fit these products.

Credit

In addition to transformations in advertising, marketing, and branding, consumer credit has expanded in recent decades. This expansion reflects legal changes in the banking industry that have allowed banks to broaden the populations to which credit can be extended (including college students, for example), as well as the consolidation of the secondary credit market via payday loan operations, rent-to-own stores, and pawnshops. Sociologist Juliet Schor (1998) expressed concern in the late 1990s that, lured by advertising, middle-class Americans were spending more than they earned in order to compete with higher-income groups. Robert Manning (2000) ties rising credit use to the growth of low-wage jobs that prevent workers from meeting basic expenses combined with aggressive marketing of credit cards to middle- and working-class Americans. Further, low-income and middle-class consumers suffered the consequences of easy credit policies beginning in 2008 when the mortgage crisis led to massive home foreclosures, unemployment, and personal bankruptcies. Since then, U.S. congressional officials have discussed placing stiffer regulations on the banking industry, though the actual results of banking reform have been disappointing to industry critics (Smart 2010; Johnson and Kwak 2011).

U.S. and European banking industries have also embarked on a global effort to increase the number of cardholders in the Global South. Additionally, as the domestically owned retail industries have expanded in these regions, local retail chains have created their own store credit cards, as have banks and travel agencies. These countries are different from those in the Global North because their precarious job bases and sharper income inequalities have led to continued demand for informal credit alongside credit cards and banking. Since large segments of their populations lack stable employment, to access credit, they must turn to street vendors and corner stores who provide credit based on trust rather than formal documentation, much as was true in the U.S. in the early twentieth century (Strasser 1989; Manning 2000). Given the higher risk of default these creditors face, they charge higher interest rates than department stores or banks. However, they also offer their clientele more flexible payment terms (Stillerman 2006; Öz and Eder 2012).

In research on credit use among low-income families in Santiago, Chile, Stillerman (2012) found that several families had defaulted on credit-card debts due to a family illness or job loss. Therefore, these families developed two strategies to access credit for daily necessities or to buy "big-ticket" appliances they could not afford to purchase with cash. First, they relied on informal credit through street markets in order to purchase food and occasionally clothing, furniture, or small appliances. Second, they turned to family members to "borrow" their credit cards. The family member would purchase an item at a department store or supermarket, and their relative would repay them in cash. Individuals lacking formal credit relied on their family members' loyalty to access credit. This practice reflects how family systems of reciprocity "domesticate" formal systems of credit to solve immediate problems (see Manning 2000 on family members borrowing credit cards or student loan funds in the U.S.).

Additionally, families whose head of household was employed would alternate the use of formal and informal credit depending on the type of purchase and time of the month. They might use informal credit to buy an appliance in a street market if they were short on cash but did not want to run up credit-card debt. In contrast, they might make monthly food or other large purchases at a supermarket but would restrict the size of their bill so they were sure they could make their minimum monthly payments. In this way, adults could stretch family finances to buy needed or desired goods without risking credit-card default. These practices underscore poor people's ingenuity when faced with financial challenges and the importance of family ties as resources that make purchases possible (compare D'Andrea et al. 2004; Gonzalez de la Rocha 1994).

Those families that defaulted on credit cards were likely targeted by department-store creditors who use the strategy of "sowing consumers" (Ossandon 2013). In this analysis, creditors use risk-analysis formulas to identify very low-income Chilean consumers to whom they offer credit. They adopt this strategy, even though they assume that half of these consumers will default on loans, because it expands the store's and financial institution's market, and they expect that those consumers who do not default will recruit other debtors, thereby "sowing consumers." The use of advanced statistical analysis has allowed Chilean department stores to reap huge profits from interest payments by low-income consumers, but this has also produced hardships for the large number of debtors who default on credit cards (compare Manning 2000 on predatory lending in the U.S.).

Contemporary Retail and Consumption Practices

In the final section of this chapter, we consider how the retail sector and consumer lifestyles have changed since the 1970s. Changes in the retail sector are in part related to the increasing centrality of lifestyles to shopping. As Sharon Zukin (2004) argues, the 1960s counterculture led to individuals' increased focus on defining their identities through consumption. This shift led consumers to seek distinctive identities through clothing and accessories that made them stand out in a crowd. This observation supports and extends Simmel's (1957) analysis of fashion as a system encouraging conformity among some and innovation among others. The rise of so-called lifestyle consumption was an important departure from the postwar era when clothing and other consumer products were standardized in appearance and functioning. This heightened interest in pursuing a distinctive style contributed to the increasing importance of design within companies producing consumer goods (compare Leiss et al. 2005).

With the growing focus on design, the 1970s witnessed the rise of designer-label clothing lines as well as brand boutiques. Hence, when walking down a shopping street or in a mall, one is likely to find stores that sell a single brand (like Victoria's Secret, Eddie Bauer, or Abercrombie & Fitch). Department-store chains such as Macy's or Sears have reorganized their stores into distinct sections featuring specific brands of clothing, kitchenware, or hardware to mimic brand boutiques. Even discount chains commission well-known figures to design appliances, as in the alliance between Target and Michael Graves. These shifts reflect the link shoppers made between individuality and distinctive design.

As noted above, some brands have also added an "experiential" component to the design and activities promoted in their stores. This is the case with Nike, ESPN, and Swatch (Lash and Lury 2007; Kozinets et al. 2004; Zukin 2004). Here, shoppers are invited to play in a store in addition to buying its products, and the store itself is akin to a tourist destination. This strategy seeks to heighten shoppers' identification with the brand, leading them to make many purchases because of this loyalty built on the excitement experienced in the store. Store personnel may also observe shoppers and use these observations to modify product and store design, so customers may unwittingly provide free labor to companies.

Technological changes have also transformed shopping. An increasing portion of transactions now occur online through the use of personal computers and mobile devices – smartphones and tablet computers. Shoppers now have much more information at their fingertips about the characteristics and quality of a given good, but no clear certainty about which information is reliable. The rising role of the Internet and mobile devices in shopping has important implications for how we find and experience goods. The appeal of mobile devices to consumers has also influenced technology use inside retail stores, as some stores, most notably the Apple Store, use mobile phones instead of cash registers to receive customers' credit- or debit-card payments, and a variety of software companies are currently developing "virtual wallets" and "virtual currencies," like Bitcoin and Google Wallet, that allow consumers to make purchases using mobile devices.

A useful example of these technological changes is provided by sociologist Chris Rojek's (2011) analysis of the music industry. He argues that in the 1960s and 1970s, record stores were important social settings where shoppers learned about new albums or artists, met other music enthusiasts, or heard about upcoming concerts. Further, it was common for people (especially teens) to get together in homes to listen to records, cassettes, and CDs. Today, most music is purchased (or illegally downloaded and shared) as single songs in a weightless, digital form. Individuals may share music online with their friends via social media or Internet radio sites, but the experience of listening to music is much more isolated than it was in the past, as most listening occurs on computers, MP3 players, and mobile phones. Further, since most individuals buy or acquire songs rather than albums or CDs, this may be a disincentive for artists to produce "rock operas" (like The Who's *Tommy* or *Quadrophenia*); high-concept albums, like some of the recordings by progressive rock bands Yes, King Crimson, Gong, and Genesis; experimental music like that of the German band Einstürzende Neubauten, or the San Francisco-based band The Residents; or album-length dance songs produced by Nigerian Afro-Pop legends King Sunny Adé or Fela Anikulapu Kuti.

Changing technologies are also altering music production and distribution. Computer software allows individuals without formal musical training to produce studio-quality music and market it without renting time from a studio or seeking out an agent. Further, some groups have chosen to market their own material on the Internet rather than work with a recording corporation (or even allow free downloads and attempt to make money on tour), in order to capture all of the profits themselves (Rojek 2011). This was the case with the 2012 rap music hit "Thrift Shop" by Macklemore and Ryan Lewis. The hip-hop duo decided to market the song independently, although they sought advice from an industry "heavy" about how to promote their song and CD (Chace 2013).

A further transformation of retail and consumption is the rising linkage between tourism and consumption. (The expansion of tourism is related to the broader phenomenon of globalization, explored in the last section of this chapter.) While tourism has existed as a mass phenomenon at least since the late nineteenth century, the expansion of road transportation infrastructure and decreasing prices of air travel have encouraged the industry's expansion. Several different factors influence the supply of tourist infrastructures and consumers' desire to engage in tourist activities. On the supply side, large global corporations run the major hotel chains, cruise lines, and all-inclusive vacation sites like those run by the French company Club Med. In addition to servicing many cities, large-scale vacation infrastructures in part reflect the crushing poverty and lack of adequate employment available in many tourist destinations, such as the Caribbean islands, the countries of North Africa, or Thailand (Sheller 2003; Wherry 2008). Additionally, many historically legitimated sites like the Egyptian pyramids or the Eiffel Tower draw tourists due to their unique and widely recognized characteristics. However, less famous places like small towns in the U.S. or ethnic neighborhoods in larger cities see tourism as a major source of economic development. Governments and businesses in these less famous settings attempt to highlight their historical importance or unique characteristics (real or fabricated) to draw in tourists (Gotham 2007).

On the demand side, many individuals today seek authentic experiences as an alternative to the standardized consumption they might find in a fast-food restaurant or a shopping mall. This desire to connect with unique or original places and peoples may lead tourists to remote places in search of authentic cultures or artifacts, as sociologist Frederick Wherry (2008) notes in his study of craft vendors and their customers in Costa Rica and Thailand.

Another branch of the tourist industry builds on a traditional theme of "sun, sand, and sex," associated with visits to the Caribbean or other warm-weather locations. Here, consumers seek out short-term, intense experiences of consumption in a pleasant environment, but it is unlikely that they seek uniqueness or authenticity. Rather, such consumers seek an expected package of amenities. This phenomenon is evident in the annual trek of American college students to Florida, Mexico, and other places in the U.S. South for spring break. Here, the goal is to engage in an expected set of (mis)behaviors around other college students without paying attention to local residents or sites (Sheller 2003; Babb 2011; Rushkoff 1999).

Another example of "standardized" tourism is the increasing popularity of the "destination" wedding. In these cases, the wedding party and their guests seek to enjoy a controlled environment where they will not have to "rough it" or "mix" with the "natives," and to have an "unforgettable" experience because of the event's location in an area of natural beauty or appealing climate. This example reflects the merging of conspicuous consumption with a consumption ritual (Otnes and Pleck 2003).

Mimi Sheller's (2003) analysis of tourism in the Caribbean contends that this phenomenon builds on a history of exploitation of native and African-origin people as well as the islands' natural landscapes. Tourists may be unaware of the privilege they bring with them when they travel to impoverished locations or of the history of Westerners' exploitation of the islands' people and resources.

Tourists also travel from the Global South to the Global North. Maureen O'Dougherty (2002) studied middle-class Brazilians' visits to Disney World. She found that visiting the theme park was an expected ritual for middle-class families. In addition to visiting the park, many families purchased small items and electronic appliances to give to others as gifts or to resell upon their return to Brazil. While some might interpret these trips as evidence that Brazilians are becoming "Americanized," the author argues that her interviewees go to Disney World to gain status among their peers in Brazil. The Disney visit is thus meaningful in the Brazilian national context.

Another interesting example of how tourism and migration have intensified national identities in the Global South is provided by anthropologist Richard Wilk's (2006) study of the history of food in the Central American country of Belize. Wilk argues that as a former colony of Britain, middle-class Belizean colonial employees had historically preferred imported foods to local dishes and ingredients. Several factors beginning in the 1970s combined to promote a revival of Belizean food. Americans living in Belize "rediscovered" local cuisine. Additionally, Belizeans who migrated to Chicago and Los Angeles opened restaurants because they missed national recipes. Some of these individuals returned to Belize when job opportunities improved and opened restaurants serving local recipes to tourists who sought an authentic experience. Here, globalization has led to the intensification of national identity.

The growth of tourism in recent decades also reflects the growing significance of "experiential consumption." As societies become wealthier and material goods become overabundant, affluent individuals may give greater importance to meaningful experiences than to material goods. These experiences might include an unforgettable vacation or activities such as "extreme sports," whitewater rafting (Arnould and Price 1993), spiritual retreats, or family reunions. This accent on experiences has created a new market for specialized goods and activities, but it has also affected the nature of the retail industry, which increasingly seeks to focus on the shopper's experience as a way to keep her or him in the store and spending money, and to weave unique or appealing experiences into the shopping event. Incorporating entertainment into a retail venue, as in the ESPN Zone, is an important example of how retailers have sought to refocus consumers away from experiences that occur outside stores and back to the purchase of material goods (Zukin 2004; Kozinets et al. 2004; Jantzen and Fitchett 2012).

Another form of experiential consumption is that of individuals' focus on "self-improvement." One dimension of the growing focus on lifestyle is the idea that each person has the opportunity (or even the obligation) to improve her/his health, appearance, and skills. This tendency is evident in the increasing popularity of exercise, yoga, meditation, psychotherapy, New Age spirituality, "life coaching," plastic surgery and body modification, tattoos and piercing, and other means to enhance body and mind. Each of these activities likely entails purchases – of gym memberships, athletic clothing, or medical attention. It also encourages individuals to "work" on their bodies and minds to achieve goals such as attractiveness, health, or a sense of well-being (Sassatelli 2007; Illouz 1997).

This focus on self-improvement is of course prompted by many media sources (television, magazines, the Internet), our peers, and our own individual desires. Hence, the improvement of body and mind has become another site of consumption beyond the purchase of traditional goods or experiences (Milestone and Meyer 2012; Lury 2011). This relatively new focus on activities is illuminated by practice theorists' argument that the purchase and use of physical products results from participation in specific activities, e.g., bicycling, yoga, mountain climbing, or book clubs. To engage in these activities, a given individual must purchase or acquire a package of goods (Warde 2005; Ingram et al. 2007).

Some authors focus on a relatively new phenomenon called "prosumption" (the integration of production and consumption). While there is historical precedent for current-day prosumption, authors are particularly interested in how the Internet 2.0 (social media sites like YouTube, Facebook, Twitter, tumblr, Instagram, Pinterest, and digital music file-sharing sites) provides a platform for consumers to produce goods for others to consume. This phenomenon offers a different twist on our traditional understandings of consumption. We assume that companies produce products and services, advertise them, and then consumers buy them. With these new Internet platforms, individuals have a greater opportunity to produce their own media content for others to view. At times, these images and messages have a small-scale, do-it-yourself (DIY) style, like the "how to do a French braid" or "look at my dog do tricks" videos that are popular on YouTube. However, some DIY songs become international hits launching musicians to stardom, as in the case of the South Korean hip-hop artist Psy, whose "Gangnam Style" video "went viral" on

YouTube and converted him into an international pop star (Ritzer et al. 2012; Rojek 2011; Smart 2010; Strangelove 2010).

These new media platforms are significant in two respects. First, they have a democratizing effect on the production and distribution of media content, undercutting the monopoly previously held by media companies and advertisers (Strangelove 2010). As Chris Rojek (2011) contends, the major recording companies have been unable to eliminate illegal music downloads and file-sharing, and these represent the vast majority of music consumed today. However, social media users often unwittingly provide free advertising for products or musicians they favor by "sharing" a YouTube video on Facebook, for example. Further, companies have been quick to capitalize on these platforms by inserting advertisements into the content we see on these sites, and mimic the music file-sharing culture with legal downloads and subscription radio sites like Pandora, Last.fm, and Spotify. Turow and Draper (2012) describe the sophisticated methods market research companies use to analyze and scrutinize individuals' use of social media to tailor ads to those individuals. Further, companies encourage consumers to use their own social media platforms to provide testimonials and narratives that speak positively and sincerely about the brand. Consumers' narratives and experiences become a source of profit for brands (Foster 2011). Hence, the shift to prosumption heralds new opportunities for creativity for producers of digital content and new opportunities for large producers, market researchers, and advertisers to study, analyze, target, and profit from individual consumers, often without their knowledge.

A final area of change in consumption since the mid-1970s is the phenomenon known as globalization, which refers to the growth and intensification of connections and flows of people, money, goods, organizations, and cultural images across regional and national borders. Historians point out that globalization is not new: global empires have existed since the Middle Ages and international trade between Europe and the Far East dates back at least to the Roman Empire (Abu-Lughod 1991; Straubhaar 2007). However, the current stage of globalization follows a period of greater control and influence of national governments over the operation of economies, cultures, and societies. Further, our contemporary era has experienced an acceleration of contact and influences across local sites, due to rapid changes in communications and transportation technologies that have reduced the "friction of distance" (Harvey 1990), thereby permitting a faster and larger movement of people, goods, money, ideas, and organizations across borders.

There is a sharp debate regarding the consequences of globalization for consumers in the Global South. One view argues that globalization has meant the rise of U.S. economic and cultural influence in the Global South (Ritzer 2003; Smart 2010). Here, researchers argue that the expansion of American retailers or entertainment companies such as Walmart, McDonald's, and MTV, and the export of branded products from the U.S. and Europe around the world, have led to the diffusion of American-style consumer practices and lifestyles to the Global South.

Another perspective focuses on the idea of hybridity (cultural mixture) and glocalization (the integration of the global and the local) (Appadurai 1996; Straubhaar 2007; Watson 1997). In this view, any large corporation must adapt to local cultural settings in order to successfully sell its products, and the ultimate outcome is a combination of external and internal cultural elements. A third view focuses on resistance to globalization (Caldwell 2002). In this view, segments of local populations reject foreign goods and companies as representing a threat to local and national cultures; or organized consumers seek to challenge the reputations of large corporations (Foster 2011; Cova et al. 2007). A final view suggests that the global and the local are two sides of the same coin. Richard Wilk's (2006) study of the history of food in Belize shows that "Belizean food" was a product of British and Spanish colonial rule and settlement – the "local" was produced by the "global."

What evidence supports each of these perspectives? An examination of food provides a clear illustration of each perspective. George Ritzer (2003, 2008) argues that the efficiency and uniformity of McDonald's (and other corporations in the fast-food, tourism, and credit industries) makes it very popular among consumers and also has permitted its global expansion. Given McDonald's success in many places around the world, Ritzer argues that the company has succeeded in changing local eating habits in many places. James Watson's (1997) study of McDonald's in Hong Kong illustrates the idea of cultural hybridity. He found that McDonald's had to adapt to local eating styles (the view that anything served without rice is a snack) and cultural rules (the rejection of service with a smile and customers' refusal to bus their tables) in order to be successful there. Caldwell's (2002) study of McDonald's in Russia found that older, lower-income Russians rejected McDonald's as contrary to local eating traditions and the company was only successful with this population when it advertised itself as part of the local and national culture. Finally, Wilk (2006) found that Belizeans only came to embrace their own cuisine after they had migrated to the U.S. and missed "home cooking." Demand from tourists in Belize allowed Belizeans to create restaurants that sold "authentic" local food.

A further twist on the globalization story refers to the appeal of foods from Asia in the U.S. and Europe. Theodore Bestor's (2000) study of the sushi industry is instructive. He found that sushi became popular in the U.S. in the 1970s after business executives visited Japan, alongside increasing health consciousness among U.S. consumers that led them to favor fish over red meat. Japanese companies control every stage of the production process of sushi. They control the fishing in New England and Spain. After fish are caught, they are flown back to Tokyo's traditional sushi market where sushi chefs, who developed their skills through a traditional apprenticeship process, cut and sell the fish in response to individual bids. The purchased fish is then sent back to the U.S. or Europe where trained sushi masters prepare it for restaurant customers.

In some ways, this story sounds like McDonald's except for the fact that the center of operations is in Japan. However, there are important differences that call for a more nuanced understanding of globalization. Japanese sushi companies use traditional craft principles and organizations to capture the fish, prepare it, and sell it. Hence, globalization has reinforced the power of a traditional, non-Western craft organization whose functioning does not follow the modern bureaucratic form.

A further example refers to television production and consumption in a global context. Some argue that the expansion of Hollywood films into countries of the Global South has led to the global consumption of standardized shows (Smart 2010). However, Straubhaar (2007) argues that most television-watching tastes are shaped in national settings, subnational regions, or cultural-linguistic zones (like Latin America, East Asia, or the Middle East). Following the work of Arjun Appadurai (1996) and Nestor García Canclini (1995), he argues that local cultures are hybrid phenomena that mix together domestic and foreign elements, and individual and national cultural identities contain multiple layers. The phenomenon of hybrid cultures predates the sixteenth-century rise of European empires as evident in the expansion of Chinese, Middle Eastern, and South Asian empires. The expansion of U.S. and European media technologies and products continues this process of cultural mixture. Additionally, the growing availability of broadcasting technology has allowed emerging economies like Brazil and South Korea to produce and export their own television content.

Viewers in a given country consume a range of different television shows, reflecting their multilayered identities. Action films and animated shows are the most popular global genres, and these were first exported by the U.S. but later developed by Japan and other East Asian nations. While viewers may enjoy these imported shows and films, they also lean toward cultural proximity (content that approximates the viewer's culture) for shows that require a more sophisticated understanding of dialogue from viewers (Straubhaar 2007).

In this context, while U.S.-based cable and satellite stations export their programming, the most popular shows, which require a greater degree of cultural knowledge to decipher, are nationally or regionally produced soap operas, variety shows, or local adaptations of global formulas like the reality show. Indeed, American soap opera producers look to Mexican and Venezuelan soap operas (which dominate the U.S. Hispanic market) for ideas and formulas they can apply to their own shows. Further, only a tiny segment of local populations in the Global South, the economic elite, define their identities primarily in relation to Europe or the United States (compare Üstüner and Holt 2010; Lash and Lury 2007). Straubhaar (2007) argues that working-class and poor television viewers in Brazil interpret television through a local prism and tend to contrast their lives with those of the sophisticated upper-class characters seen on TV. Finally, in some African countries, much of the population is too poor to acquire televisions and/or television and radio signals do not reach these remote locations.

Thus, in contrast to the above discussion of food that tends to contrast the global with the local, Straubhaar's (2007) discussion suggests that television must be classified into different genres and segments. Viewers outside the U.S. and Europe consume some imported content, but, where it is available, they prefer to view shows that are closer to their own cultural experience. Hence, it makes sense to talk about hybrid and multilayered identities and to question the idea that only the U.S. and Europe export mass-media products. There are growing and powerful media industries in Latin America, East Asia, India, and the Middle East that serve their own cultural-linguistic zones and export some shows to the U.S. and Western Europe.

A third perspective on globalization revisits our discussion of advertising in India and other areas outside the U.S. and Europe. Discussions of local advertising industries examine how advertisers attempt to make global products and brands appealing to a culturally distinct population (Mazzarella 2003; Cayla and Peñaloza 2011; Miller 2012). These professionals may have a vested interest in emphasizing the "difference" between their own population and the West to sell their services to multinationals (Mazzarella 2003), they may need to reformulate the brand's message to make it understandable and appealing to local populations (Cayla and Peñaloza 2011), and they may also need to create messages that appeal to culturally diverse populations (Miller 2012). Advertisers are on the front line of companies' "glocalization" strategies whereby they adapt global products and messages to distinctive local settings. They play a crucial mediating role between large multinational corporations and culturally distinct local populations.

These three different ways of thinking about globalization suggest that no single theory or debate adequately captures this process. We need to look at the reception of imported goods and messages, the changing landscape of production (particularly mass-media products), and the challenges global companies face when penetrating local markets outside their traditional home. In each of these arenas, we find evidence against the hypothesis that globalization leads to greater standardization of the products consumed and the ways individuals use and interpret these products.

Conclusion

In this chapter, we have explored the rapid and intense changes in the world of consumption since the 1960s. Complex cultural processes of individualization and the rise of subcultures and consumer tribes have coincided with changing and more sophisticated patterns of advertising, marketing, and branding that focus on market segmentation, emotion, and experience. Technological changes have transformed the production and distribution of goods and media content, with implications for the relationship between production and consumption and the arenas in which advertising operates. The current phase of globalization has also intensified the reciprocal influences of companies, goods, and lifestyles across borders. In the next chapter, we consider the intersection between consumption and class inequality in today's fast-changing world of consumption.

4

Consumption, Status, and Class

Introduction

Thus far, we have focused on the behaviors and attitudes of consumers that are broadly shared across individual societies. This is the first of three chapters that demonstrate the significant ways different groups of individuals vary in their approaches to and experiences of consumption. In this chapter, we examine how consumption varies in both quantity and quality across social classes. We understand classes as groups of people with similar incomes, educations, and professional statuses.

If we look at an entire society, we find that many individuals can be classified together based on their income, education, and profession so that it makes sense to divide society into the rich (investors, executives, political leaders, and celebrities), the middle classes (college-educated professionals, middle managers, or small-business owners), the working class (individuals with high-school educations who engage in physical rather than mental labor), and the poor (the unemployed, marginally employed, or those unable to work and who cannot achieve the standard of living considered acceptable within their society).

There is an extensive discussion about how members of each category differ in their education, income, and profession; but also how their position within these categories shapes consumption. We begin with the origins of modern class societies and how this large-scale transition set the stage for the role of class in consumption. We continue with early concepts of status developed by Max Weber and Thorstein Veblen. Status is related but not identical to class. Nonetheless, discussions of status continue to powerfully influence our understandings of consumption and class. We continue with the work of sociologist Pierre Bourdieu, who attempted to integrate the concepts of class and status to understand consumption in France. He argued that an individual's family-based class origins, educational experiences, and occupational position as an adult shape how they consume and that consumption is a field of symbolic conflict between members of different social classes and class fractions, each of which seeks to dominate the status game. Bourdieu's work has been enormously influential but also highly controversial, and so we explore some of the criticisms of his work, including ideas of individualization explored in chapter 3. We conclude with analyses of poverty and consumption, as well as a discussion of class differences in the retail and housing markets.

Historical Origins of Modern Class Divisions

To understand differences in consumption across social classes in modern societies, we first need to consider how social inequality shaped consumption in the premodern era. Under feudalism, society was divided into estates based on birth: the nobility, the clergy, and the commoners (or peasants). Social inequality was reproduced across generations based on primogeniture (inheritance). In addition to the transfer of property and social status through inheritance, feudal societies also controlled access to consumption through sumptuary laws. These laws restricted access to luxury goods to the nobility. Hence, for example, peasants were prohibited from hunting because meat was considered a luxury good. Thus, there were clearly defined differences in consumption between members of different estates, but this system was stable because peasants were legally prohibited from consuming luxury goods (Slater 1997; Sassatelli 2007; McKendrick et al. 1982).

A further source of stability resulted from the fact that most transactions were based on non-monetary exchanges, and peasants satisfied most of their needs through home-based production, while the nobility's survival depended on taxes on goods accessed through war or tribute from peasants, and the Church's survival was based on donations from the nobility (Douglas and Isherwood 1996). Hence, peasants were self-sufficient and did not seek out goods through the market, and the other two estates relied on taxes in order to satisfy their needs and desires. The market was not the main means of exchange.

The rise of a commercial bourgeoisie or business class in European cities disrupted the stability of consumption under feudalism. As these merchants gained wealth, they could define their social status based on conspicuous consumption rather than birthright. This opened the doors to status competition via consumption, which had only existed within the nobility before then. However, the bourgeoisie were a small segment of the population and so this change had symbolic importance rather than signaling a massive shift in consumer practices (Slater 1997; Sassatelli 2007; McKendrick et al. 1982).

Marx (1967) argued that, over several hundred years, segments of the nobility, merchants, and governments "liberated" the peasantry from the land. Feudalism was a social system based on customary rights and responsibilities between different social groups. Thus, kings granted lords title to massive farms and the noblemen permitted peasants to live on the land in exchange for paying the lords a share of their crops. Under this system, peasants had the right to remain on the land across generations, to retain control over their tools, and to receive protection from the lords (although this was more in principle than in fact).

As landlords and governments began to see the advantages of cutting the ties between lord and peasant, the latter were gradually removed from farms and converted into wage laborers. Landlords threw peasants off their land while governments passed vagrancy laws that made it illegal for peasants to circulate in public. Businessmen took over craft workshops and ran them as profit-making firms rather than guilds designed to provide for their members.

The gradual elimination of feudal institutions had important implications for wage laborers. First, to survive, these individuals needed to identify employment that would pay an adequate wage to satisfy their needs for food, clothing, and shelter, and to support their families. Second, because employers were not required to provide peasants with food and shelter (or the land on which to build it), and peasants no longer controlled their work tools, they were compelled to buy whatever they needed on the market. Modern class divisions in consumption coincided with the creation of a working class as well as the efforts of artists, craftsmen, and manufacturers to create and supply noble, bourgeois, and working-class markets (Slater 1997; Mukerji 1983; McKendrick et al. 1982).

While Marx's work was primarily focused on the production of goods directed toward profit-making, he also sought to explain how production and consumption are part of a single system that depends upon workers to make and purchase goods. Marx (1978b) argued that production and consumption are two mutually dependent phenomena. Workers use up their physical energy, raw materials, and machinery in the act of production, thus creating demand for food and factory supplies. Further, products do not exist as such without a market of users who add the "last finish" to them when they use them. Consumers also create further demand for new production. Finally, producers shape needs by developing new products. Hence, Marx saw production and consumption (as well as distribution and sales) as elements of a unified and self-reproducing system.

However, Marx (1978c) was pessimistic about the ability of capitalism to satisfy workers' needs. Because in nineteenth-century Britain (the main focus of his analysis) work was exhausting and unsafe, housing was inadequate, and wages were low, consumption could only be a momentary respite from the dull monotony of work. He argued that just as workers were alienated from the means of production (the tools they use to make things), they were also alienated from the goods they purchased. Hence workers could only satisfy their "basic, animal needs" through consumption due to their low wages, insufficient leisure time, and the fact that, for them, consumption is just a means to the end of producing for their employer.

Status

Both Weber and Veblen examined consumption as a social process that is independent from production. In his essay "Class, Status, Party," Weber (1946b) looks at three systems of ranking and power under modern capitalism. He argues that while Marx understood class as based on whether or not individuals own the means of production (tools, factories, land, or banks), Weber understood class as an individual's market position, which might include skills or assets (like a house). Individuals with different market positions have different life chances, which in part refer to what they can or cannot consume. Access to leadership positions in parties or government was another source of power.

Weber's (1946b) discussion of status is directly relevant to consumption. He understood status as the social honor or prestige an individual or group receives within a given society. He linked status to premodern systems of ranking based on birth or group membership. In his argument, social elites attempt to retain their dominance by monopolizing access to luxury goods and participation in specific rituals. Outsiders to this group, however, try to usurp the elite's monopoly of prestige goods.

The concept of status is useful for understanding consumption in that it demonstrates that we cannot classify different groups' consumption patterns only based on their income or assets. Rather, consumption varies based not only on monetary resources but also the social honor a group enjoys. These two systems of ranking often overlap. Those with more money, like corporate executives or celebrity athletes, also enjoy social honor. Likewise, the homeless, who lack assets, are a stigmatized group. However, income and status may not coincide. A mafia boss might be a millionaire, though he would unlikely be admitted to an elite country club due to his outlaw status and modest origins. In contrast, a successful painter, who may not earn a stable income, might find those same country-club members at her art gallery opening due to the high status of the visual arts among the wealthy. Hence, class and status fit together uncomfortably.

Thorstein Veblen (1979) developed the concept of status into a full-fledged theory of consumption, which continues to influence scholars today (Schor 1998; Smart 2010). Veblen attempted to understand the consumer behavior of the new rich during the "Gilded Age" in the U.S. (roughly 1870–1930) when the country experienced increased concentration of wealth in the hands of bankers, oilmen, steel entrepreneurs, and railroad magnates. Veblen also looked for historical precursors to the dominant class of his day.

Veblen (1979) argued that throughout human history, consumption styles differed between the honorable elites who were exempted from menial labor and subordinate groups engaged in dishonorable manual labor. He first identifies this division between male hunter/warriors who enjoyed ceremonial luxuries like tobacco and alcohol, and female or male slaves who engaged in farming and other necessary manual labor. This division, he argued, was based on concepts of social honor and dishonor, which favored those not tainted by menial labor. In his mind, this division continued through ancient Greece and Rome and into the Middle Ages. He notes that during the Middle Ages, members of the nobility held opulent parties and bestowed gifts upon their guests, dressing servants in elaborate uniforms to display their wealth.

This pattern changed in the modern era with the rise of wage labor. Workers promoted the value of craftsmanship, taking pride in their labor. To justify the fact that they did not work, elites engaged in rituals of conspicuous consumption (hunting parties, philanthropy) and developed cultural rules (like etiquette) to pretend to be productive. For Veblen, conspicuous consumption and waste justify the elite's social dominance and exemption from manual labor. Further, the majority of the population looks up to and seeks to imitate elite consumption. Therefore, while the elite is distinct from the general population, the latter try to imitate them and hence there is a tendency for class-based consumption differences to be diluted. Nonetheless, once a particular consumption pattern spreads to the broader society, elites abandon it for other products or lifestyles they can more easily monopolize (compare Simmel 1957).

There is evidence that some of the dynamics Veblen envisioned are still at work. For example, the actress and heiress, Paris Hilton, began to appear in public with a tiny Chihuahua in her purse. Several other celebrities followed suit. After many people viewed her on television, there was a craze for tiny dogs, designer handbags, and a line of pet jewelry that Hilton created. The handbag dog craze spurred an industry focused on breeding the tiny dogs (Warren 2008). Juliet Schor (1998) similarly argues that during the 1990s, middle-class Americans tended to compare themselves with the next higher-income group and to television celebrities.

Status competition is not limited to the U.S. O'Dougherty's (2002) analysis of middle-class Brazilians' ritual visits to Disney World, discussed in chapter 3, supports Veblen's ideas. Additionally, Van Bavel and Sell-Trujillo (2003) found that low-income Chileans who live near the wealthy accumulated debts to imitate their consumption habits.

However, Campbell (2005) challenges Veblen's theory. First, he argues that today's elite is much more diversified than in 1900; there is no one elite that sets fashion trends for all individuals. Some may wish to imitate business leaders (Veblen's example), others may imitate actors or musicians, while still others may look to other reference groups (such as family members, religious officials, teachers, or other close social contacts) for guidance on consumption. Some celebrities come from very modest backgrounds and hence do not match the business elite that Veblen studied.

Second, Campbell (2005) argues that members of the middle class have more influence on tastes than do business leaders. Here, he is thinking of the cultural intermediaries studied by Mike Featherstone (2000) – media professionals, interior decorators, and fashion designers. These individuals shape tastes, but they do not do so because they are the wealthiest members of society. Third, Campbell argues that individuals are not solely motivated by envy and greed; our consumption decisions may be motivated by generosity, religious values, or political beliefs. Additionally, many consumption patterns "bubble up" from low-income groups to middle- and upper-income groups. A contemporary example of this phenomenon is hip-hop music. This musical style was first developed in the 1970s by low-income Caribbean immigrants and African Americans in the Bronx, New York. As the musical style became more popular across income and racial groups, various companies drew upon the style in their advertising and product design. Athletic shoe companies like Reebok have utilized hip-hop styles to give their shoes an image of authenticity and "edginess," popular among white, middle-class youth. Status "trickles down" from the wealthy, as Veblen argues, but it also "bubbles up" from innovative cultural producers like African American youth (Goldman and Papson 2000; Klein 2010).

Research in developing countries has raised similar questions about Veblen's claims. For example, Daniel Miller (1994) found in his research on the Caribbean island nation of Trinidad and Tobago that many people he interviewed liked American soap operas such as *The Young and the Restless* because they felt the characters embodied cultural characteristics they associated with being Trinidadian, namely, the idea of "bacchanal," which means "drama" or "scandal," rather than out of a desire to imitate Americans. Further, Stillerman examined poor (2012), working-class (2004), and middle-class (2010) Chileans' consumer behavior, finding that these groups feel ambivalent about status competition in their society. The poor are concerned with their immediate survival needs, working-class people try to exercise "self-control" to avoid spending beyond their means, and some middle-class people reject the materialism they observe among others, favoring crafts over standardized goods or exercising self-control in consumption behavior based on religious beliefs. Members of each of these groups reject status as a motivation for their own consumption and express scorn toward the status-oriented consumption of other groups.

Richard Wilk's (2006) study of food in Belize offers another critique of Veblen's model of status. During the nineteenth century, middle-class colonial employees favored imported British foods over those made with local ingredients, which they scornfully labeled "bush food" due to the rural origins of many ingredients and recipes. Middle-class people distanced themselves from the poor by rejecting their preferred foods. This pattern supports Veblen's model of status imitation. However, Wilk finds that upper-class Belizeans enjoyed "bush food," which they obtained from rural relatives or domestic employees. Members of the elite did not fear being associated with the poor, and hence could eat bush food and maintain their social status. Wilk describes this pattern as a "style sandwich," whereby poor people's tastes skip the middle class to jump up to the elite. Hence, the poor and the elite represent the "bread" and the middle class symbolizes the "meat" of the sandwich. This pattern is intriguing in that tastes neither trickle down from the elite to the middle class and the poor nor do they bubble up from the poor to higher social classes. Rather, styles jump from poor to rich. While several scholars have identified flaws with Veblen's theory, it remains influential among scholars of consumption as a powerful analysis of status competition.

Pierre Bourdieu's Concept of Cultural Capital

Pierre Bourdieu (1984) offers a more complex understanding of variations in consumption between different classes and class fractions than does Veblen. As such, Bourdieu has developed the most influential (and controversial) model of class and consumption to date. Bourdieu's analysis of consumption builds on his earlier anthropological research in Algeria, as well as his studies of how the French educational system favors upper-class students while penalizing those from the working class. In his work on Algeria, he developed the idea of habitus, which he describes as a set of durable dispositions (or attitudes) developed in childhood. He argues that parents teach their children the values and attitudes specific to their class background. These values, attitudes, and skills allow children to navigate their immediate social surroundings, but make them ill-prepared for survival among other social classes with distinct attitudes and skills. Habitus gives children an identity and skills but also marks them as members of a specific social class. Bourdieu's point is illustrated by the differences in speech patterns among children from different social classes, ethnic/racial groups, and regions of the U.S. (Bourdieu 1977; Bourdieu and Passeron 1990).

His work on education added the concept of capital. While economists understand "capital" as money that is saved or invested, Bourdieu argued that individuals can save, accumulate, and invest knowledge (cultural capital) and social connections (social capital). Further, he argued that as adults, individuals can attempt to convert one form of capital into another. For example, individuals might use their personal acquaintances (social capital) in order to get a job and hence increase their economic capital (Bourdieu 1983; Bourdieu and Passeron 1990).

Bourdieu argued that children from distinct social classes start school with different quantities of cultural capital based on their parents' class backgrounds. Middle- and upper-class parents tend to have more formal education than their working-class and poor counterparts and they also have more money to invest in preschool, tutoring, or other enrichment activities. Further, schools promote the values held by upper- and middle-class parents. As a result, children from these classes are steered toward advanced classes, while working-class children are directed toward classes likely to lead them into a life of manual labor.

Bourdieu (1984) added the third concept of "field" to his analysis of consumption. He argued that within any area of consumption, or any profession, different groups have dominant and subordinate positions depending on the quantity and type of capital they possess. For example, the field of wine drinking is divided among sommeliers (professional judges of wine quality), connoisseurs (individuals who learn about fine wines in order to enjoy them), and the vast majority of wine drinkers. Sommeliers define the field, connoisseurs display their knowledge by enjoying specific types of wine while rejecting others, while most wine drinkers may find the search for the perfect wine a pointless endeavor when the point of drinking wine is to get drunk. The notion of field allowed Bourdieu to understand consumption as a form of status competition within and across classes, based on a more complex classification of consumers than "elites" vs. everyone else as defined by Veblen.

Building on the concepts of habitus, class, and field, Bourdieu and his collaborators conducted a significant amount of survey and interview-based research during the 1960s on patterns of consumption and leisure in France. He also used a data-analysis technique developed by French mathematicians, known as multiple correspondence analysis (MCA). Unlike much survey data analysis, which uses mathematical formulas to find the independent variable that affects the dependent variable, MCA is an inductive method – it matches together variables that coincide without looking for a single causal variable. Using MCA, Bourdieu attempted to see how different professions (whose members had different levels and types of education) displayed different forms of consumption (Bennett et al. 2009).

Based on the concepts of habitus, capital, and field, and his analysis of survey data with MCA techniques, Bourdieu developed a "map" of tastes across social classes, as well as an explanation for the inequality between classes (and class fractions) with regard to who gets to define what is "good" and "bad" taste and what is "refined" and "tacky." The map has a vertical axis that defines social classes in terms of economic capital (income and investments) that looks like our traditional image of the lower, middle, and upper classes. The map also has a horizontal axis that depicts capital composition within classes (the proportion of economic and cultural capital members of each profession possess). For example, within the middle classes, teachers have more cultural capital but small businessmen have more economic capital and their capital composition shapes their divergent tastes, according to Bourdieu.

Bourdieu identified different principles of taste within and across social classes. He was mainly interested in symbolic conflicts within the dominant class between intellectuals (university professors and artists) and businessmen. (When Bourdieu was writing, French intellectuals had enormous prestige, especially in Paris, in contrast to the U.S., where business owners have always held a more dominant status position.) In his view, intellectuals emphasized both aesthetic tastes (appreciation and knowledge of artistic goods and/or the aesthetic qualities of goods) and asceticism (appreciation of spiritual or intellectual rather than material values), while businessmen displayed more hedonistic tastes (a desire for expensive and luxurious goods). In contrast to the dominant class, the working class developed a "taste for necessity" in which they took a functional approach to goods, favoring quantity over quality (think of the popularity of buffet restaurants among working-class consumers in the U.S.).

Bourdieu argued that members of the middle class consumed imitations of what was popular among the upper class (again echoing Veblen), but were never in a position to define taste in the way upper-class fractions can. Thus, for example, small businessmen might enjoy sparkling wine instead of champagne, and school teachers might listen to light classical music rather than opera. For Bourdieu, the working class occupy a subordinate position in the class system. Rather than attempting to imitate the upper class, members of the working class withdraw from the status game, valuing simple pleasures over the efforts toward self-improvement adopted by members of the middle class. He argues that working-class people are pragmatic – they realize that they have little chance of upward mobility and hence opt out of the status game. Further, imitating the middle class would mean rejecting their own roots and expressing disloyalty toward their peers, another disincentive against competing for status via consumption.

This map of tastes differs from Veblen's model. First, not all social classes seek to imitate the elite. Members of the working class reject middle- and upper-class tastes as frivolous, effeminate, or boring. Further, differences within each social class reflect variations in capital composition across individuals and groups. Members of the same social class may reject the tastes of their peers in different occupations. Second, unlike Veblen, who argues that the upper class defines taste and other social classes observe and imitate them, Bourdieu argued that each social class has a greater influence on its own members than does the leisure class, principally through the family and schools. Hence, members of each social class learn to enjoy certain clothes, foods, and music through family members and teachers. Third, because Bourdieu places such emphasis on class-based socialization, he is interested in how each class reproduces tastes across generations and hence contributes to the reproduction of inequality across classes.

According to Bourdieu, this reproduction occurs via different mechanisms. First, family members and teachers inculcate in children a class-based habitus that becomes the basis of their tastes as adults (though this may be modified in adulthood through professional socialization). Second, taste is also an investment strategy through which parents seek to maintain or elevate their children's class positions. For example, a parent might give their child piano lessons with the idea that their music education might give them a common language with others from the upper class or help with their college applications. He argues that parents' inculcation of taste among their children is an example of a reconversion strategy. His idea is that middle- and upper-class parents invest in enhancing their children's cultural capital so they can convert their education into a higher-paying job as adults (see Lareau 2003; Pugh 2009).

He contends that not only do middle-class parents or intellectuals (what he called the dominated fraction of the dominant class) make educational investments in their children, but businessmen do so as well. Hence, new class fractions have emerged because of these investment strategies. He argued that a new bourgeoisie was emerging in France as a result of parents using the scholastic mode rather than the family mode of social reproduction. He observed that businessmen feared the employment competition for their children from university-educated adults who do not come from business families, so to retain their class position they increasingly sent their children to college. Thus, college-educated adults from the upper class displayed new tastes that combined the intellectuals' aesthetic approach with businessmen's focus on luxury. This new bourgeoisie displayed a taste for elite sports (skiing and tennis) and travel, for example.

He also observed the emergence of a new middle class, which was distinct from the traditional middle class comprised of small businessmen. This class resulted from the overproduction of university graduates that generated employment troubles for young adults. Many members of the new middle class were downwardly mobile children of the economic and intellectual elite. Given the absence of adequate jobs, many of these individuals created new fields of consumption that came out of "hippy" subcultures such as organic foods and handmade clothing, rock music, alternative lifestyles, and expert knowledge in "middle-brow" creative genres like comic books and jazz music. As we noted in chapter 3, these individuals also became involved in the culture industry as "cultural intermediaries," and others have explored how their own tastes influenced the broader public (Featherstone 2000).

Thus, Bourdieu was interested in how a specific group's consumption patterns might be part of their strategies to gain employment or take advantage of educational opportunities. He was also interested in how the "symbolic struggles" between classes and class fractions were carried out largely through expressions of taste and distaste. So, for example, an intellectual might view a bourgeois woman donning a fur coat as "tacky," preferring a knowledge of the history of clothing design. Similarly, a businessman might criticize abstract painter Jackson Pollock's work (in which he created spontaneous designs on canvas by spraying paint from tubes, likening his creative process to jazz musicians' improvised solos) as "ugly," preferring the more familiar portrait paintings he purchased at an art gallery. Finally, a member of the working class might prefer watching a football game on TV to looking at any painting. Bourdieu's point was that in making these statements about any consumption (art, food, or electronics), a person (intentionally or not) justifies their class position while pronouncing a negative judgment about other social classes. Hence, status conflict need not be visible solely in possession of goods displayed by the elite (as Veblen argued); rather, each class or class fraction makes judgments of others based on the familiar and unfamiliar, and these judgments contribute to status inequality within and across classes.

Bourdieu's approach to class and consumption is interesting in that it brings to light how an individual's identity emanates in part from the tastes they have developed throughout their life, as well as the ways that members of different social classes use taste as one among several strategies for seeking status, money, and power. For Veblen, all social classes imitate the elite as a means to increase their social status. In contrast, Bourdieu contends that each class and class fraction has its own tastes and strategies, thus making consumption patterns more diverse than Veblen would suggest, and the jousting between social classes more dynamic than his model proposes.

Through Bourdieu we can observe ongoing battles within social classes over what form of consumption is more "worthy" as well as see how members of a given social class might choose to reject the tastes of other classes. To take a familiar example, a working-class individual might drink Budweiser beer because it is inexpensive but also because it represents a familiar taste and is what "everyone drinks" within her or his social circle. When offered a "microbrew" or a European specialty beer, they might contend that it tastes "disgusting" or that it's a "waste of money." In contrast, a member of the middle class might describe the "working man's beers" as "piss water" or revolting, while describing the intricate details and "flavor notes" of the different types of beers, ales, and stouts produced by their local brewery. These judgments reflect the class-based nature of tastes, how taste is a weapon in the status warfare between social classes, and the complexity of these differences. "High-status" tastes do not merely trickle down from the elite – some social groups reject these tastes.

Critiques of Bourdieu

Bourdieu's model has been enormously influential in the study of consumption and class, but it has also generated considerable controversy. I begin by exploring a few of the criticisms of Bourdieu's work and then examine some authors who have sought to extend his ideas through new research. Michèle Lamont (1992) sought to test Bourdieu's theory by examining the "status signals" adopted by upper-middle-class men in small and large cities in the U.S. and France.

This focus on status signals (see also Lamont and Lareau 1988) is narrower than Bourdieu's interrelated concepts of cultural capital and habitus. Bourdieu sees an individual's strategies in the status game as resulting from her/his entire body of experiences in the family, school, and workplace – these are "embodied" elements of her/his identity that are much more deeply rooted than the "status signals" they send to others for strategic gain.

Lamont (1992) argues that Bourdieu's focus on cultural capital as the key status marker missed other ways that upper-class men signal social status. She points to socioeconomic divisions (income and wealth) and moral boundaries (ideas about worthy or unworthy individuals and behaviors) as sources of status that may overshadow cultural capital in some contexts and for some groups. She found that an individual might emphasize any of these three sources of division when marking boundaries with others, and that the status signals used varied across cities and countries. In her view, Bourdieu's focus on cultural capital only applies to the Parisian intelligentsia, and hence he overstates the role of class socialization in shaping taste and status strategies. She argues that status conflicts take diverse forms that are much more open-ended than Bourdieu claims.

Some researchers in dialogue with Bourdieu's ideas focus on *cultural consumption* – consumption of arts, music, and media – rather than consumption as a whole. Bourdieu applied his ideas to all forms of consumption, though many of his followers and critics have focused on his argument that individuals with high cultural capital consume the arts because they are "legitimate," highly revered forms of culture. In this context, David Halle (1993) took aim at Bourdieu's view that art is a principal indicator of divisions in taste based on social class. In his study of the artwork displayed in upper-class and working-class homes in the New York metro area, he found more similarities than differences across social classes. He did not see a deep understanding of art among the upper-class residents who displayed abstract art in their homes (a minority within his sample), and that even those who did have abstract paintings tended to view them much like the landscapes that working-class families displayed in their homes. He further questioned the idea that an individual's cultural capital improves their job prospects. He argued that technical training and connections are more relevant to job opportunities than cultural capital.

A third criticism of Bourdieu comes from French sociologist Bernard Lahire (2003, 2008). He takes a more individual approach to understanding taste than does Bourdieu. He argues that Bourdieu views taste as consistent across individuals within social classes, and tastes in different goods as consistent in each individual (e.g., if I like micro-brews, I probably will like abstract art). Lahire uses survey data to show that each individual has a wide variety of tastes that cannot be reduced to a coherent "package." As a result, he argues that Bourdieu goes about studying taste in the wrong manner because we cannot "read" individual taste from class taste, as taste varies across individuals and each person has a wide range of tastes. We should focus on individuals rather than social classes when studying taste and consumption.

Perhaps the most influential critique of (or alternative to) Bourdieu's model comes from sociologist Richard Peterson (Peterson and Kern 1996). In examining musical tastes in the U.S., he argues that the high status accorded classical music has declined in recent decades and the focus on specific forms of high culture (fine arts, opera, classical music) among the wealthy has dissipated in the U.S. However, he argues that there is still a class-based division in musical taste, but it takes a different form than Bourdieu argued. He contrasts the upper/middle-class "omnivores" with the working-class "univores." Rather than limiting their tastes to "high" culture, upper-class people now show their cultural knowledge through the diverse types of music they consume – classical, jazz, rock, and rap. In contrast, working-class people show an intense loyalty to a single style – like heavy metal or country music – rather than displaying knowledge of or interest in other styles.

Chan and Goldthorpe (2007) attempt to further specify Peterson's thesis. In doing so, they largely follow Weber in arguing that class and status follow two separate logics, thereby departing from Bourdieu's view that class and status are intimately linked. Class refers to occupational position and is the principal determinant of life chances, while status refers to the degree of social honor conferred on differently positioned individuals. Status is operationalized as friendship ties and is found to map closely on to the occupational structure. The authors find that status is most important to understanding differences in cultural consumption, calling into question Bourdieu's view that an individual's tastes reflect their class position.

Savage and Gayo (2011) challenge the omnivore thesis by using multiple-correspondence analysis to study musical tastes in Britain. Rather than seeing an omnivore vs. univore pattern based on class differences, they find that musical tastes are divided by age groups and this division reflects the intensity of different groups' investment in music more than a division between groups who like different types of music. Thus, "expert" listeners might like a variety of styles, but they differ from "pop voracious" listeners who consume vast quantities of music, and "classical enthusiasts" show no particular musical expertise and look more like Peterson's "univores." In sum, they see changing boundaries between and among musical genres that reflect generational rather than class differences.

In an interesting twist on this discussion, Lizardo and Skiles (2012) return to Bourdieu to explain Peterson's findings. Recall that Peterson argued that high art had lost its appeal to the upper class and was replaced with an omnivorous orientation. Lizardo and Skiles

(2012) seek to explain how individuals become omnivores. They propose that early childhood experiences and formal education give individuals high in cultural capital the skills to make risky choices in their tastes, and this "risk-oriented" attitude is increasingly valued among highly educated adults. Thus, while they agree with Peterson that high culture no longer defines "good taste," they contend that Bourdieu's understanding of how cultural capital is generated and used best explains this more recent phenomenon of omnivorous taste (see DiMaggio and Mukhtar 2004 for a similar view that the omnivorous orientation in part reflects class-based differences in cultural capital). With this last approach in mind, we turn to authors who have attempted to extend Bourdieu's insights.

Extensions of Bourdieu's Ideas

While several authors have challenged Bourdieu's theory, methods, and findings, others have sought to defend and expand upon his thesis. Doug Holt (1998) interviewed working-class and upper-middle-class Americans in a U.S. college town. He contends that many of Bourdieu's critics rely on an outdated model of class developed by W. Lloyd Warner to study status differences in American small towns in the middle of the twentieth century. Since Americans move frequently and are exposed to the mass media, Holt contends that they do not only look to their neighbors to assess their own and others' status. Further, because consumer goods are widely available to members of different social classes in the U.S., differences between classes are more visible in how individuals consume rather than from what they purchase. Following Bourdieu, he suggests that today "embodied" cultural capital (what an individual knows) is more important than objectified cultural capital (the prestige of the goods they own).

Holt (1998) continues that many of Bourdieu's critics focus too heavily on what individuals consume rather than how they consume it – what Bourdieu called the "mode of appropriation" of consumer goods. He finds that individuals with high and low cultural capital vary systematically in what they consume and how they consume it. For example, working-class people tend to shop in big-box stores and chains, enjoy watching television, and engage in hunting and fishing for leisure; while upper-middle-class people prefer independent restaurants, handmade goods, and boutiques. Further, members of the upper middle class focus more on the aesthetic aspects of goods and experiences and their sophisticated knowledge about them than do their working-class counterparts. These findings support Bourdieu's claim that members of the upper class take an "aesthetic" approach to consumption while those in the working class adopt a "functional" approach.

The most systematic effort to assess and extend Bourdieu's model is Bennett et al.'s (2009) study of tastes in the United Kingdom. The authors conduct a national survey, using the same methods as did Bourdieu, but engage with all of the critical work that was developed after the publication of *Distinction*. The authors generally support Bourdieu's view that class structures consumption, but it does not do so as universally or exactly the same way as he argued.

They find that some areas of consumption, like artwork and books, are much more class-based than others, like music. Nevertheless, they reject Bourdieu's notion that working-class people have a "taste for necessity." Rather, they found unique and rich forms of consumption among working-class people based in their social networks, musical performance, and DIY (do-it-yourself) projects.

They also found different sources of inequality in taste. Differences in musical taste are largely based on age, with younger people consuming more than older people. Hence, the division between classical and popular music does not hold today. Further, gender is an important source of division focused on outer or inner orientations toward consumption. Women also tend to be more versatile in their styles of consumption than men. The authors also found that ethnicity was a source of division between different groups within the U.K.

Bennett et al. (2009) are part of an ongoing research program in Europe (but also elsewhere), which seeks to explore how cultural consumption and leisure practices vary across social groups. Using survey data and MCA, researchers have attempted to test and make more complex Bourdieu's and Peterson's claims in contemporary Europe and Chile. Gayo and Teitelboim (2009) found results consistent with Bourdieu's claims in Chile; Bihagen and Katz-Gerro (2000) argue that the main division in cultural knowledge and participation in Sweden is between women and men rather than between different social classes, with women displaying more cultural participation and knowledge than men; while, in contrast, Lizardo (2006) found no gender differences in cultural participation and knowledge among intellectuals ("the dominated fraction of the dominant class"), supporting Bourdieu's findings.

In addition to this largely survey-based research on class and consumption, others have applied Bourdieu's ideas through qualitative interviews in different countries. Tuba Üstüner and Doug Holt (2007) found that first-generation migrants to Istanbul, Turkey, retained their rural cultural identity, while second-generation women attempted unsuccessfully to participate in modern consumer culture. In a second study (2010), the authors found that middle-class Turks with higher cultural capital attempted to flawlessly imitate American cultural styles, while those with lower cultural capital preferred Turkish goods. These studies use Bourdieu's ideas to identify the class bases of consumption, but also point to the distinct position of Turkey in the global economy in contrast to France, the U.K., or the U.S. Turkey has its own domestic consumption traditions and has recently experienced the growth of Western products and retail formats. Hence, consumers from different social classes need to negotiate their identities in relation to the class system in Turkey, as well as to national and international cultural models.

Stillerman's (2010) study of middle-class fractions in Chile found divisions among high cultural capital professionals who work in different fields and between these first two groups and members of the lower middle class who possess less cultural and economic capital. Intellectuals and public employees favored crafts and Latin American or European artistic products, private-sector professionals were more comfortable with American movies and artworks by Chilean producers, and members of the lower middle class favored family-based consumption like barbecues and parties. These horizontal and vertical divisions in taste are similar to those Bourdieu identified, but these individuals articulate their tastes in relation to what they perceive as "authentically" Chilean versus what they view as foreign (often products coming from the U.S.).

Amy Hanser (2008) extends Bourdieu's ideas in her study of clothing stores in China. She examined female staff at a state-owned store, a high-end retailer, and a bargain-oriented market selling imitation goods or knock-offs. Following Bourdieu (1984), Hanser (2008) explores the "distinction work" sales employees engage in to differentiate their store from competitors and attract their target clientele. Workers in the state-owned store attempted to distance themselves from the stigmatized bargain market. Those in the high-end store dressed as "respectable" women and showed deference to their upper-class customers. Finally, vendors in the bargain market modeled their stores' sexually provocative styles while countering customers' disrespectful comments or attitudes. Thus, in her study, retail workers (and managers) seek out customers from a specific social class, but they also defend their class- and gender-based honor against customers' prejudices toward lower-class women.

Alternative Conceptions of Class and Consumption

Other discussions of class and consumption depart from the debate regarding Bourdieu's or Veblen's analyses of class and status. Many of these discussions use the concept of individualization. While Giddens, Beck, Lash, and Bauman note that harsh inequalities still exist in many societies (and these differences have worsened in recent decades), they suggest individuals no longer perceive themselves as belonging to class-based communities as Bourdieu and others argue they did in the 1960s and earlier. These changes result from post-Fordist design and employment systems and the fragmentation of traditional identities (Lury 2011).

Bauman's (2007) analysis of the "new poor" exemplifies this approach. He argues that, since the 1970s, the loss of stable employment and the intensification of consumption have undermined traditional bases for group belonging and political identity. He contends that individuals increasingly shape their identities through consumption rather than through work. Those who can afford to be in the "status game" experience stress and anxiety as they participate in a rat race to keep up with changing styles and social judgments. However, the situation is worse for the unemployed or those with weak labor market ties. Bauman argues that employed workers view those who are too poor to participate in the status game as "flawed consumers." Thus, the shift to a consumption-based society has cruel consequences for the poor.

Consumption and Poverty

Bauman highlights the fact that many studies of consumption ignore the working classes and the poor because they saw much of the dynamism in consumption as operating among the middle classes and the wealthy. In principle, this perspective is logical, but it also runs the risk of ignoring an important segment of the population. Furthermore, the consumer practices of the poor often "bubble up" to the wealthy via brands and marketing, as in the examples of hip-hop music and clothing brands like Tommy Hilfiger (Zukin 2004; Holt 2004; Holt and Cameron 2010).

A long-standing literature examines the consumption practices of low-income consumers. Studies of low-income consumers address how families struggle to satisfy their basic needs and participate in culturally valued consumption activities. When families lack adequate income, they may look to a variety of small-scale income-generating activities to increase their resources, use various sources of credit to buy daily goods and appliances, and share resources and services with extended family or friends. Hence, while recent discussions of consumption emphasize processes of individualization, which imply that each consumer feels the need to construct her or his identity via consumption, low-income consumers struggle to survive by pooling resources, labor, and goods between individuals and households. These consumers operate within a web of reciprocity or sharing that helps them stay afloat (Stack 1974; Gonzalez de la Rocha 1994).

Class and the Retail and Housing Sectors

Thus far, we have focused on how tastes for goods and services differ across social classes. It is important, however, to consider how retail and housing sectors differ by class across neighborhoods and urban–suburban divides. Poor and wealthy neighborhoods include specific businesses targeted to their respective income groups. Every high-rent district in a city's downtown or exclusive suburb includes expensive hotels, restaurants, investment firms, and luxury goods stores targeted to office workers, residents, or tourists. In contrast, low-income communities are filled with businesses that both target and exploit those populations, such as dollar stores, secondary lending sources (checks-cashed stores, rent-to-own stores, and payday lenders), pawnshops, and liquor stores. Hence the retail landscapes inhabited by individuals from different social classes reflect businesses' calculations about the class background and tastes of residents and others passing through (Dreier et al. 2004; Zukin 2004; Cohen 2003; Manning 2000).

Class divisions are also central to the structuring of the housing market. Adults' housing decisions are often linked to school choices because, where possible, parents seek housing in neighborhoods or municipalities where they believe their children will receive a high-quality education. We note those links here, but focus on housing in this chapter and school choice in chapter 6.

In the U.S., we can identify several patterns in which housing and education decisions are linked. Since World War II, primarily white middle-class residents have selected suburban homes based on a desire for safety and privacy, and have "bought into" a quality school system. Given the racial segregation in housing, which we will discuss in chapter 5, and decentralization of local government (cities, towns, or villages control the types of housing or businesses built), cities and suburbs were "color coded" (defined by racial composition) and also tended to be homogeneous in class terms. Growing suburban areas could filter residents by social class, for example, by restricting or eliminating the construction of apartments or public housing.

When parents move to a suburb, they are also selecting (consciously or not) the race and social class of their children's classmates. In this sense, public schools are in fact "private" insofar as parents "buy into" a school district if they can afford the housing and tax costs. In Bourdieusian terms, for more affluent or highly educated parents, this represents a reproduction strategy as their children will attend schools with more resources and more affluent peers, improving their opportunities for admission to college and highly remunerative careers. Lower-income and minority families tend to send their children to local urban or rural schools due to lower housing costs, greater availability of rental units, the ease of transportation to school, and lack of resources and knowledge that would facilitate the selection of better-performing schools located further from home (Cohen 2003; Dreier et al. 2004; Lacy 2007; Pugh 2009; Lareau 2003).

Western Europe diverges from the U.S. with regard to the spatial organization of cities and suburbs and the role of government in planning. Apartments represent a much higher percentage of the market than in the U.S., and apartments are located in the core of cities. Further, governments tended to construct public housing in the periphery. With a premium paid for apartments, a larger segment of the housing market in public hands, and education primarily in the public sector, it is less likely that parents might buy into a public-school district; rather, affluent parents might send their children to elite public or private schools (Raveauda and van Zanten 2007; Ball et al. 1995).

In much of the Global South, the structure of the housing market is different from that in the U.S. or Europe. In most major cities, the home builders could not keep pace with rural to urban migration. Thus, most cities are surrounded by shantytowns composed of "self-help" homes – houses constructed by their owners on vacant land. Squatters initially build homes with makeshift materials and later improve them as they accumulate savings (Gilbert 1998; De Oliveira and Roberts 1996).

Only in the last two decades have US-style suburbs appeared in the guise of gated communities in low-income areas. Affluent families may seek traditional elite housing areas or new suburban "enclaves," depending on their preferences for older housing in upper-class communities or greater space in mixed-income areas. Authors note that gated communities and shopping malls in countries such as Brazil have changed an earlier pattern of the mid-twentieth century when residents from different social classes were more likely to cross paths in residential neighborhoods and retail areas, and raise concerns that the increasing use of armed guards and surveillance cameras in gated communities and shopping malls will undermine full access to public spaces.

This critique actually began in the U.S. through analyses of the privatization of public space in Los Angeles, New York, and elsewhere (Davis 1990; Zukin 1995). Teresa Caldeira (2000) argues that gated communities in São Paulo, Brazil, have created more harsh inequities between upper-middle-class residents who live inside and the poor people who work in the buildings or live in slums outside the gates. Murray (2011) and Selzer and Heller (2010) develop a similar analysis in Johannesburg, South Africa, in a different historical context in which many residents and spectators expected that the end of white rule would bring residential racial integration. However, gated communities linked to schools, jobs, and retail insulate the middle class from poor, inner-city blacks. In contrast, Gonzalo Cáceres and Francisco Sabatini (2004) argue that because gated communities in Chile were built in formerly poor settlements, they provide local poor residents with jobs and increased opportunities for street interactions with the rich, thus reducing class-based segregation.

Gentrification is a recent trend in urban housing markets in the U.S., Europe, and some areas of the Global South. While the postwar mass wave of suburbanization in the U.S. led to cities' economic decline, some suburbanites began returning to cities at the beginning of the 1980s. Initially artists and members of sexual minorities, and later "mainstream" families, began to "colonize" abandoned warehouse districts, historic districts, and other urban areas. Artists wanted cheap space, while other groups wanted a more "authentic" urban experience in contrast to the "bland" suburbs (Lloyd 2006; Gotham 2007; Zukin 1995).

Gentrification did not reverse suburbanization in the U.S. Today more than half of the population lives in the suburbs. However, it has important implications for cities and our understanding of consumption. Gentrification is connected to urban governments' strategies to increase employment and tax revenue given the loss of residents and jobs. City officials hope that investments in real estate, entertainment, and services will generate economic solvency and growth. Individuals' desire for authenticity reflects the processes of individualization and the aestheticization of everyday life. Moving to the city is a form of personal expression for many new urban residents who seek to be part of the "authentic" aspects of city life, which include the presence of racial and ethnic minorities and the availability of arts and entertainment. Many authors argue that white, middle-class families' return to cities makes these areas unaffordable for lower-income racial and ethnic minorities, some of whom have become homeless while others have moved to declining inner-ring suburbs that offer fewer services for low-income inhabitants (Florida 2003; Zukin 1995; Harvey 1990; Dreier et al. 2004).

Gentrification has encouraged cities and neighborhoods to "brand" themselves to attract new residents. Realtors invent new names for neighborhoods, which they think will appeal to buyers. City officials promote their school districts to attract parents to the housing market. Further, city governments invest in bike paths, arts activities, and entertainment that they hope will attract affluent residents and tourists. The promotion of the city as a commodity with a recognizable brand has led to an increasing role for private business in funding infrastructure like sidewalks and parks. All of these efforts to boost real-estate values and tax revenues have also made cities less welcoming to the poor, particularly the homeless. Hence, cities that seek to make their downtowns more appealing to tourists and affluent residents have passed anti-panhandling ordinances or built "bum-proof benches" at bus stops to keep the homeless out of entertainment districts. Gentrification is a double-edged sword (Davis 1990; Zukin 1995; Gotham 2007).

Individuals seek out different aspects of specific neighborhoods and homes, based on their tastes and the visual and textual messages they receive about these neighborhoods and homes. Sometimes these taste-based choices are rooted in adults' class backgrounds, but they may also reflect other attitudes, beliefs, and orientations weakly connected to class. For example, educated middle-class adults might seek a "historic" home with exposed wood because it matches their desire to be "authentic." Upwardly mobile individuals might seek a newer house in the suburbs, which symbolizes their success. Others with more limited means might focus on living close to extended family due to their feelings of emotional attachment to their place of origin and need for support to care for children (Bourdieu 2005; Pugh 2009; Ball et al. 1995).

New housing developers and realtors seek to satisfy different groups of home seekers' desires and to persuade them that amenities and features they did not previously consider are what they really want. Developers of large housing complexes design and describe homes based on extensive market research. Based on these results, they utilize specific code words and stylistic features to appeal to their target market. As Mark Gottdiener (1997) argues, many of the names of housing developments and the designs of suburban homes reflect potential buyers' nostalgia for the medieval estate that never existed in the U.S. (with the exception of Southern slave plantations, which were only a regional pattern). Suburban homes' large lawns, which are not used to produce food, are a small-scale copy of landed rural estates that existed in the past and that most Americans could never afford.

Duany et al. (2010) contend that the annual home builders' convention is characterized by displays of luxury appliances like Jacuzzis that vendors believe most customers want in new homes. Many of these "estate-like" homes are new constructions. They also note that names of new housing developments that refer to natural or agricultural habitats (orchards, brooks, and creeks) appeal to home buyers' nostalgia for the rural America that the suburbs have destroyed.

Urban developers may use different messages to attract home buyers or renters. Many neighborhoods have received designations by the National Registry of Historic Places. Neighbors have appealed to the U.S. Department of the Interior to intervene when homes in older neighborhoods are in danger of demolition to permit new development. Historic designation protects these homes from destruction, but it also becomes a marketing appeal to buyers interested in finding a "historic" home that they can "restore" to its original state (Gotham 2007). This desire reflects a different kind of nostalgia than that evident among suburban residents, as these individuals are attracted to historic home designs rather than the size and stature of a rural estate or images of the natural environment. Occupants of historic homes may find the visual aspects of newer homes to be unattractive or even tacky. These tastes and distastes reflect differences in cultural capital possessed by members of different class fractions (Bourdieu 1984, 2005).

Urban realtors or neighborhood associations may promote neighborhoods as "hip" to attract young people interested in the arts and entertainment who may wish to be part of a "scene." Richard

Lloyd (2006) found that many new middle-class residents found the formerly low-income Polish and Hispanic Chicago neighborhood of Wicker Park appealing after artists had moved in and created a gallery and performance scene alongside the growth of restaurants, bars, and music venues where many of the artists worked "day jobs." Hence, the allure of cool also figures in the real-estate market.

Conclusion

In this chapter, we have explored the different ways scholars understand the relationship between consumption and social class. Veblen's model of conspicuous consumption and emulation continues to influence academic and popular understandings of status competition, though several scholars challenge the view that all consumption is driven by individuals' desire to imitate the wealthy. Bourdieu's understanding of class-specific patterns of consumption and symbolic conflict has inspired a substantial research agenda and provoked considerable criticism. In some cases, authors argue that class has a declining influence on consumption. Scholars focused on individualization suggest that individual consumption or lifestyle projects may have sidelined class as a basis of identity, while Bauman notes that our individualized societies harshly exclude the poor. Poor people must rely on one another to make ends meet and develop complex strategies for satisfying day-to-day financial needs and planning for culturally expected gift purchases.

Class differences are evident in patterns of metropolitan segregation, whether in the form of large-scale segregation between cities and suburbs or small-scale segregation between "hip" young people moving to "unique" urban neighborhoods and poor people with longer-term roots in these communities. Globalization has meant increasing polarization of incomes in the Global South as evident in the cheek-by-jowl location of wealth and misery reflected in the rise of shopping malls and gated communities in poor communities. However, scholars are divided about whether these new settlement and shopping patterns further divide or bring together the rich and poor.

In this chapter, we have considered the continued relevance of class to consumption. While some argue that class is no longer a collective identity that shapes consumption, many scholars agree that an individual's class background shapes their consumption, even if they do not consciously see themselves as members of a class. Nonetheless, as we shall see in chapter 5, a singular focus on class is deceptive. Gender, sexuality, race, and religion are axes of inequality and difference that intersect with class. Hence, inequalities are expressed in complex ways through individuals' combined subject positions based on class, race, gender, sexuality, and religion.

5

Gender and Race at the Margins and Center of Consumption

Introduction

When considering consumption, we often think in terms of generic individuals that are roughly equivalent in their identities and resources. As the last chapter suggested, this approach is deceptive because it does not address the important ways that class and status differences among individuals lead to differences in their orientation toward consumption and their access to resources that allow them to purchase or access goods.

This chapter takes this focus one step further by examining how gender, sexuality, race, and religion intersect with consumption. An exclusive focus on class does not address the extent to which consumers are also differentiated based on other axes of inequality. In this chapter we will not only look at differences between men and women, racial/ethnic groups, religious groups, and those based on sexual orientation; we will also consider how gendered and racialized symbols used in advertising, marketing, and design influence how consumers think of themselves and others.

The chapter begins with a discussion of gender as a category of analysis and a set of symbols attached to men and women. Gender is relevant to our understanding of consumption in two ways. First, it is crucial to understand how men and women consume differently, and how masculinity and femininity have been symbolically represented through consumer culture. Second, it is essential to explore how women have been positioned as "objects" within consumer culture, namely, how the female body becomes an object of the heterosexual male gaze via its adornment with cosmetics and clothing and "improvement" via dieting, exercise, and plastic surgery. Women have a dual role as consumers: to satisfy their needs and desires (and often those of their families), and to serve as objects of male desire. Women's objectification through consumer culture underscores how consumption produces inequality through its commodification of the female body. In an analysis of global variations in gendered consumption, we consider the role of Islam in shaping women's consumption in different ways than do other religious traditions. We conclude this section by considering whether or not gay and lesbian consumers represent a distinct market from heterosexuals.

The discussion of race has a similar format to the analysis of gender, though racial and gender inequalities operate in different ways. In the U.S. and Europe, African Americans (and to a lesser extent Latinos, Asians, and Native Americans) have faced and continue to endure institutionalized discrimination in retail and credit markets. African Americans still struggle to be accepted as consumers, placing them in a distinct position from other ethnic and racial groups. Nonetheless, in spite or perhaps because of their exclusion from white-dominated consumption settings, African Americans have developed innovative styles of cultural production and consumption that have significantly influenced Western and global culture.

Distinctive African American consumption styles connect to how members of this group have been objectified to promote "cool," particularly in the fields of clothing and music. Ironically, as Sharon Zukin (2004) notes, a group that has faced systematic discrimination as consumers has been utilized by producers and media outlets as a symbol of style and cool to be consumed by whites. This objectification of blackness reflects African Americans' historical relegation to the occupational fields of entertainment and sport, as well as the "exotic" image of non-Westerners that resulted from European colonial rule in Asia, Africa, and the Americas. We also consider the distinctive consumption patterns of Hispanics and Asian Americans. We conclude the section by considering the racial dynamics of consumption in the Global South through an analysis of native peoples as consumers in Latin America and Africa.

The chapter ends with consideration of theoretical discussions of "intersectionality." The concept of intersectionality was developed by black feminists interested in understanding how the experiences of black women are different from those of other women. Others have used this concept to look at the interlocking pattern of inequalities based on class, race, gender, sexuality, age, and ability, and on how an individual's subject position includes multiple dimensions. We examine some recent work on intersectionality in consumption to consider how we might integrate insights on these different axes of inequality to better understand consumption.

Gender and Consumption

Before entering into the role of gender in consumption, we must first define "gender." Unlike "sex," which describes the biological differences between men and women, gender is a wholly cultural category. Gender refers to the meanings a given society attaches to masculinity and femininity, which are qualities we associate with men and women, respectively. Gender is a social construction: it is a product of human imagination rather than nature (Milestone and Meyer 2012).

A focus on gender allows us to examine how our beliefs about men's and women's characteristics affect how we view and treat one another. These beliefs have varied across time and space, so that the "proper" roles of men and women 100 years ago in the U.S. are different from their expected roles today; and contemporary gender roles in the U.S., Sweden, Saudi Arabia, and Japan, for example, are distinct. These historically evolving and culturally diverse concepts of gender have shaped consumer culture. Conversely, consumer culture, in turn, has shaped gender ideas.

Women and modern consumption

We begin with a discussion of gender in the early development of modern consumption. During the nineteenth century, women had an ambiguous but central role in the early development of modern consumption because of their position in society and how it related to received ideas about production and consumption. In modern economic and philosophical thinking and law, men were expected to play public roles as workers, businessmen, and family managers. Additionally, Western thinking tended to consider production as useful and consumption as trivial. Hence, within the cultural constructs of the time, women were relegated to the domestic sphere and associated with the trivial activity of consumption (Slater 1997; Milestone and Meyer 2012).

However, women's involvement in consumption was contradictory. Until late in the nineteenth century, middle-class women were legally dependent on their husbands and hence could not hold their own bank accounts. Further, these women were expected to stay indoors if unaccompanied in order to be protected from vice and to maintain the family's good name. In this context, the first phase of "triangulation" was developed, according to Juliet Schor (2004), summarizing the work of Erika Rappaport (2001) and others. Middle-class women shopped by using their husband's credit, and merchants encouraged them to run up large tabs, knowing that husbands were legally responsible for paying the bills. Hence, merchants allied with women against their husbands (compare Leach 1993: 128–30).

A second early pattern of consumption, mentioned in chapter 2, is that of department stores' efforts to cater to women while respecting men's concerns that women should be protected from immoral influences in public (Nava 1997; Leach 1993). Thus, while women had little economic or political power, they became central targets for early retailers and marketers, and women were increasingly perceived as specialists in consumption (Fiske 2000). Early twentieth-century marketing extended the initial pattern of triangulation by selling the virtues of foods and children's goods to women, highlighting women's sense of responsibility for their children (Schor 2004).

Women's involvement in consumption periodically produces "moral panics" – intense reactions from politicians or activists via the media or political organizations. Dick Hebdige (2000) describes how European scooter producers modified their product's design in the 1920s to allow women to ride them without pulling up or soiling their skirts or dresses. The scooters became popular among women, leading to a moral panic as some men feared that women's independence signaled their sexual freedom and hence the decline of the family.

Women's role as "expert" consumers continued in the post-World War II era, as social pressures to leave wartime workplaces and return to domestic roles coincided with an economic boom. With rising incomes and homeownership, women were targeted for purchases of new labor-saving devices like vacuum cleaners, blenders, and dishwashers (Cohen 2003). During the 1950s in the U.S., women were encouraged to stay out of the labor market yet many women found this stifling. Tupperware's successful direct sales model helped some women balance their domestic roles with their desires to earn money and gain satisfaction through work. Women hosted evening parties that were appealing social events and also allowed them to generate an independent income by using their relational skills (Clarke 1999).

During the 1960s and 1970s, the women's movement, growing availability of reliable contraception, relaxation of divorce laws, and women's massive entry into the workforce transformed their involvement in consumption. Women could be financially independent, delay or avoid marriage, and more easily regulate fertility. Thus, women could shift the focus of their consumption. Historically, women's consumption had been organized around the needs of husbands and children. Often women consumed on behalf of others rather than for themselves. Once they became economically independent, women could enter the world of consumption to satisfy their own needs and desires (Pahl 1989; Zelizer 1989; Cohen 2003; Milestone and Meyer 2012; Zukin 2004).

As Illouz (1997) argues, women have also played a central role in modern consumption because of the strong cultural connections between romance and consumption that advertisers appropriated and promoted. Beginning in the early twentieth century, advertising and film connected romantic love with consumption, and the emergence of dating linked romance with purchases (such as restaurant meals or films), or the use of consumer goods (like cars). Dating emerged as romance replaced religion as the main focus of everyday life. The author contrasts ads focused on romance during 1900–30 with those from the late 1980s and notes a shift in focus from products to experiences, like travel. This shift reflects the emergence of postmodern consumption, described in chapter 3.

Illouz (1997) also conducted interviews with working- and middle-class couples and found a contrast between their ideas about romance (as present in dating and extramarital affairs), and their understandings of how to identify the ideal partner and reignite passion in marriage. Ideas about romance are linked to consumption rituals (meals, travel, luxury), while discussions of committed relationships use the metaphor of work to describe making lists of the ideal partner's qualities or developing strategies to reinject romance into marriages. Interviewees drew ideas about committed relationships from women's magazines. Following Bourdieu (1984), the author argues that middle-class couples (especially women) have more cultural capital than their working-class counterparts and hence are more familiar with the therapeutic discourse present in these magazines and more skillful in developing strategies to find romance in everyday experiences rather than consumption, or in negotiating with partners to better satisfy their emotional needs. She demonstrates the close linkage between romance and consumption, and how the contradictory demands of work and consumption under capitalism are reflected in ideas about and practices of love and romance.

Women, men, advertising, and the media

Advertisements, product design, and marketing for women have changed since the early 1970s in that they increasingly position women as individuals who seek to satisfy their own needs and desires, although some advertisements continue to view women primarily as consumers on behalf of their families. Ads have attempted to address women's desire to be treated as individuals by drawing on feminist themes such as the 1970s Virginia Slims cigarette ad that adopted the feminist slogan, "You've come a long way, baby," speaking to progress in women's rights within society (Bordo 2000). As the second-wave feminist movement waned, the focus shifted to personal care and adornment in what some scholars see as an embrace of post-feminist attitudes focusing on female professional independence and sexual assertiveness. Several scholars criticize these ads for reinforcing traditional ideas regarding female beauty. Women appear more assertive in these ads but they seem to promote traditional female images and roles as subservient to men (McRobbie 2008; Milestone and Meyer 2012; Gill 2009).

Katie Milestone and Anneke Meyer (2012) provide an overview of the role of gender in the media and entertainment industries since World War II, which traces changing gender roles in the West. They examine work in the advertising and entertainment industries; the changing images of men and women in advertising, television, and film; and how men and women consume media products.

The authors find that men dominated creative work in music, film, and information technology industries in the postwar era and continue to do so today, despite the women's movement's impact on cultural attitudes and the passage of anti-discrimination laws in the U.S. and Europe. They find that cultural assumptions going back to early modern Europe position men as "creative geniuses" and women as producers of "crafts." These attitudes, along with women's primary responsibilities as caregivers for children, led to men's dominance in "frontline creative" roles in advertising and information technology. This idea of creative genius being a uniquely masculine quality has also meant that men dominate the popular music industry (as producers and instrumentalists), and key creative roles as film directors. Hence, in all of these industries, the images of women produced for popular consumption tend to reflect male perspectives and to reinforce stereotypes of women as sexual objects or driven by emotion.

The authors note important changes since the 1960s in images of men and women in television, advertising, magazines, and film. In the postwar era, men were represented as rational, in control, powerful, and sexually assertive; while women were depicted in domestic roles that supported men. Recently, new images of women and men have emerged. In the new femininity, women are depicted as professionally successful and sexually assertive, which represents an important shift from traditional views of women. However, in television shows, ads, and film, women are portrayed as attractive and ultimately seeking true happiness through romance and family. Hence, the new femininity does not represent a radical break from traditional views of women, who are largely still viewed in relation to men.

Two new images of men have emerged, particularly in men's magazines – the "new man" and the "new lad." The new man is viewed as focused on style and fashion and emotionally expressive, while the new lad is stuck in adolescence and views women as objects. The new man, or metrosexual, reflects a softening of traditional male stereotypes. The authors argue that men are still depicted as having dominant roles in society through both of these images (compare Tuncay 2006). The authors build on Sean Nixon's (2003) study of male copywriters and art directors in a British advertising agency. He found that the "new lad" image reflected the modest origins of those male advertising professionals who identified with this image, agencies' interests in targeting young men, and creative workers' tendency to "work hard and play hard," which brought them in contact with prototypical "new lads" in London's pubs.

Finally, the authors explore differences in how men and women consume media products. They find that teenage boys and girls read magazines differently: boys tend to read magazines alone, while girls read and comment on magazines in groups. Additionally, men and women may accept or reject the gender images they observe in the media. For example, women may criticize the association of thinness with beauty in the media, while some men reject the objectification of women in men's lifestyle magazines. Finally, the authors explore how most video games are designed to appeal to heterosexual males, making it difficult for girls to participate in them.

Milestone and Meyer's (2012) overview of gender and popular culture offers a sobering view of the unequal positions of men and women in the production and consumption of popular entertainment. They demonstrate that while we might assume that women have made great strides in society, the images of women in popular culture reinforce negative stereotypes and women have little influence on the images produced in the entertainment industry. The production and consumption of television, music, film, and the Internet play a role in reproducing the unequal positions of men and women.

In their analysis, Milestone and Meyer (2012) reflect on studies of women's and men's magazines. McRobbie (1997) considers the evolution of feminist analyses of teen girls' magazines and their changing foci over time. Feminists initially argued that these magazines offer girls negative images because they repeatedly assert that girls should focus solely on romance and boyfriends. Scholars later asked why magazine authors felt the need to constantly reinforce these ideas; their reiteration implies that traditional patriarchal ideas were under challenge and hence need to be asserted. Later, researchers asked how and why girls find the magazines appealing. Most recently, scholars have expressed concerns about current magazines' sexually explicit content. McRobbie suggests that rather than criticizing magazines' sexual content, feminists should begin to study and build alliances with female journalists.

Stevenson et al. (2003) examine the content of men's magazines and male readers' interpretations of them. They explore the discourses of the new man and the new lad described above. In contrast to some scholars who express concern that lads' magazines reinforce old-fashioned patriarchal norms in which men dominate sexual encounters and ignore women's feelings and experiences, they find that the magazines and their readers evoke contradictory messages. They promote patriarchal messages in which the goal of sex is men's pleasure, but also offer young men advice about improving their sexual performance to attract women, thereby implying that men are not always able to sexually please women, and hence undermining their sexual dominance.

Several studies explore men's magazines in non-anglophone or non-Western locations. Kosetzi and Polyzou (2009) examine a Greek men's lifestyle magazine. They find that the magazine consistently asserts and promotes traditional masculinity, while attacking men who digress from these ideals and feminist ideas that challenge male dominance. The authors hypothesize that this assertion of "hegemonic masculinity" may be a reaction against women's growing rights in Greece. Schneider et al.'s (2008) analysis of the South African magazine, *Men's Health*, explores the publication's advice to men about how to achieve "ideal sexual experiences" and argues that this advice implicitly notes that men may not live up to this ideal, in line with Stevenson et al. (2003).

Song and Lee's (2010) analysis of men's magazines in China diverges from the Greek and South African examples, which seem to parallel British and U.S. magazines. The authors contrast current Chinese men's magazines with earlier Confucian and communist models of masculinity. Premodern Confucian masculinity was represented by images of the intellectual or the warrior, and was asserted among other men rather than toward women. Hence, it contrasted with Western conceptions of masculinity. Communist ideals represented working-class revolutionaries as asexual. Further, the authors argue that lads' magazines like *Maxim* and *FHM* target a different socioeconomic group than their British counterparts. While pornography and frank discussions of sex are associated with working-class males in the U.K. and U.S., these genres and attitudes are connected to the economic elite in China. Sexual prowess and success with women are today associated with wealth and power and men's consumption of soft-porn lads' magazines is a sign of "the good taste of the gentleman," thereby serving as a form of cultural capital. The authors show that current models of hegemonic masculinity in China reflect the evolution of Confucian, communist, and post-communist ideals more than they do the post-feminist discourses evident in U.S., U.K., Greek, and South African magazines.

Thus far, we have considered the evolution of women's and men's involvement in consumption without exploring how producers and marketers attach gendered meanings to objects. Much of the production and promotion of products and services is bifurcated by gender. If you, the reader, visit the toy section of any store, you will find a "boys" and "girls" aisle. Each aisle will be color coded (normally red for boys and pink for girls) and the boys' section will be filled with cars, sports items, and toys representing war; while the girls' section will include dolls, princesses, and toys focused on the caring work associated with women (childcare, food preparation, and cleaning) (Schor 2004).

These patterns continue into adulthood. We have coded different consumption items as male or female. This does not mean that some men or women do not cross these boundaries, but we still carry these categories in our minds. Hence, machinery and technology are coded as masculine, while clothing and cosmetics are coded as feminine. This coding is also expressed in subgenres or types of a given product. Consider film: action and war films are coded as masculine while romantic comedies are colloquially known as "chick flicks" (Lubar 1998; Milestone and Meyer 2012).

In addition to the gendered coding of particular objects or services, the design, marketing, and advertising of these commodities attempt to attach positive gendered meanings to these goods, with the notion that possession of the product will make an individual a more successful man or woman. Hence, car ads seek to persuade men that owning a particular brand or model will increase their strength, virility, and sex appeal. Similarly, the advertising of breakfast cereals suggests that these goods will allow women to fulfill their maternal role of maintaining their children's health and simultaneously win their love. Advertisements for perfume or cologne suggest that the wearer will have to beat back members of the opposite sex because the fragrance will give them a magnetic attraction. These examples illustrate how these inanimate objects gain cultural significance through advertising, but also how seeing the advertisements or owning the items may lead us to feel that they make us more successful in fulfilling our culturally constructed roles as men and women (Jhally 1990; Baudrillard 1996; Slater 1997; McCracken 1988).

Gender, consumption, and family decision-making

Men and women play different roles in the purchase and use of goods within family contexts. Viviana Zelizer (1989) and Jan Pahl (1989) have carefully examined men's and women's roles in allocating family budgets – decisions about how to spend money and for whom the money is spent. Zelizer (1989) examined how, at the beginning of the twentieth century, families differentiated household budgets into different "piles" or "accounts." She found that in working-class and poor families, it was common for women to administer their husbands' meager earnings, though they allowed men and working children to retain some money for personal expenses. When women worked, their earnings were considered "pin money" – insignificant sums designated for personal use. In middle-class families, men would give women a small "allowance" for family or personal needs.

Pahl (1989) examines variations in contemporary families' budget allocation, based on the family's class background and whether or not women are employed. Women use most of their earnings on the family while men retain a larger portion of their salaries for personal use. Women thus blur their own needs with those of their families. The most egalitarian decision-making occurred in families where both partners were employed. The key finding here is that, for many families, men continue to retain disproportionate control over household budgets even though we assume that women are "natural shoppers." Women tend to sacrifice their own consumption in favor of their children.

Stillerman's (2004) interviews with working-class couples in Santiago, Chile, supported this pattern. Unemployed women received an "allowance" from their husbands to cover daily shopping needs, while the husband would make monthly purchases at the supermarket and would often buy "big-ticket" items like electronics or cars. Some women would "save" money from the allowance to purchase "gifts" or needed items for children. Men and women had different priorities for large expenses, with men favoring cars and women preferring to purchase or remodel homes. Interestingly, both partners prioritized children's schooling and care for older relatives in making decisions about large expenses like homes or cars. These findings support Daniel Miller's (1998, 2012) contention that married women's shopping decisions reflect their devotion toward their husbands and children rather than an effort to satisfy their own desires. These findings contrast with the notion that contemporary consumers are primarily interested in self-fashioning through lifestyle consumption. Perhaps this focus on lifestyle is limited to single young adults without family responsibilities or affluent adults with families (compare Milestone and Meyer 2012).

Consumption: oppressive or empowering for women?

Scholars debate whether consumption has been beneficial or detrimental to women. The discussion of family budgets shows that as women gain greater financial independence, they also increase their influence over family expenditures. Several scholars build on this idea, arguing that consumption has positively influenced women's lives. During the nineteenth century, as discussed above, middle-class women were largely confined to the home and so department stores and other retail settings were among the few public venues these women had access to. Hence, they positively affected women's lives. Further, the definition of consumption as a feminine activity permitted women to develop skills and a sense of purpose and worth that was denied them until they joined the paid workforce in large numbers. Further, through consumption, women could satisfy their own needs and desires outside of the household. At home, women were largely responsible for others' needs (Nava 1997; Fiske 2000; Rappaport 2001).

Others contend that consumption has largely failed women due to their objectification in advertising and other media outlets. These authors argue that advertising and marketing have reinforced women's traditional roles as dependent caregivers at home or as sex objects. To the extent that women have bought into modern advertising and marketing, they have also bought into harmful stereotypes and roles that limit their power and autonomy (Milestone and Meyer 2012; Lury 2011; Gill 2009). While there is no consensus on this issue, it is clear that women may find identity and meaning through consumption, though in doing so they may consent to their subordinate position in relation to men.

It is important to avoid assuming that gendered patterns of consumption in the U.S. are the same as those in non-Western settings. Gender ideas vary across time and space. In this context, an examination of the rising fashion industry for women's veils in Turkey offers an interesting counterpoint to our image of scantily clad women exuding sex appeal in many television commercials in the U.S. and Europe. Scholars note a recent change in ads for veils directed toward upper-class Islamic women in Turkey. They contend that, in the past, rural women wore simple headscarves to cover their hair. However, with the growing political and economic power of Islam in Turkey, many affluent Muslim women have begun to wear scarves covering their head except for their eyes, as well as covering their bodies. As conservative Islamic women became more prosperous and some received high-paying jobs, an industry developed producing brightly colored scarves and tunics using silks and other fine fabrics.

Though some conservative Muslim men harshly criticized the fashion industry for veils and its fashion shows, the industry has been very successful. It reflects an interesting phenomenon for these women. On one hand, their religious faith requires them to cover their faces, hair, and bodies in public. On the other hand, they want to participate in the cult of style evident among prosperous secular Turkish women. However, secular Turks are uncomfortable with the increasing visibility of veiled women in a society formerly ruled by a secular government. Hence, the use of fashionable tunics and scarves is a way for these women to honor their religious beliefs while participating in contemporary consumer culture. This phenomenon reflects processes of glocalization – these fashions are specific to conservative Muslim women (in Turkey and likely elsewhere), but they also reflect broader trends toward the aestheticization of everyday life in many countries (Gökarıksel 2012; Kılıçbay and Binark 2002; Sandikci and Ger 2007).

Men, masculinities, and consumption

Scholars working within the paradigm of consumer culture theory have explored male-based consumption subcultures and how marketers have drawn on those subcultures to promote brand loyalty among men. Holt (2004) and Holt and Cameron (2010) develop numerous case studies that illustrate their overall analysis of the relationship between (mostly) male consumption subcultures and advertising creatives. As noted in chapter 3, these authors argue that the most successful brands draw source material from the media or specific subcultures to develop "identity myths" that respond to specific social groups' desires and anxieties. These myths help members of these groups grapple with the challenges they face in achieving socially valued ideals.

Many of these case studies refer to the "frontier myth" that provides an idealized image of nineteenth-century white American men. In the myth, men are rugged individualists who seek their fortunes on the Western frontier through dint of hard work and ingenuity. They save the nation by fighting against its enemies, but distrust the central government, seeing democracy as residing in individual, autonomous citizens.

The authors argue that at historical moments when economic, political, or cultural change threatens specific segments of the population, social groups or political leaders unearth or rework this myth to provide troubled populations (primarily working- or middle-class, white men) with a sense of dignity and purpose. Thus, they explain that during the 1950s, white men in the rural South rejected the growing urban middle class and its focus on office work and upward mobility. In this context, Jack Daniels, Marlboro, and Mountain Dew drew on the frontier myth to attract this population as well as other urban white men who felt uncomfortable with the implicit postwar bargain, whereby men obeyed authority at work in exchange for material success. This bargain clashed with the frontier myth's focus on independence, hard manual labor, and physical strength, threatening to emasculate these men.

In a contrasting and much-studied case, after World War II, working-class white men in Northern California developed outlaw biker clubs whose members used the last remaining American motorcycle brand, Harley Davidson, which soldiers rode during World War II. Outlaw cyclists lived as nomads, rejected political authority, attempted to be self-reliant, and gained a sense of power and identity through their domination of female bikers (compare Schouten and McAlexander 1995). Films broadcast the outlaw biker myth, but the Harley Davidson Company did not embrace the outlaw bikers until much later because management felt this group gave the brand a bad name. In the 1980s, building on President Ronald Reagan's, entrepreneur Malcolm Forbes', and other celebrities' promotion of the brand, the company created the Harley Owners' Group (HOG) to attract high-income men who admired the outlaw biker image but had a different class background from the original bikers.

Holt (2004) and Holt and Cameron (2010) argue that brands need to respond to social changes by developing new ads that often challenge the previous brand image (an example of anti-marketing), as economic and cultural changes make previously successful ads obsolete. This was the case with Budweiser. During the 1980s, when many white working-class men voted for Republican President Ronald Reagan, they faced a difficult dilemma. While these men liked Reagan's nostalgic use of the frontier myth in his call to "take back America" and militarily defeat the Soviet Union, they worried that their own jobs were becoming obsolete as the industrial base of the U.S. began to decline in the face of foreign competition and corporate decisions to move production overseas. In this context, Budweiser produced several successful ads honoring working men's dignity and skills.

However, as the economy shifted again in the 1990s, and new employment opportunities for youth declined, Budweiser's ads showing working men and Clydesdale horses drawing carriages fell flat. In this context, the company developed two series of ads, one featuring lizards telling jokes and the second highlighting a group of African American friends (discussed below), both of which used humor rather than a serious tone to describe male camaraderie and to poke fun at the previous ads.

Other studies explore how male consumers draw on a similar set of cultural materials as those adopted by advertisers. Modern-day "mountain men" also draw on the frontier myth (Belk and Costa 1998). These men plan outings in the Rocky Mountains to re-enact the early nineteenth-century fur trade. Modern mountain men feel nostalgic toward the past, and seek to return to a "primitive" time they believe is more authentic than the present. Re-enacting the myth gives participants an opportunity to engage in meaningful play, but it also reinforces romanticized images of the past. For these authors, the participants have constructed a fantasy that can only be realized through group-based consumption rituals.

Two studies depart from Schouten and McAlexander (1995) and Belk and Costa (1998), who argue that men seek to compensate for threats to their masculinity in the workplace and family through episodes of fantasy-based rebellion or a retreat to natural environments. Holt and Thompson (2004) argue that men's consumption seeks to integrate and transcend the cultural ideals of the breadwinner and the rebel, building on the idea of the "man-of-action" present in popular culture. Here, men develop leisure-time pursuits and consumption practices that include the competitiveness of the breadwinner, the rejection of societal norms of the rebel, and also incorporate more stereotypically feminine interests in romance novels or fashion design. Similarly, Thompson and Holt (2004) find that men do not seek to adopt hyper-masculine personas through consumption; rather, they incorporate competitive, communal, childlike, and emotional elements that soften masculine ideals that are difficult to achieve. These two authors suggest that men do not have a "knee-jerk" response to the challenges they face fulfilling masculine ideals; they develop creative, complex, and integrative responses to these challenges through their consumption practices.

Moisio et al.'s (2013) study of men's home-repair projects challenges earlier analyses of men's consumption that focus on activities outside the home. Further, they suggest that men's home-repair or "do-it-yourself" (DIY) projects vary based on their class position. Upper-middle-class men whose employment does not involve manual labor adopt the "suburban craftsman" ideal to show their superiority to their peers and also compensate for their inability to achieve masculine ideals of physical strength and skill in the workplace. Working-class men who have difficulty fulfilling the breadwinner role use the "handyman" ideal as a way to act as family providers through home remodeling rather than earning a salary. The authors find the home is a crucial site for men from different social classes to construct their gender identities through productive consumption.

These studies are an important complement to research focused on women's consumption and images of women in advertising, in that they point to the complex and dynamic character of men's consumption and the construction of masculinity through consumption. However, one limitation of studies that focus exclusively on men is that they miss women's experiences and voices. Martin et al. (2006) make this point in their follow-up study of female Harley Davidson motorcyclists. They argue that Schouten and McAlexander's (1995) original study was limited because it only included men's voices and experiences. By focusing on female riders, Martin et al. (2006) learned that in contrast to men, who tended to conform to gender stereotypes in their practices and identities as riders, female riders *challenge* gender stereotypes by engaging in a traditionally masculine activity as a way to assert their female identities. These riders adopted the "hyper-masculine" ethos of male riders while accentuating their femininity. Female riders thus engaged in unexpected identity work as participants in the biker subculture. Their study underscores the value of studying gendered *relationships* in consumption rather than examining women or men in isolation.

Sexuality and Consumption

The intersection of sexual orientation and consumption follows in some respects from the discussions of gender, both because of similar forms of discrimination experienced by heterosexual women and members of sexual minorities (Lesbians, Gays, Bisexual, and Transgendered individuals, LGBT), and because the field of sexuality studies emerged from analyses of gender inequality.

LGBT individuals share with heterosexual women the situation of being both subjects and objects of consumption, but their experiences are different. Within popular conceptions of gay and lesbian identities, members of each of these groups dress differently and adopt different consumption habits from their heterosexual counterparts due to their rejection of gender stereotypes, their adoption of distinct sexual identities, and their participation in LGBT subcultures centered around bars, clubs, and other consumption settings. However, research does not consistently support this commonsensical notion. One study about "gay innovativeness" found that gays' and lesbians' consumption is no more innovative than heterosexuals' consumption (Vandecasteele and Geuens 2009).

The idea that LGBT individuals consume in different ways than do heterosexuals may reflect stereotypes about these groups fostered by representations in literature and the media, as well as the increasing role of lesbian and gay entertainment districts as "tourist destinations" for heterosexuals. While lesbians and gays were largely invisible in television and film until recent decades, except for occasional caricatured or satirical depictions (as in the French 1970s film, later remade in English, *La Cage Aux Folles*), recent films like the 2013 Oscar-winning *Dallas Buyers' Club* and television series (like *Queer Eye for the Straight Guy*, *Queer as Folk*, *Glee*, and *Modern Family*) have made gay and lesbian characters more visible, though viewers debate whether or not these characters and images are believable (Milestone and Meyer 2012; Gill 2009).

Recent studies highlight the emergence of a "gay market" of consumers who are targeted by both "gay-identified" producers and mainstream brands. Scholars note that LGBT social-movement organizations may be resources for marketers seeking to tap into an increasingly lucrative market. Further, some traditional brands attempt to attract LGBT customers by marketing themselves as "gay-friendly" employers and services. Some LGBT activists regret that the LGBT community has become another niche market to be exploited by profit-oriented businesses, while others applaud the fact that some businesses are finally paying attention and catering to gay customers after decades of ignoring or discriminating against them. In contrast, scholars find that LGBT-identified individuals continue to face discriminatory treatment in retail settings (Walters and Moore 2002; Um 2012; Gudelunas 2011).

Kates (2002) provides a detailed study of a gay consumption sub-culture centered in the "gay ghetto" of a U.S. city. He argues that the gay male subculture is different from others analyzed in previous research (bikers, *Star Trek* fans, dance club enthusiasts, or mountain men) in two ways. First, because gay consumers are part of a stig-matized group, adopting gay consumption behaviors is more than a lifestyle choice; it reflects fundamental aspects of a person's identity that cannot be lived only on weekend getaways. Second, unlike other scholarship that sees subcultural norms as homogeneous, Kates finds that gay subcultural styles are contested and community members value innovative individual expression.

Being a member of this community entails accepting or finding alternatives to dominant standards of beauty within the subculture (like muscular bodies), learning how to be a gay consumer and iden-tify other gay men via consumption cues (developing "gaydar" or gay radar), participating in group rituals like Lesbian and Gay Pride parades that promote highly visible displays of difference, and engag-ing in status competition based on adoption or critique of dominant beauty norms in the group. Kates (2002) concludes that the gay male subculture is relevant for understanding other subcultures whose members have stigmatized identities, see themselves as different from the mainstream, and engage in individual competition with other group members.

Race and Consumption

Much like gender, race is a socially constructed category. Common-sense views of race assume that this category merely reflects bio-logical differences in skin color and visible physical characteristics. However, these physical characteristics only matter in social life when they are socially recognized and understood in specific ways. Systems of racial classification vary across countries and even within regions of the same country. (Consider differences in racial attitudes between the North and the South in the U.S.) (Omi and Winant 1994).

While we often think of the "generic" consumer as white and middle class, racial differences have been integral to modern consumption since its inception. As Sidney Mintz (1985) observes, Afro-Caribbean slaves harvested many of the luxury goods (coffee, tea, sugar, and chocolate) consumed by Europeans during the "commercial revolution" of the early modern era. Mimi Sheller (2003) further argues that Europeans have "consumed" the Caribbean (its natural environment, goods produced by slaves, and people's bodies) for several hundred years. Hence, non-Europeans need to be integrated into the story of modern consumption.

Much as is the case with women, we need to understand ethnic/racial minorities as subjects and objects of consumption. Much of the discussion of minority consumers in the U.S., Europe, and South Africa focuses on persons of African origin. There are occasional references to Latinos and Asians in the U.S. literature. Research on race and consumption in Latin America focuses on indigenous people and persons of African or mixed heritage. Before examining members of minority groups as subjects of consumption, we first need to examine discrimination against these groups in the past and present.

Discrimination and African American consumption

The history of discrimination is particularly illuminating in that it points to the blind spots in our understanding of "consumers" if we assume that all consumers are free to participate in consumption in the same way. In the U.S. and European contexts, consumers classified as "white" and "middle class" can move freely in retail or other consumption settings without generating suspicion on the part of retail staff or mall managers. Hence, for these groups, consumption is a mundane task with few inherent difficulties. This is far from the case for members of ethnic and racial minorities, especially African Americans.

African Americans, and, to a lesser extent, members of other ethnic minorities, have experienced systematic discrimination in credit and retail sectors in the past and present. In the credit sector, until the 1970s, banks and federal agencies denied African Americans access to home mortgages through the practice of "redlining," whereby residents of segregated African American communities could not access mortgages because investments in these neighborhoods were viewed as too "risky." More recently, African Americans and Hispanics were disproportionately targeted with predatory mortgages (including large fees and variable interest rates that increased the likelihood of default) in the run-up to the 2007–9 subprime mortgage crisis that began in the United States and spread to several other regions. From the 1940s until the 1970s, realtors and white residents also attempted to keep African Americans outside white neighborhoods through various tactics later deemed illegal. Hence, African Americans were restricted in their ability to purchase that quintessential American consumer good, the single-family house, unless they could buy it with cash or purchase it via an intermediary (through a land contract) (Dreier et al. 2004; Cohen 2003; Johnson and Kwak 2011).

From the late nineteenth century until the 1964 Civil Rights Act, so-called Jim Crow laws in the U.S. South differentiated whites' and blacks' access to public facilities, including privately owned consumption venues like movie theaters and stores. While this discrimination was legally binding in the South, it also occurred in practice in many places in the North. Additionally, African Americans were systematically overcharged in home rental and retail markets, rarely had opportunities to work in independent white-owned retail stores, and were charged usurious interest rates in local stores. Between the 1930s and 1960s, and to some extent until the present, African Americans engaged in a wide range of protest actions to open up retail markets, as we explore in chapter 7 (Zukin 2004; Cohen 2003; Dreier et al. 2004; Chin 2001).

While laws today require retail stores to serve African American customers, other forms of discrimination persist. It is common for store or mall personnel to follow black customers as a matter of policy, based on the suspicion that they are more likely to steal than are white customers (Zukin 2004; Chin 2001). In 2013, a black customer alleged that upscale New York store Barney's asked police to follow and arrest him after he bought an expensive belt with cash. Further investigation indicates that discrimination against African American customers was a store policy. Macy's was later criticized for similar policies. To dramatize the injustice of this practice, critics dubbed it "shop and frisk" in a reference to the New York Police Department's policy of "stop and frisk," recently judged illegal by the New York State Supreme Court, in which police stop and often arrest minority males on the street based on suspicion. Barney's later paid a 500,000 dollar settlement after a nine-month investigation by the New York State attorney general (Gardiner 2013; O'Connor 2013; Santora 2014).

Malls commonly utilize curfews to restrict access to teens and African Americans (Staeheli and Mitchell 2006). The upper-middle-class black individuals that sociologist Karyn Lacy (2007) interviewed in the Washington, DC, suburbs said that they often wore suits or formal attire when they went to the mall, to insure that they would receive respectful service. Further, African Americans brought a successful class action suit against the Cracker Barrel restaurant chain for insisting on seating them away from white customers (Feagin et al. 2001). Hence, "shopping" is an often laborious and sometimes humiliating experience for many African Americans.

Shaping African American identities through consumption

Given these external constraints, what, if anything, is distinctive about the tastes and consumption choices of African Americans? Here, the boundaries are blurred between African Americans as subjects and objects of consumption in that many of African Americans' distinctive consumer orientations have later been broadcast to and absorbed by the broader population in the U.S. and globally. This is so because African Americans have been innovative producers of consumer goods and styles that broader portions of the population have later adopted. The most obvious examples of this phenomenon are music and fashion.

African Americans developed unique musical styles that originated in work songs and spirituals developed under slavery and continued with jazz, blues, rhythm and blues, disco, funk, hip hop, and house/electronic music. These musical styles utilize distinctive linguistic codes and describe experiences that are meaningful and valued within the black community (Jones 1963; Dyer 2009; Rojek 2011; Gotham 2007).

However, other racial and ethnic groups have always consumed black music. Further, in the U.S. and U.K., white musicians have adapted African-origin styles to gain fame in the broader market, as in the case of rock and roll. Hence, African Americans and other members of the African diaspora have produced commodified cultural forms that have gained national and global appeal (Rojek 2011).

Another field of cultural innovation and consumption is the area of clothing. Throughout the twentieth century, African Americans have developed styles of dress and tastes for specific types of clothing and brands that were distinct from those worn by the general population. Examples include jazz musicians' use of sunglasses beginning in the 1940s, and black men's use of low-hanging, baggy jeans, which originated among ex-convicts prohibited from using belts in prison. Each of these styles originated with a segment of African Americans before whites adopted it (Klein 2010; Zukin 2004).

Additionally, because of African Americans' distinctive experiences of discrimination, their everyday shopping practices often reflect the ideologies (or worldviews) that have guided African American politics. In their study of African Americans living in a segregated community in Milwaukee, Wisconsin, Crockett and Wallendorf (2004) found that black liberals (those seeking racial integration and equal citizenship) and black nationalists (those promoting the development of a separate black economy) reacted differently to the poor-quality products and housing options available in their segregated neighborhood. Liberals favor living outside segregated neighborhoods while remaining loyal to black-owned businesses, while black nationalists criticize those who leave the black community and form their own businesses to serve blacks. In both cases, African American consumers see their consumption decisions as intimately tied to their political commitment to support the black community, not just a means to satisfy their individual needs or desires.

Many African Americans use specific consumption practices, styles, and tastes to demonstrate their racial authenticity and group membership. In her studies of low-income African American youth, Prudence Carter (2003, 2006) found that different individuals deployed black cultural styles in distinct ways depending on the social context. Many youth used their taste for hip-hop music, clothing tastes, dance forms, and speaking in black English as markers of in-group identity, a source of pride, and a boundary that excludes non-blacks or those African Americans perceived as inauthentic. However, school authorities think these consumption practices reflect individuals' lack of academic preparation. Thus, some individuals used these styles, which Carter sees as a non-dominant form of cultural capital ("black cultural capital"), only among their peers, while displaying dominant forms of cultural capital (use of standard English, wearing mainstream attire) at school to advance academically and in the job market. She describes those who use both forms of cultural capital as "cultural straddlers" (2006) and argues that these "code-switching" behaviors allow students to gain respect in school while maintaining their status among their peers and families. However, other children do not possess these code-switching skills, or opt to stay true to their heritage, and hence face rejection by school authorities. Hence, for low-income African Americans, consumption is not only an individual lifestyle choice, but a symbol of group membership. Further, some individuals possess dominant and non-dominant forms of cultural capital and thus are able to consume strategically in different social settings to achieve competing goals of class mobility and social acceptance among peers.

Warikoo (2007) extends the idea of cultural straddling to South Asian youth who live in multiracial communities in New York and London. These young people receive pressure from family, other South Asians, and members of other ethnic groups to consume in ways that reflect their Indian heritage to show that they are authentically Indian. These individuals would like to listen to the hip-hop music their African American peers enjoy, but they feel awkward doing so because it might make them appear inauthentic. They resolve this conflict by listening to Indian hip hop or bhangra music that mixes traditional Indian melodies with motifs from Western electronic dance music. These youth thus have blurred boundaries with African Americans that allow them to enjoy specific musical styles while retaining their status as "authentic" Indians. Warikoo and Carter show that black and South Asian youth define group membership based on specific consumption practices, and their definitions of group membership and boundaries with others are constantly negotiated within their group and with other racial and ethnic groups.

African Americans' consumer tastes in part reflect black advertising professionals' efforts to create and legitimate a black market, which date back to the end of World War II. Brown (2011) describes how black advertising agencies attempted to convince white-owned companies that African Americans had purchasing power and hence it would be profitable for these companies to target the black population. Black advertisers and emerging modeling agencies reacted against the racist images of African Americans that regularly appeared on product labels between the two world wars. To depart from this practice, black-owned modeling agencies promoted "respectable" images of middle-class black women that offered a sanitized version of their sex appeal. The idea was to depict an image of "glamorous beauty" to rebut stereotypical images of black female servants or overly sexualized women, and hence appeal to black consumers who were tired of seeing stereotypical images of themselves.

Lamont and Molnár (2001) examine similar issues in the contemporary period. They argue that middle-class African Americans construct their identities based on how others view them as well as their self-perceptions and group identities. They find that African American advertising professionals seek to promote positive images of African Americans that would improve their public image. In this regard, these professionals argue that African Americans can gain full citizenship in the U.S. by exercising their purchasing power while simultaneously strengthening their collective identities. African American consumers make purchases as a way of claiming group membership and demanding inclusion in society. The authors argue that advertisers positively influence the lives of African Americans by opening up consumption opportunities for them, but the equation of citizenship with purchasing power is problematic because poor people are thereby excluded from full membership in society. The modification of the category "black consumer" through advertising also gives African Americans the opportunity to change what it means to be black through their consumption.

African Americans as objects of consumption

As noted above, like women, in addition to their roles as consumers, African Americans are also "objects" of consumption for other ethnic and racial groups. With the aftermath of slavery in the U.S. and widespread employment discrimination, entertainment and sports were among the few fields of employment that remained open to African Americans. Consequently, members of other ethnic groups often perceive African Americans through the stereotypical lens developed in the media. One early example of this phenomenon is "blackface minstrelsy" whereby whites adopted black dance and entertainment routines and performed them in "blackface" as a satirical imitation of blacks. Blacks also blackened their faces in performance. Many early branded goods and home decorations included stereotypical images of African Americans in servile or slave-like representations. The most obvious contemporary example of this phenomenon is Aunt Jemima pancake syrup. Films and other entertainment media depicted African Americans in stereotypical fashion at least until the middle of the twentieth century, and yet African American musicians and athletes have gained significant white audiences since the nineteenth century (Riggs 2004; Saxton 2003; Rojek 2011).

The most recent stage of this phenomenon refers to the associations between "cool" and "black" in marketing. Scholars argue that it is common for advertising agencies to seek new trends among consumers and then utilize them to promote styles to the broader population. Many times this "cool hunting" involves identifying and adapting African American clothing and music styles and promoting them to non-blacks. This process is also evident in the "branding" of African American athletes such as Michael Jordan, Tiger Woods, and LeBron James. Major brands have used these athletes' fame to promote their products, while the athletes have used their exposure to promote themselves as a brand. Similarly, hip-hop musicians like Sean Combs and Jay Z have used their musical success to create branded lines of clothing, restaurants, and other consumption venues. Hence, the triumph of "cool" and its associations with African Americans have benefited a few artists, though many of the indignities and injustices experienced by African Americans in retail venues continue (Klein 2010; Zukin 2004; Rojek 2011; Schor 2004; Goldman and Papson 2000; Rushkoff 1999).

Recent analyses of the representation of African Americans in advertising demonstrate their association with "cool" and efforts to depict a mythical world in which racism does not exist. Crockett's (2008) analysis of over 200 advertisements featuring African American actors argues that advertisers use two strategies to sell products. The first diminishes references to racial difference between whites and blacks, implicitly arguing that these two racial groups have equal opportunities in the consumer marketplace. The second emphasizes the differences between the black actors and a presumably white audience by referencing stereotypes of African Americans as cool, athletic, and as culturally distinct from whites. The analysis indicates that advertisers (and presumably white viewers) cannot imagine African Americans outside the legacy of stereotypes and discrimination that continue to affect this population.

Watts and Orbe (2002) reach a similar conclusion in their analysis of a well-known Budweiser "Whassup?" commercial in which several black male friends joke about Black English while talking to one another on the phone. Based on focus group research with white male viewers, the authors argue that both the advertisement and the audience response reflect whites' ambivalence toward African Americans. On one hand, focus group participants felt they could relate to the "male bonding" evident in the commercial, while also enjoying its depiction of "authentic" black culture. The authors argue that white viewers seek out similarity with and difference from blacks when viewing commercial media, speaking to their discomfort regarding interactions with blacks (compare Holt 2004).

Marketing and consumption among Latinos and Asian Americans

While research on other ethnic minority groups in the U.S. is limited, studies offer a window into the distinctive consumption experiences of Hispanic and Asian Americans. Each of these groups occupies a distinct position in the ethnic/racial hierarchy of the U.S. in contrast to African Americans, as they encounter less overt discrimination but also face unique challenges because many of their members are immigrants or children of immigrants who may speak English as a second language. Hence, members of the white majority tend to perceive these groups as "forever foreign," a view that affects their everyday treatment and representation in advertising, television, and film.

Peñaloza (1994) conducted an influential study, examining how Mexican immigrants in California adapt to the different consumption environment of the U.S. The author found that these individuals lived in Mexican-American communities and shopped in Mexican-dominant retail settings where Spanish was spoken. Hence, the challenges they faced in the consumption setting were less related to language barriers than the need to learn different patterns of consumption in the U.S. environment. In this regard, low-income immigrants from rural Mexico had a much more difficult time adapting to new products and their uses than did urban, middle-class migrants. The immigrants went through a learning process that drew on their peer groups in Mexico as well as family, friends, and co-workers in the U.S. Their consumer behaviors and attitudes varied, based on class, place of origin, generation, and gender.

Peñaloza (1994) found that while these immigrants did purchase many goods they had not previously accessed in Mexico, and they were influenced by Spanish-language marketers, they also retained traditional food habits and criticized some aspects of U.S. consumer culture. Therefore, she describes them as "border consumers." Peñaloza's study demonstrates how the consumption patterns of members of immigrant and ethnic minority groups differ from the majority population due to their distinct economic situations, legal status, and cultural backgrounds. Additionally, these groups are internally differentiated, much as was noted by Chin (2001), Pugh (2009), and Lacy (2007) on African Americans.

Dávila (2001) examines the other side of the coin – Hispanic marketers and how they define Hispanics as a unified market. She shows that Hispanic marketers have functioned as intermediaries between white-dominated companies and Hispanic consumers, much like local advertisers in India as discussed in chapter 3. In order to effectively persuade companies to spend advertising dollars targeting Hispanics, marketers needed to first sell an appealing image of this highly diverse group to companies. In order to do so, they drew on both the ideas of Latin American nationalist intellectuals of the nineteenth century who viewed Hispanics as different from Anglos (English speakers), as well as the 1970s decision of presidential administrations and the Census Bureau to create a unified category of "Hispanics."

Dávila notes that it is very problematic to label individuals from Mexico, Central America, the Caribbean, and South America, as well as those of Latin American ancestry born in the U.S., as fundamentally the same based only on a shared language. As such, marketers had to both minimize cultural and historical differences between these groups but also offer companies a sanitized image of Hispanics as hard-working, family-oriented, and religious, to persuade these corporations that they were "worthy" of marketing attention in light of widespread negative stereotypes regarding Hispanics. Hispanic marketers convinced companies that Hispanics are indeed "profitable," and they also convinced those of Latin American ancestry that they were part of this pan-ethnic group. Hence, marketing was crucial in promoting a new group identity. However, she argues, the Hispanic label ignores the complex realities of individuals with Latin American ancestry, this group's internal diversity, and what many Hispanics share with other Americans. She concludes that the creation of Hispanics as a "market" reflects parallel moves with African Americans and Asian Americans. The common source of these marketing efforts is whites' view that these groups are "foreign" or "different," and marketers play the role of persuading companies and consumers that members of their groups are both worthy and culturally distinct. One cost of this strategy, she argues, is that the construction of culturally distinct ethnic markets makes it more difficult for members of these different groups to find common cause in the political arena. Hers is a sobering assessment of the negative political consequences of "successful" multicultural marketing to ethnic minorities.

Shankar (2012) finds somewhat similar challenges to those Dávila notes with regard to Asian American "niche" advertising agencies. Like the Hispanic agencies Dávila studied, these companies must sell a unified image of Asian Americans to corporate clients to gain lucrative contracts. However, unlike Hispanic agencies, the Asian American agencies cannot direct the same advertisement to all target populations (those of Chinese, Korean, Filipino, South Asian, and Vietnamese descent) because of the language and cultural differences between these groups. Hence, the agency is often charged with making distinct translations of the same "general market" ad for different ethnic groups, but must make sure to communicate the same meaning as is present in the English-language ad while making it intelligible and appealing to each ethnic group. Hence, advertisers need to maintain the "brand message" developed by the corporate client while making the ad linguistically meaningful and culturally appealing to the target audience.

In addition to the language and cultural barriers these ad "creatives" have to bridge, they must also construct an image of the target audience that is appealing to the corporate client and the target market. To do so, agency professionals draw on the well-known "model minority" stereotype that depicts Asian Americans as hardworking, highly educated, and professionally successful. On average, Asian Americans have higher educational achievement and incomes than whites, and this stereotype effectively targets the highest-income segment of Asian Americans. However, the ads ignore working-class Asian Americans as well as smaller ethnic groups who are less profitable to ad agencies and corporations. Hence, much like the Hispanic example, these agencies ignore or hide Asian American ethnic groups' internal diversity. Both the Hispanic and Asian American examples point to the complexities of developing marketing appeals that "translate" across cultural boundaries. They reflect our earlier discussions of "glocalization": consumption is embedded in specific cultures, and corporations that seek to tap a new market can only do so by making their product meaningful and appealing within the culture and lifestyle of the group they seek to target, which often means modifying the product or message so that it "fits" a given cultural group. Scholars have also considered the consumer behaviors and identities of Asian Americans, and we review their findings in this chapter's final section on intersectionality.

Race and consumption in Ecuador and South Africa

Racial differences take on a distinct character in other national settings. Rudi Colloredo-Mansfeld's (1999) study of Ecuador's Otavalo Indians is instructive. This group has a long history as merchants and craft producers that predates Europeans' arrival in Ecuador. After Spain's conquest of the region, Europeans and their descendants perceived the Otavalo ethnic group as occupying an intermediate racial position between Europeans and the so-called "savage" Jibaro Indians who occupied the Amazon jungle.

While they had a relatively impoverished existence through much of modern Ecuador's history, a segment of Otavalo traders became prosperous during the 1980s and 1990s as a result of their travels to the U.S. and Europe to sell crafts they had produced or those made by members of other native populations in Latin America. The wealthier Indians have reinvested in the town of Otavalo, building large homes.

One might anticipate that this increased wealth would lead this group to assimilate into the dominant cultural styles of European-origin and mixed-race (mestizo) Ecuadoreans, but their increased wealth has had two unanticipated effects. The first has been the resurgence of native culture as evident in traditional festivals, dress, and craft production. The second is a widening class divide between poor Otavalans who continue to engage in farming (a traditional source of indigenous identity) and wealthier Otavalans who earn their living from craft production and trade and engage in the most "authentic" indigenous rituals. Hence, globalization has permitted a cultural resurgence of native peoples expressed in part through their distinctive consumption activities. This resurgence has boosted ethnic pride among members of a group that had long faced racial discrimination.

Annika Teppo and Myriam Houssay-Holzschuch (2013) explore the economic and political ramifications of the installation of a shopping mall in a poor, black suburb of Cape Town, South Africa. For decades, South Africa was ruled by the white-run apartheid government that severely repressed blacks. Since the 1990s, the black-dominated African National Congress (ANC), an organization that fought for democracy and civil rights, has ruled the country. While many poor blacks hoped the ANC government would resolve the country's severe inequalities, the results have been ambiguous at best.

In a context in which the ANC has pushed the country in the direction of free-market policies but many blacks feel attached to the pro-democracy struggle, building a new mall is a complex affair. A local black businessman with political connections lured white investors with advertisements showing all white shoppers. However, the mall's clientele consists of working-class blacks from the surrounding neighborhood. To attract the mall's target consumers, the mall is decorated with poetry and images celebrating the anti-apartheid movement. The authors argue that the mall's founder played a crucial role as a successful black businessman who was respected by white investors but had credibility among black consumers. Further, to make this business venture profitable, the mall needed to symbolically acknowledge black political identities. While the mall attracted local customers due to its low prices, residents were disappointed that it did not provide job opportunities to unemployed residents.

Further, the mall's construction led to the eviction of local black business owners, one of whom successfully sued the developer and was awarded a locale in the mall. The authors contend that neoliberal policies have allowed large white businesses to enter this poor black community, although, to do so, investors needed to acknowledge the area's history of political struggle. Nonetheless, the owners still faced local businesses' resistance. Mall development takes shape within South Africa's conflictive racial and political context.

Integrating Gender, Race, Class, and Sexuality: Intersectionality and Consumption

This chapter's final goal is to consider intersectionality – the idea that different axes of inequality mutually influence one another in shaping individuals' life chances. Feminist sociologist Patricia Hill Collins (1998) initially developed this idea. She sought to understand how the experiences of women of color were qualitatively different from those of white women due to their subjection to both sexism and racism as well as their common experience of poverty. The concept of intersectionality helps us avoid reducing individuals to a single position (e.g., their class or race) and shows that individuals in specific social locations (such as working-class Latino males) will have specific subjective attitudes, experiences, and opportunities that differ from those in other social locations (working-class Latina women or middle-class black men).

Ann DuCille's (2000) analysis of the "black Barbie" doll exemplifies this approach. DuCille describes the complex ways race and gender are expressed in toys. She notes that Mattel, the company that produces Barbie doll products, decided in recent decades to produce "multicultural" Barbie dolls to appeal to non-white girls. Initially, the dolls were merely dyed different colors without changing the shape of their bodies. After protests that the black dolls did not look "black," the manufacturer altered the doll's shape to make their behinds appear larger, which generated more criticism that the dolls reinforced stereotypes regarding black women's bodies. A further complication was that black girls tend to prefer "real" (meaning "white") Barbie dolls because they have "good" hair and these girls do not want to be perceived as "different" from white girls.

This case illustrates the complexities of racial and gender ideologies and experiences. The manufacturer initially perceived that they could increase their profits by targeting niche markets through the sale of identical dolls with different skin colors (much like Alfred Sloan's early use of different colors in General Motors cars or Benetton's use of "multicultural" models to sell clothing – see Lury 2011) and learned that they had completely misunderstood African American girls' preferences. In a complementary discussion, Elizabeth Chin (2001) found that the low-income black girls she interviewed would braid their white Barbie dolls' hair much as they braided their own hair – they made them "black."

Rosalind Gill (2009) develops an intersectional analysis of advertising focused on gender, class, and sexuality. She looks at ads focused on "six packs" (used as a metaphor for male actors' muscular bodies), midriffs (referring to thin, attractive female models), and "hot lesbians" (ads in which two attractive women kiss or hug). In the first ads, she finds that most actors are white or look "Latin," drawing on exotic stereotypes of the "Latin lover." Because advertising has traditionally positioned women as sex objects to be looked at by heterosexual men (Milestone and Meyer 2012), the new penchant for showing men's bodies in ads faced the challenge of appealing to heterosexual men, heterosexual women, and gay men without making heterosexual men anxious about the homoerotic nature of the ads or about the power women had to look at them as objects. To avoid these potential problems, the ads included highly muscular, young men who looked unquestionably masculine, as well as humor to undercut sexual anxieties that might emerge if heterosexual male viewers took the ads seriously.

Gill argues that the "midriff" or sexually assertive "new woman" (Milestone and Meyer 2012) is a response to feminism and women's growing workforce participation. Ads needed to depict women as active and independent if they sought to sell them goods. These ads emphasize women's beauty and sexual desire rather than their role as objects for men's pleasure. She notes that these images are predominantly of young white, heterosexual women. Black women tend to still be depicted as passive sexual objects in ads. Further, she argues that they represent a middle-class, respectable sexuality, rather than a "trashy" working-class sexuality. Hence, the ads exclude lesbians, older women, working-class women, and women of African origin.

Finally, Gill argues that the "hot lesbian," visible in numerous ads showing women kissing, hugging, or locked in an embrace, is mainly designed to appeal to heterosexual men. The women in the ads are conventionally attractive and many of the scenes borrow from images in soft-core pornography. In this regard, the ads nod to the hipness of lesbianism while creating an image of women which assumes that the viewer is a heterosexual male, making lesbianism invisible. Gill's analysis of "new" forms of advertising underscores how they seek to reinforce traditional ideas about gender, class, and sexuality, and how, through doing so, they exclude several segments of the population.

Stacey J. Lee's and Sabina Vaught's (2003) comparison of the consumption patterns of two groups of Asian American young women illustrates how an intersectional approach can illuminate consumer behavior and identities, in contrast to the above-mentioned studies of product design and advertising. The authors first examined the consumer behaviors of working-class Hmong high-school students in California. Second-generation girls distinguished themselves from FOBs ("fresh-off-the boat") new immigrant girls. They criticized these girls for being uninterested in fashion, as a way to distance themselves from the stigmatized category of the "forever foreign" used by many whites to classify Asian and Hispanic Americans. To distance themselves from recent immigrants, these young women adopted hip-hop clothing styles because they felt excluded from the broader society and hence preferred to adopt what they viewed as an oppositional identity. To do so, they relied on racial stereotypes that associate African Americans with poverty, describing their clothing styles as "ghetto." However, some of these girls engaged in dieting in order to achieve the white middle-class beauty ideal of thinness.

The authors also interviewed affluent Asian American college students in the South. These young women sought to assimilate to white middle-class beauty norms by using blue or green contact lenses, dying their hair, dieting and exercising, and using push-up bras. Further, these women sought white, middle-class male partners because they found Asian men unattractive, drawing on stereotypes of Asian men as asexual. To attract white male partners, they attempted to downplay their cultural difference to avoid frightening them.

This study illustrates how Asian American women from different class backgrounds attempt to adapt to U.S. society through specific consumer behaviors. These practices involve stereotypical assumptions about immigrants and different ethnic and racial groups. They also reflect their class positions. In this regard, specific consumption choices reflect their identities and aspirations, which in turn build upon their gender, class, ethnic, and immigration status. Consumer practices and identities diverge within and across ethnic, racial, class, and age boundaries, and are produced within complex and dynamic systems of power.

Conclusion

This chapter has examined how our understanding of consumption is both enriched and complicated through an analysis of its intersection with gender and race. We have learned that modern consumption is intertwined with the history of women. Further, women have the peculiar position of being both subjects and objects of consumption: they shop for themselves (and their families), but are also represented in advertising as sex objects to appeal to the male gaze. Gender also becomes an important dividing line between the different products marketed to men and women. Received ideas of masculinity and femininity permeate the marketplace, but new products and images also contribute to changes in gender ideas. Specific products and brands are developed to serve members of white male subcultures and figure in the ongoing construction of masculinity. Constructions of femininity shape consumption in different ways in distinct national contexts, as evident in the fashion for veiling in Turkey.

Race is also a fundamental dividing line in consumption. For whites, shopping is a mundane practice in which individuals can focus on their own desires and needs with little interference. This is not the case for African Americans, whose access to the principal channels of consumption has been and continues to be restricted through institutional forms of discrimination. However, African Americans have developed distinctive consumption styles that also reflect unique forms of cultural production, especially in the fields of music and entertainment, and consumption is essential to the construction of racial authenticity and the erection of boundaries between blacks and other ethnoracial groups. These styles have bubbled up to white consumers, artists, and advertisers, and hence African Americans have fundamentally influenced consumer culture although they have rarely profited from these contributions. Hispanic and Asian Americans face distinct forms of discrimination and also function within segmented markets built on the assumption that they are "forever foreign," even though significant segments of these populations were born in the U.S. Racial hierarchies and their effects on consumption take on distinct forms outside the U.S., as in our analysis of the cultural renaissance of indigenous consumption rituals among the Otavalo people of Ecuador, and the conflictive racial politics of consumption in South Africa.

We concluded with a discussion of intersectionality in which we tried to illustrate how class, race, gender, age, and sexuality combine in unpredictable ways to shape the consumption of specific individuals and groups. It is not enough to argue that class or race shape consumption because each individual occupies a subject position that includes their class, race, gender, sexuality, and age, which influence both their access to consumer goods and their subjective experience of consumption. In the next chapter, we further consider the differentiation of consumption across groups by analyzing consumption and the life course. How does consumption vary between children, teens, adults, and the elderly? How does each of these stages of life become a field for the deployment of marketing and product development?

6

The Life Course

Introduction

In the previous two chapters we have considered how distinct axes of inequality shape consumption. These chapters offered an important starting point for considering variations in consumer behaviors and identities based on economic resources or ascribed characteristics, namely, gender and race. In this chapter, we consider another axis of difference – an individual's stage in the life course.

When we think about one's stage in the life course, it is tempting to describe this simply as one's chronological age. However, this view is deceptive for two reasons. Demographers have demonstrated that life expectancies have been increasing since the early modern era. Hence, what we call old age today did not even exist a century ago when many people died in their forties or fifties. Furthermore, changes in life expectancy often interact with changing cultural views of specific stages of life, or the definition of new stages. For example, in the U.S., people began speaking about "teenagers" after World War II. Increasing wealth allowed teens a great deal of leisure time as well as the resources to develop distinctive clothing styles, musical tastes, and to produce music themselves, for example (Cohen 2003).

Today, sociologists and other social scientists have begun to see that individuals who are chronologically and legally "adults" (aged twenty-one and older) are waiting to make the transition to what we have commonly defined as adulthood (marrying, having children, and purchasing a home) until their late twenties or later. How do we define the period between college graduation and marriage? These individuals are no longer teenagers and yet they do not behave like adults. To answer these questions, scholars have developed the new category of "emerging adulthood" to describe those living in this stage of the life course. These two illustrations lead us to avoid thinking of biological age as necessarily the same as social age.

With those caveats in mind, this chapter explores how consumption practices and ideas about consumption take shape in relation to different stages of the life course: childhood, adolescence, adulthood, and old age. We find that at each stage individuals develop different attitudes toward and habits of consumption, and those in other age groups also have distinct expectations for and interpretations of the consumption of individuals in a given social group. Hence, consumption is a way that we define ourselves as part of a specific age group, but it is also a means through which others define us as members of that group.

In this context, we explore how the meanings of childhood have changed during the twentieth century and how those changes influenced and were influenced by advertising, marketing, and specific consumption patterns. Various social groups, including sociologists, have expressed concern about what they call the "commodification" of childhood – the excessive role of consumption in children's lives. Today, marketers attempt to initiate children's loyalty to brands that they hope will continue throughout their lives (Schor 2004).

Following this discussion, we examine adolescence. Adults are often suspicious of adolescents as they may carry out rebellious behavior via their consumption practices. This phenomenon has inspired research on how adolescent consumption (particularly musical and clothing taste) may hold the potential to serve as a form of rebellion against broader patterns of authority and injustice. However, many of these same authors demonstrate how effectively companies and advertisers have co-opted youth rebellion.

Our discussion of adulthood focuses on the changing modes of consumption that accompany the shift to adult roles. We return to the ambiguity of emerging adulthood mentioned above. Those adults who have not yet married or become parents may have the opportunity to intensively engage in the consumption of clothing, travel, and gourmet food before facing the financial challenges of adulthood. These single adults fit the image of the new petite bourgeoisie whose members are much discussed as "style-makers" in the literature on consumption and class (Featherstone 2000; Bourdieu 1984). After adopting traditional adult roles, these individuals increasingly focus on developing educational opportunities for their children. We explore how parenting through consumption varies by social class and the implications of these processes for our understanding of adults and families.

We conclude with a discussion of consumption and aging. Marketers have described aging "baby boomers" (those born between 1946 and 1964) as a potential goldmine because of their high incomes, reduced parental responsibilities, and intense focus on consumption. However, two factors limit marketers' abilities to reap the "rewards" of this goldmine. First, marketers have tended to ignore this population in part because of discriminatory attitudes toward the elderly and the cult of youth that marketers promote. Second, baby boomers tend to be "brand loyal" and skeptical about purchasing new types of goods. Hence, they may resist marketing appeals. Nonetheless, marketers have focused on this population with an emphasis on pharmaceuticals and healthcare products as well as incitements to participate in tourism. We consider how the marketing industry represents and targets the elderly and what this says about how the rest of society views this age group.

Childhood

We begin this discussion with Daniel Cook's (2008) assertion that, until recently, children have been largely absent from theories of consumption. He contends that the main focus of theories has been on adult consumers, which reflects the flawed assumption that women and children are incidental to consumption. In fact, as noted in the previous chapter, women have often been viewed as the prototypical consumers and their consumption often entails making purchases and using goods on behalf of spouses and children. He argues that this fact raises doubts about theories that argue that consumption is motivated by individual desires or competitive strategies. Rather, he asserts that altruism motivates women's consumption on behalf of their children. Further, the fact that women and children often make purchases together challenges our view that consumption is an independent activity. Finally, the assumption that adults consume on behalf of children and that the latter are passive recipients in this process ignores children's active role in shaping consumption practices. Cook persuasively argues that theories of consumption must take women and children into account to effectively interpret and explain this phenomenon.

To understand children's role as consumers, we must first consider their evolving role in society over time. In an influential account,

Zelizer (1985) points to the changing role of children in the U.S. that began in the early twentieth century. Prior to this point in time, adults had viewed children as having value mainly based on their financial contributions to the household. In a primarily agricultural society, adults had large families with the idea that children could work to contribute to the family economy and support parents in old age. With rapid urbanization and government regulations that restricted or eliminated child labor, children no longer fulfilled this role. At this time, adults began viewing children as "priceless" and emphasized their "moral" rather than "economic" worth. Hence, adults increasingly focused on protecting children from harm and investing in their well-being. With this changing conception, children became increasingly important as consumers and as targets of marketers. This was so because parents have increasingly felt that they can improve children's emotional and educational development through purchases.

Juliet Schor (2004) suggests that marketing to children has gone through distinct phases based on the idea of "triangulation" noted in chapters 2 and 5 – marketers allied with one group in order to gain access to a target market. The first stage of triangulation entailed an alliance between women and merchants against the women's husbands. Second, for much of the twentieth century, marketers adopted a "gatekeeper" model whereby they directed their messages to mothers when seeking to sell goods and services to children. In this model, mothers had discretion over which commodities and images their children had access to. Drawing on the belief that mothers' primary concern was their children's well-being, advertisers focused on the health-giving qualities of foods and other ways that their goods could enhance children's lives.

Schor (2004) argues that this model started to change in the 1980s, as marketers communicated directly with children. Through television shows and advertisements, advertisers and marketers promoted "child empowerment," whereby children could feel that they can and should make their own decisions and that parents represent an unwanted obstacle to their independence. Marketers hoped to short-circuit parents' discretion over expenses for children to increase sales and promote children's brand loyalty throughout their lifetimes.

Parents' vulnerability to these strategies is indicative of changes in parent–child relations in recent decades that reflect the increasing symbolic value of childhood. Many parents reject the traditional model of parenting they experienced in which children are "seen but not heard," preferring to discuss and negotiate decisions with children, thereby giving children greater influence over shopping decisions. Additionally, as more women have entered the workforce, parents face a time crunch and often purchase goods for children to assuage their guilty feelings because they lack sufficient time to spend with them.

Schor argues that marketers have developed numerous techniques that allow them to speak directly to children, like promoting "pester power," whereby children beg their parents for goods; and age compression, in which they market goods designed for teens to pre-teens, drawing on younger children's desires to be more mature and independent. Further, marketers use "stealth marketing" techniques like asking children to secretly test products on their friends and then report the results to the company. Schor fears these techniques disrupt children's relationships with parents and peers and will ulti-mately affect children's mental health, as she demonstrates through statistical analysis about the relationship between children's media exposure and their emotional well-being.

Schor (2004) also explores the effects of food marketing on chil-dren's physical health, focusing on breakfast and fast foods. She explores strategies marketers use to associate food with toys and fun, including market tie-ins (adding a toy promoting a movie to a fast-food restaurant's children's meal), and trans-toying (giving food toy-like qualities, like cereal that makes milk change colors). These techniques effectively increase sales of foods that harm children's health due to the large quantities of sugar, salt, fat, and chemical additives they contain.

Further, she argues that when health advocates challenge com-panies for creating unhealthy products, they respond by denying their products' negative health effects and also blaming parents for purchasing the goods. These arguments are questionable because considerable scientific evidence indicates that these foods are harmful and the companies make sustained efforts to sell the goods to parents.

While Schor demonstrates the risks children face as a consequence of their participation in contemporary consumer culture, Allison Pugh (2009) focuses on how perspectives and practices related to consumption differ between parents and children and among parents of different social classes. In contrast to Schor, she suggests that chil-dren's consumption is prompted by their peers more than by adver-tisers. She argues that, at school, children construct an "economy of dignity" through which they feel included by their peer groups if they have or know about specific goods or experiences their class-mates value. While upper-class children face few restrictions in their access to goods, poor children in mixed-class settings need to develop strategies that demonstrate their knowledge of these goods. They may study the goods in grocery stores or at parties so they can demonstrate their knowledge to their peers. If they lack the goods or knowledge about them, they may assert their self-worth based on other knowledge or characteristics they possess that other friends lack.

As children tell their parents what goods are "essential" to their peer group, adults from different class backgrounds respond in distinct ways. Upper-class white parents use a strategy of "symbolic deprivation" whereby they express a desire to limit their children's consumption (by offering allowances or restricting the amount of time children use video games), but largely fulfill children's requests out of concern that they will face social exclusion if they lack particular goods.

Low-income African American parents, in contrast, develop a strategy of "symbolic indulgence." Given their limited means and the knowledge that they could never fulfill all of their children's desires for goods, these parents might buy a child a single large gift during the course of the year that will be meaningful to them. They acquire the funds to buy these goods by saving during the year, purchasing goods during the off-season, or making purchases when a sudden "windfall" of money (such as a tax refund) becomes available. These parents are less fearful than wealthy parents that material goods will harm their children; rather, they want to shield their children from the sense of deprivation they felt during their own childhoods.

Affluent African American parents tend to accede to their children's wishes to soften the blow of discrimination they may face in the primarily white schools they attend. Pugh concludes her study by arguing that both the economy of dignity and parents' fears that their children will be socially excluded result in children's intense involvement in consumer culture.

Karyn Lacy's (2007) study of the black middle class complements Pugh's findings. She argues that middle-class African Americans with working-class origins encourage their teenage children to seek jobs to purchase goods they desire and to pay for their college expenses. In their view, children need to gain work experience and to learn the value of money to be prepared for adulthood. Hence, these parents do not discourage children's purchases per se; rather, they insist that they must be financially independent. In contrast, upper-middle-class African Americans want their teenage children to stay out of the workforce and hence they seek to satisfy their children's desires. They hope their children will focus on education and extracurricular activities so that they will gain admission to highly selective colleges or universities and secure high-paying jobs. They anticipate that satisfying their children's desires until they complete college will deter them from seeking jobs that would distract them from their studies.

Hamilton and Catterall's (2006) study of poor families in Northern Ireland had similar findings to Pugh (2009). They contend that children in low-income families had considerable influence over their parents' purchases of items used in "public consumption," namely, goods that will be seen by others. These goods were most commonly name-brand clothing. Parents often acceded to their children's requests for expensive branded items to satisfy their desires and to avoid the stigma they would likely experience if their classmates knew they were poor. To purchase these goods, parents reduce their own food and clothing expenses, based on the assumption that others were unlikely to see this evidence of poverty. This study illustrates Cook's (2008) argument that much of parents' consumption on behalf of children is motivated by altruism.

Elizabeth Chin's (2001) study of poor African American children in New Haven, Connecticut, contrasts with the above studies in that it shows children who have little interest in purchasing consumer goods for themselves. These children live in poor families. They are very involved in trading small goods, like food, with friends at school. Further, they express a great desire to provide siblings and parents with gifts above and beyond their own personal desires. Chin argues that these children defy stereotypical representations of poor African American children attacking their peers to steal their name-brand shoes or clothes. They embody the ethic of reciprocity characteristic of poor families mentioned in chapter 4.

Sharon Zukin (2004) argues that parents often view consumption as a setting that allows them to offer children moral and practical education. The author observes that parents take children shopping and use the occasion to teach them about the value of a dollar, thrift, comparison shopping, budgeting, and self-control. Teens often see their first shopping trips without parental supervision as symbolizing their growing autonomy from adults and use these trips as raw material for shaping their identities. Thus, consumption is an important site for the development of parent–child relationships and children's socialization within the family.

James Watson (1997) examines Hong Kong children's and teens' consumption at McDonald's. He argues that young children have adopted a role similar to their U.S. counterparts in their visits to fast-food restaurants. In Hong Kong, parents traditionally ordered food for their children in restaurants. In contrast, younger children assert greater independence by asking grandparents for specific items, in a parallel to the "symbolically valued" child characteristic of the West. Further, teens have appropriated McDonald's as a place to study and snack rather than to get a quick meal. Consequently, Hong Kong residents spend more time at McDonald's on average than do their U.S. counterparts.

Adolescence and Youth

Since the 1950s, adults have viewed adolescents as vulnerable to a variety of risks and as potential threats to society through their "delinquent" behavior. As Slater (1997) notes, many of these concerns reflect adolescents' allegedly "excessive" use of consumer goods like cars, music, alcohol, and drugs, and adults' belief that these fields of consumption are linked to sexual freedom. As such, adults often express concern about adolescent consumption and teens see consumption as an arena of self-definition and rebellion.

Marketers' and other adults' interests in teen consumption are primarily linked to changing teen lifestyles since World War II, expressed through clothing and music. Beginning with early rock-and-roll, teens began to assert greater independence from adult supervision and expectations in part due to their growing resources and leisure time. This self-assertion became more politicized during the 1950s, 1960s, and 1970s as the student movements and youth counterculture took hold. As noted in chapter 3, the counterculture was framed as a rejection of consumerism but actually fueled the intensification of lifestyle consumption as a form of personal expression and a marketing formula. Hence, the youth rebellions beginning in the 1960s informed the "marketing of rebellion" that has characterized the music and clothing industries as well as advertising since the 1970s (Zukin 2004; Smart 2010).

We can identify two broad approaches to youth rebellion via consumption: the "Birmingham School" studies of youth subcultures, and analyses of the marketing of rebellion. The two approaches overlap, though the first emphasizes commodified youth rebellion, while the latter stresses how marketers have co-opted and taken over youth cultures.

The Birmingham Centre for Contemporary Cultural Studies (CCCS) brought together a group of British scholars who began research on primarily male, working-class youth subcultures during the 1960s. The initial goal of these studies was to explore the potential of forms of youth cultural expression to spark widespread social change, as working-class movements had declined in the UK and much of the West. These authors were interested in how young people came to question dominant social beliefs and attitudes through their appropriation and modification of consumer goods. Youth subcultures are important because, at least in their origins, members of these groups develop unique ways of using goods that are not shaped by the goals of producers or marketers. Furthermore, these groups are significant because they demonstrate the embeddedness of consumption in meaningful social relationships.

Dick Hebdige (1979) examines British subcultures from the 1950s to 1970s. He explores teddy boys, mods, skinheads, rude boys, and punks, each of which asserted a distinctive musical preference and clothing style. He suggests that each of these groups in one way or another reflects racial inequality between white British natives and Jamaican immigrants and their progeny. Hebdige argues that these groups used commodities (clothing, musical recordings, and motorcycles) in unique ways to symbolically comment on and at times challenge some aspect of British society. He sees the punks as the most radical in their challenge to social authorities and rock culture. Nonetheless, he argues that punk, like all of these earlier movements, was eventually "hijacked" by marketers who learned they could profit by borrowing images from these groups and repackaging them for sale to a broader audience.

In a later article, Hebdige (2000) revisits the mod subculture as part of a study of the evolving significance of the Vespa scooter in European society during the twentieth century. He finds that after World War II, the Italian producers of the Vespa scooter promoted it to women and teenagers as groups who might use it for leisure rather than as a merely functional means of transportation. During the 1960s, the mods adopted the scooter as their preferred mode of transportation and fashion accessory. Members of this group modified the scooters by removing their engine covers and adding numerous mirrors. This decision was symbolically meaningful as it involved these young men's use of the scooters as emblems of personal and group identity. Further, their decision to expose the scooters' engines was a symbolic effort to make them seem more "masculine" because Vespa originally added the engine cover so that the scooters would appear more stylish and thereby appeal to women. Indeed, the mods developed a rivalry with "rockers" who preferred riding ostensibly more "masculine" motorcycles.

Milestone and Meyer (2012) revisit McRobbie and Garber's (2006) critique of studies of working-class youth subcultures because of their exclusive focus on young men. Building on this earlier study, Milestone and Meyer argue that girls and young women were participants in the subcultures catalogued by Hebdige and others, but they often played subordinate roles due to the broader system of gender inequality in Britain. Two important exceptions to this generalization are the mods and punks. The authors hypothesize that because male members of the mods had an androgynous style, women had more opportunity to participate in this group and dress in ways that did not reinforce their roles as passive sex objects. This was even truer for punk. The music's egalitarian ethos made it possible for some women to front bands and use songs and lyrics as vehicles of self-expression outside the tropes of love and romance. Nonetheless, the authors argue that women never achieved an equal role in any of these subcultures, largely due to patriarchal ideologies and practices.

Thornton's (1996) study of the "rave" scene of dance clubs, in 1980s and 1990s London, moves beyond this early work. She is less interested in subcultures as sites of resistance than with how members of subcultures interact with popular media, how they change over time, and internal status competitions within subcultures. She argues that members of the dance-club scene she studied develop "subcultural capital," adapting one of Bourdieu's concepts. DJs and dancers develop insider knowledge of dance styles as well subculture-specific clothing styles and slang, and they use this knowledge to compete for status within the subculture, to police the group's boundaries with outsiders, and for some (like successful DJs) to earn economic profits. Members of the dance scene focus on divisions between the authentic and inauthentic, the hip and the mainstream, and the underground and the media. Members seek to maintain the exclusive character of their tastes and practices with regard to the surrounding society, while the very success of particular artists or styles makes this quest challenging. Thornton's conception of subculture points to the fluid and contested meanings of in-group identities for their members.

Best's (2006) study of contemporary youth car cultures in the U.S. points to the important roles of race and gender in shaping the characteristics of subcultures. In examining low-riding and illegal car racing in California, she finds that Mexican-American youth cruise in low-rider cars to identify with their parents and as an expression of ethnic pride, even though they often face police discrimination while driving. Cruising as a means of self-expression is less available to young women, who attempt to participate in the subculture, but who often do so as spectators and need to protect themselves from young men's harassment. Further, the illegal racing culture is divided between native-born white, African American, and Latino men, on one hand; and Asian American youth, on the other. These two groups compete and clash, often deriding their counterparts in racial terms. Best sees car culture as an important means of self-expression for young people, but participants often reinforce pre-existing inequalities through their participation in this subculture.

A second body of work examines how pre-existing subcultures are repackaged and marketed to a broader population. In this process, any critical tendency within youth cultures is removed and they serve to reinforce the power of brands and consumption. Douglas Rushkoff (1999), Juliet Schor (2004), and Naomi Klein (2010) all discuss companies' strategy of "cool hunting" and branding, noted in previous chapters. As Klein (2010) argues, during the 1990s, older corporate executives hired younger people to go out and research what was "cool" so they could sell it to the broader population.

Klein (2010), Goldman and Papson (2000), and Zukin (2004) argue that "cool" is often strongly associated with "black," as noted in chapter 5. Companies have carried out product testing with poor black youth (a practice known as "bro-ing"), and have drawn on the styles of hip-hop music and dress in the design and promotion of their products. As hip hop originally emerged as an expression of Afro-Caribbean and African American youth, the lyrics initially included strong political messages criticizing racial segregation, poverty, and violence, and it was performed by a group with whom much of the white youth population had little contact, offering the perfect formula of "resistance," "cool," and "edge." Hence, brands like Reebok, Sprite, Nike, and Tommy Hilfiger have profited handsomely from their associations with hip-hop music and artists.

However, the marketing of rebellion is not limited to hip-hop or African American artists. It is common to hear songs from "classic" rock bands such as the Rolling Stones or The Beatles in the background of commercials. Further, songs and individuals linked to the post-punk, grunge, and rave music scenes have been linked to marketing campaigns for specific goods or large-scale concerts such as the annual event, Lollapalooza (Rojek 2011).

While various authors have considered the involvement of youth in "spectacular subcultures," and the marketing of those subcultures as products to adolescents, adolescents also participate in mundane consumption activities like shopping. As several early studies of mall visitors found, youth and the elderly have an ambiguous position in shopping malls. On one hand, they are the most consistent mall visitors. On the other hand, teens and the elderly use malls as social gathering places or for exercise rather than for purchases. Additionally, teens often engage in horseplay in malls, which may deter the adult shoppers who tend to spend the most money in malls. Thus, mall administrators have attempted to restrict teens' movement in malls through curfews and other forms of surveillance to limit the negative effects they may have on sales (Lewis 1989, 1990; Ortiz 1994; Matthews et al. 2000; Cohen 2003).

Teen behavior in malls has been a topic of considerable interest to researchers who have focused on Venezuela, Chile, and Trinidad. Studies in Venezuela suggest that teens use malls as settings to express their affiliation with different subcultures like skaters or punks (Bermúdez 2008). Stillerman and Salcedo (2012) found that teens in Santiago, Chile, use malls as settings to gain autonomy from adults for romantic encounters, to skip school, or to engage in horseplay; and, as in the U.S., teens engage in a constant, low-level conflict with mall administrators. Miller (1997) finds that groups of Trinidadian youths use malls as safe spaces to hang out in contrast to the street.

In addition to their role as shoppers, teens are important early adopters of new technologies and have also developed new practices of sharing photos and digital music files that have "bubbled up" to the adult population. Through their use of cellphones, social media sites, and music file-sharing sites, teens have developed new consumption practices focused on creating or sharing digital content rather than consuming or using material goods. This culture of sharing has created a crisis for the music industry because it has been unable to control illegal downloads and file-sharing, and, as a result, CD sales have plummeted. While the industry continues to try to punish those involved in illegal downloading, it has largely followed the trends set by youth consumers by creating legal download and sharing sites. Through their use of these new technologies, teens have invented new forms of consumption and also created new arenas that can be colonized by advertisers and brands, such as advertising on cellphones. Industry and marketers have learned from teens' innovative use of these devices and Internet platforms, and use them as new vehicles for generating profits (Rojek 2011; Smart 2010; Ritzer et al. 2012).

As we consider teens as "rebels," "conformists," and "innovators," it becomes clear that no one characterization adequately fits adolescent consumption. Teens are not universally rebellious, conformist, or innovative. Rather, different groups adopt these roles, and, at times, the same individual might fit into more than one category. The fluid nature of teen consumption makes this age group one of the most dynamic groups of consumers.

Adulthood

As noted in the introduction to this chapter, reaching the legal age of adulthood may not coincide with the adoption of the traditional signs of adulthood, such as marriage and parenthood. In the Global North and some areas of the Global South, young adults are delaying marriage and parenthood in response to a variety of social changes. Women are no longer economically dependent on men, and hence may wait to marry until they identify an individual who satisfies their emotional needs. Men may wish to postpone marriage and fatherhood out of a desire to find a perfect match as well as concerns about their capacity to serve as an adequate "provider" for a family. Some heterosexual individuals may choose to remain single given the weakened force of traditional obligations to marry. Further, members of LGBT minorities may wish to postpone long-term commitments, and in many countries are unable to legally marry (Gerson 2010).

This delay of marriage and parenthood, or decision to avoid these traditional signs of adult status, have important implications for consumption. Most importantly, if young adults are employed, the absence of financial responsibilities for others makes resources available for a variety of expenses. Further, young adults may see this phase of life as one in which they may explore and experiment with their identities before "settling down" to the socially recognized identities of "father," "wife," or "parent."

In this context, this population may best reflect the qualities associated with the new middle class noted by Featherstone, Bourdieu, and others in discussing the "aestheticization of everyday life." Lacking the attachments and responsibilities that might limit their freedom of movement and liberty to spend money, these young adults may seek unique or intense experiences through international travel or "extreme sports."

Furthermore, particularly for those individuals who are not in committed relationships, a focus on physical care and personal improvement may be present, specifically with a focus on gym memberships; music concerts; or language, fitness, and New Age religion classes or activities. Each of these activities implies the purchase of a range of accessories and reflects many young adults' desire to engage in "self-fashioning" before they settle into conventional adult roles. Members of this population have also become increasingly involved in different forms of food connoisseurship with their interest in craft beers and specialty cocktails.

Zavisca and Weinberger (2013) examined young college graduates and found that their consumption focused more on unique or intense experiences than material goods. These young adults anticipate that, later in life, family and career commitments will limit their available time for travel, relocation to new cities, or cultural consumption. Therefore, they focus on obtaining these experiences as young adults for the skills and knowledge they may provide. Hence, these middle-class youth use experiential consumption to accumulate a type of cultural capital they may pass on to their children or use in the working world later in life. The authors argue that middle-class emerging adults engage in particular forms of consumption to build their portfolio of cultural capital for use later in life.

For those who move on to socially recognized adulthood, consumer culture has become deeply intertwined with weddings. Following Colin Campbell's work on the role of romanticism in modern consumer culture, Cele Otnes and Elizabeth Pleck (2003) explore the appeal of ostentatious weddings to young women. They argue that this event combines the "sacred" character of a traditional ritual with the key characteristics of modern consumer culture. They argue that this apparent contradiction between "sacred" and "profane" is resolved via the role of romanticism in modern consumption.

In their argument, young women seek lavish weddings based on their goal of having a "perfect" consumption experience. Interestingly, the "magic" of this experience results from both its lavish qualities and its adherence to specific rituals and objects such as "cake toppers" and specific routines in the ceremony and reception. The authors also argue that weddings have become even more ostentatious in recent years as reflected in the growing popularity of "destination weddings" that combine tourism with the wedding ritual.

For those married couples who become parents, a host of consumption decisions ensue from the onset of pregnancy. Purchases for babies have become increasingly specialized and customized above and beyond the gender-typed clothing and toys whose origins date back to the 1930s (Schor 2004). Middle- and upper-class parents are encouraged to begin working on their children's physical and cognitive development from the point of conception through advice manuals and companies producing children's goods. These appeals build on the symbolic value of childhood noted above.

As we discussed in chapter 4, parents' educational decisions are often intertwined with their choices in the housing market. We now consider how parents from different class backgrounds select schools for their children. With the rise in gentrification in the U.S. and Western Europe, noted in chapter 4, educational choices have become more complex for those middle-class parents living in cities. In the U.S, urban-school districts face declining funding due to large-scale population shifts to the suburbs, and the children who attend urban schools are overwhelmingly poor and members of minority groups. In part as a response to the small growth in the population of affluent white residents, urban-school districts have created a two-tiered system whereby magnet or "gifted and talented" schools attract high-performing students while neighborhood schools serve poor and special needs children. Further, some countries have experimented with the creation of independently administered charter schools that receive public funds (Ball et al. 1995; Ball and Vincent 1998; Carnoy 1998; Saporito and Lareau 1999; Raveauda and van Zanten 2007).

The creation of a quasi-market for public education (which in the U.S. already existed if parents could buy into suburban districts) has been controversial. On one hand, political leaders have promoted choice as the solution for parents with children in failing schools who lack the resources to send their children to private school or move to the suburbs. On the other hand, critics note that choice systems do not improve the quality of education for all students; they merely sort students by social class. According to this view, middle-class parents have more skills, time, and resources to navigate choice systems to their children's advantage; while low-income parents lack the skills, resources, and desire to send their children to distant schools. Further, some argue that choice systems actually increase parental dissatisfaction (Smart 2010; Carnoy 1998; Ball et al. 1995; Saporito and Lareau 1999).

Chile's school system has taken the idea of school choice the furthest. In 1980, during the military rule of General Augusto Pinochet, Chile changed its educational laws, permitting the creation of charter schools and establishing locally funded school districts. Under democratic rule in the mid-1990s, Congress allowed charter schools to charge tuition while still receiving public subsidies. The result has been that almost half of the educational market now consists of charter schools, though the quality of education has not improved as a result of competition between schools, and schools are increasingly

segregated by social class. In a micro-level analogy to the U.S. suburban model, parents can now "buy into" an individual school based
on its infrastructure and the social class of students, though they need
not "buy into" a specific local housing market (Carnoy 1998; Hsieh
and Urquiola 2006).

The introduction of choice into educational systems is significant
in that it extends the logic of the market to an area of services that
was formerly considered a public good which every child had the
right to enjoy. As such, choice systems reflect the broader shift in the
Global North and Global South from a model in which citizens can
assert their rights to government-provided services, to one in which
consumers exercise choice in a market. As is evident from the discussion above, schools do not operate in a market the way tennis shoes
or stereos do, and hence this creates a set of complex problems for
the "consumers" seeking the educational "product" for their children
(Smart 2010).

Parents also engage in significant investments in their children's
education, which go beyond the time investment of finding a school
(or in a small percentage of cases, paying for a private school). For
many middle- and upper-class parents, it is important to supplement
their children's classroom education with tutors, arts and music
classes, and organized sports. These activities are designed to prepare
children for academic achievement but also reflect the idea (particularly among those with more formal education) that it is important to
raise children who are "well rounded." There is a significant market
in each of these areas with substantial advertising and competition. In
addition, each of these activities requires a range of accessories such
as uniforms, musical instruments, and art supplies (Lareau 2003;
Pugh 2009).

Apart from their activities in the housing and education markets,
adults also need to make a wide range of choices regarding "healthy"
forms and quantities of consumption for their children. Here, adults
receive a barrage of messages from different sources regarding how
to raise physically and emotionally healthy children. As such, adults
are increasingly persuaded or pressured to conduct research regarding the types of media their children could or should consume and at
what age, what and how much they should eat, what kinds and what
quantity of consumer goods they should have access to, and so on.

In this context, Cairns et al. (2013) found that there are important
class-based differences among mothers regarding food consumption. Higher-income mothers with more formal education tend to
focus more on conducting research regarding the links between

consumption and their children's well-being, and develop more elaborate schemes for what types of and how much food they consume. Lower-income parents with less formal education tend to place fewer restrictions on the types of foods children consume, opting for a mode of parenting involving less direct structuring and supervision of activities. The authors argue that in the context of neoliberal (free-market) ideologies and ideas about motherhood, middle-class mothers come to believe they are personally responsible for their children's well-being and that they can best care for their children via individual choices that often entail specific purchases.

Dedeoglu's (2006) analysis of middle-class Turkish mothers' blog posts offers an interesting contrast to Cairns et al.'s (2013) study of Canadian mothers. While the former study focuses on the differences between middle-class and working-class mothers' food shopping for their children, Dedeoglu (2006) finds differences among middle-class women. Most participants in the website she studied articulated a "good mothering" discourse through which they described their total devotion to their children and purchases of organic foods and other goods that maximize their children's comfort, health, and growth. A less common discourse articulated by less traditional women and career women is summarized as "motherhood as a personal achievement." These women seek to satisfy their children's needs, but also purchase convenience foods and balance their own personal and professional needs with those of their children. The author suggests that although, in both these discourses, women perceive motherhood as traditional and natural, these ideas are relatively recent phenomena that result from Turkey's post-1980 urbanization and economic growth. Interestingly, organic food purchases reflect women's desire to be perfect mothers rather than their research on health outcomes that figured in the Canadian study.

Lindridge and Hogg (2006) offer a third perspective on childrearing in their study of young British women whose parents are Indian immigrants to that country. They found that fathers and brothers encouraged daughters to assimilate into British culture via consumption and to express their individuality. In contrast, mothers acted as guardians of tradition, encouraging daughters to speak in their native tongue, to eat traditional foods their mothers prepared, and to use traditional dress that supported mothers' notions of sexual propriety. Mothers responded to grandparents' enforcement of traditional norms and expressed concern about gossip within the South Asian community. This study's focus on the influence of ethnic communities on the consumption practices of children of immigrants echoes Warikoo's (2007) research on South Asian youth in London, discussed in chapter 5. Further, in contrast to the two studies noted above that focused solely on mothers, it highlights the distinct influences of fathers, mothers, grandparents, and community members on children's consumption in South Asian immigrant families. (Lai 2001 also highlights how, in Taiwan, members of extended families make purchases for other family members for everyday needs or celebrations, thereby questioning the applicability of the "individualization" thesis to that country.)

Consumption also figures in the ritual activities organized by adults for children and extended families such as family meals, birthdays, holidays, and religious ceremonies. As Douglas and Isherwood (1996) argue, these rituals are significant in that they help individuals to mark the passage of time in a meaningful fashion and to locate themselves within broader family and social groups. Nonetheless, status competition and marketing figure importantly in many of these activities, as evident in increasingly elaborate birthday, Sweet Sixteen, Bar/Bat Mitzvah, and other celebrations that may be held in dedicated entertainment facilities, and often (particularly for children) include "gifts" offered to those who attend the celebration, in addition to the person celebrating the birthday.

Family-based consumption rituals take different forms in distinct national and regional settings. One important example is the role of fictive kin (or godparents) in weddings and other celebrations among the indigenous peoples of Otavalo, Ecuador, discussed in chapter 5. In this community, godparents are financially responsible for young adults' weddings, in contrast to the U.S. and Europe, where parents are expected to finance weddings. Further, compadres (co-parents) may be a source of capital or loans for business enterprises. Finally, compadres are expected to participate in volunteer work for the community, like digging trenches for water access. Consumption rituals are rooted in these quasi-family ties, and consumption implies sets of reciprocal obligations directed toward a broad web of individuals (Colloredo-Mansfeld 1999).

Along this line, adults' consumption often involves negotiating relationships across boundaries such as work/family, nuclear/extended family, and different generations. The workplace is an important consumption site as it includes certain basic requirements for entry (formal attire, transportation) and also includes numerous consumption events that figure in workers' possible upward mobility in organizations (office parties) and in daily sociability (lunches, farewell parties, baby showers). In addition to meals and consumption during travel required at specific jobs, the workplace is an important site for social comparison where individuals determine whether or not their consumption is in line with or diverges from their peers, as evident in dress, cars, and verbal comments (Schor 1998).

Older Adults

Older adults have an ambiguous role in the world of marketing. On one hand, many market researchers recognize that the population in the U.S. and many other countries is aging and that the aging population is increasingly affluent. On the other hand, negative attitudes toward the elderly, known as *ageism* and rooted in the broader society and the marketing profession, have discouraged marketers from focusing on this group with the same intensity that they have focused on other age groups (Wassel 2011).

Advertising often reflects and promotes stereotypes about older adults being weak, unattractive, and less capable of decision-making than members of younger age groups, as well as stereotypes regarding older women. In a content analysis of advertisements across age groups, Baumann and De Laat (2012) found that women over the age of 50 are under-represented in advertising. Men dominate ads showing individuals in this age category and they are depicted in occupational roles. Further, those women in this age category who do appear are depicted either as frail and diseased or as youthful, active, and successful. The authors argue that these images reflect broader stereotypes about the appeal and sexual vitality of youth and the unattractiveness and asexuality of older people, particularly older women. They also argue that older viewers studied in market research do not share these views of themselves and hence the messages were not designed to appeal to older adults; rather, they reflect broad-based prejudices against this population.

Marketers and producers target older adults in some specific product categories. In addition to products focused on health conditions or physical limitations, newer areas of focus are recreational industries and products designed to slow the aging process. Recreational and housing industries have specifically targeted seniors with the time to travel and the resources to participate in longer-term recreational activities. Hence casinos, time-shares, condominiums, and housing/recreational complexes in warm-weather areas have specifically targeted seniors (Chaney 1995). In this context, Manning (2000) notes that credit card companies have increasingly targeted seniors, many of whom accrue debts they are unable to pay, thereby compromising the goals of having a financially secure retirement.

Additionally, with the availability of new pharmaceuticals designed to improve sexual function, drug companies have promoted the idea that seniors should remain sexually active for their entire lifespans. This idea contrasts with traditional views that older adults are not (or should not be) sexual beings. On one hand, marketing drugs like Viagra and Cialis to men is predicated on the idea that "erectile dysfunction" is a "disease" that needs to be treated with medication, rather than the view that not all men at all ages display the same sexual drive or function. Further, the idea that erectile dysfunction is a disease reflects the assumption that heterosexual sexual activity is limited to intercourse. Men's use of these drugs may also have severe side effects for both men and women. Some might argue that this instance of treating aging with a drug reflects a view of human sexuality in which the body seems like a machine. Others argue that appropriate use of these drugs can allow adults to continue to enjoy a healthy sex life well into old age and hence improve their quality of life (McGann 2011; Katz and Marshall 2003).

The idea that the body and its functions should be "ageless" if maintained and medicated appropriately reflects processes of individualization explored throughout this text, through which individuals feel pressure to shape, mold, and "perfect" their lives through consumption. A similar conclusion could be drawn in relation to the conversion of old age into a life stage defined by pleasure, recreation, and self-actualization.

Conclusion

In this chapter we have examined how consumption changes across the life course both in terms of what and how individuals consume, but also in relation to cultural beliefs about appropriate behavior and activities for individuals at different stages of life. One important insight from this discussion is that different stages of the life course have evolved in response to changing cultural attitudes; and producers and marketers have participated in that process of change. We have also considered how consumption is embedded in a distinct set of social relationships at each stage of the life course that influence its form and meaning.

In our analysis of different stages of the life course, the interconnection between family relationships and consumption rituals is evident. In the context of relationships within and across age groups, consumption is a crucial means through which individuals construct, maintain, repair, and transform meaningful and valued relationships (Zelizer 2005a; Miller 1998). Additionally, consumption within and across generational groups is a crucial field for status competition and the reproduction of class boundaries (Schor 1998; Bourdieu 1984). Finally, we can observe how processes of individualization, particularly in the Global North, have affected emerging adulthood and old age, particularly among the affluent. Members of these groups have adopted the notion that each person is in charge of constructing her or his life project and narrative through practices of self-actualization, participation in meaningful experiences, and efforts at self-perfection (Lury 2011; Sassatelli 2007).

In the next two chapters we shift our attention to the relationship between consumption and politics. We will continue to examine how consumption intersects with distinct axes of social inequality, but we will do so in the context of discussions of how consumption operates within the political sphere and if and how consumers can also function as citizens.

7
Consumer Citizenship and the Nation-State

Introduction

Thus far, we have focused on how individuals or groups satisfy their desires, needs, or social obligations through consumption. In these last two chapters, we reconsider this view by examining how consumption intersects with citizenship.

We normally regard citizenship as a set of rights and responsibilities accorded to members of a national community in relation to government. This chapter modifies that idea by considering how consumers acted as citizens through actions in the marketplace, participation in governmental agencies, and demands to governments; and how, at certain historical moments, government officials encouraged citizens to participate in government agencies as consumers. Each of these phenomena expands the idea of consumption beyond the desire for, purchase, use, display, exchange, and disposal of goods and services to the realm of politics. While we have already looked at power in relation to how consumption produces and reinforces inequalities, we have not yet explored the exercise of power in the political realm.

To examine this dimension of consumption, we consider how, during the nineteenth and twentieth centuries, individuals banded together to create consumer co-operatives and to support boycotts and buycotts of companies they either criticized or supported. We then look at the distinct waves of twentieth-century consumer citizenship in the U.S. Finally, we examine alternative models of consumer citizenship in Europe and Asia. This chapter and the next one demonstrate how some segments of publics see consumption not only as a means of personal, family, or peer-group satisfaction, but also as a tool of political expression and struggle. Further, governments at times seek to harness the power of consumers to help achieve their political and economic goals.

The idea of consumer citizenship has broader implications for our understanding of consumption. First, this phenomenon illustrates how, in some settings, consumers can express and enact the values and goals of solidarity and social change, as well as assert collective identities, in contrast to our understanding of consumption as largely revolving around immediate social relationships, social status, or individual identity. Second, the history of consumer citizenship demonstrates how less powerful groups like women and African Americans have used the arena of consumer citizenship to assert their collective rights, as well as to demand equality in the marketplace and in the political sphere. The concept of consumer citizenship leads us to consider the complex ways that consumption can be the medium through which citizens link their personal needs and desires to their membership in political communities and to ideas of morality and justice.

Early Models of Consumer Citizenship

Consumer citizenship dates back to the era of the American Revolution. American colonists boycotted British products (as in the Boston Tea Party) to undercut the British Crown's undemocratic authority. During the nineteenth century, Britons participated in boycotts linked to anti-slavery campaigns (Gabriel and Lang 2006; Soper and Trentmann 2008). These first examples of consumer citizenship are important not simply because they were examples of innovative social protest tactics, but because the boycott became a crucial tactic in many consumer protest campaigns from the eighteenth century until the present.

A second form of consumer citizenship emerged as a reaction to the rise of industry and wage labor in Britain. Following the ideas of utopian thinker Robert Owen, working people in Rochdale, England, formed producer and consumer co-operatives. By 1830, they had already created 300 co-operatives (Williams 2007). Workers own these organizations and they seek to guarantee low prices and quality goods to members, while eliminating the exploitation of employers and high prices and uneven quality associated with the retail trade. Producer co-operatives became a major segment of the British economy until the 1990s, when many co-ops sold their assets because they had difficulty competing with private companies that separated production and retail functions and subcontracted labor to other firms (Gabriel and Lang 2006).

During the 1960s, in Japan, *seikatsu* clubs were founded as consumer co-operatives. The clubs have expanded in recent decades due to consumers' desire to purchase environmentally friendly products and because their non-profit character fit well in the context of Japan's stagnating economy in the 1990s and 2000s. In the U.S. and Europe, co-ops represent a niche marketplace for organic, vegetarian, and other specialty foods unavailable in most large grocers. Further, co-ops attract "ethical consumers," discussed in the next chapter. Ethical consumers seek to limit the negative effects of their consumption decisions on workers and the environment and also reject the standardized retail model that dominates many Western societies. Hence, while today co-operativism lacks its nineteenth-century stature, it continues to attract a segment of consumers who seek to opt out of mainstream retail environments (Gabriel and Lang 2006).

Co-operatives developed in distinct historical circumstances in the Global South. Agricultural and credit co-operatives emerged in India and Bangladesh to help poor farmers to eke out a living. In Latin America, co-operatives have roots dating back to the early twentieth century. Labor laws allowed workers to create consumer and housing co-operatives in the 1920s and 1930s. Governments and religious organizations promoted agricultural co-operatives as economic development tools after land reforms divided large rural estates in the 1960s and 1970s. Finally, progressive political movements organized co-operatives as tools designed to achieve economic development and social justice. Hence, unlike the nineteenth-century United Kingdom, where co-ops were an economic response to industrialization, in the Global South, co-operatives have been social and political responses to poverty (Williams 2007; Phillips 1998; Morris 1966).

Consumer Citizenship in the Twentieth-century U.S.

Lizabeth Cohen's *A Consumers' Republic* (2003) is a powerful and complex analysis of the evolution of consumer citizenship in the twentieth-century U.S. She identifies three waves of consumer movements that developed: from the 1890s to the 1920s; the 1930s until the 1940s; and the 1960s to the 1970s. Each wave had different characteristics and goals, and the second and third waves were led by white women and African Americans, both of whom had limited access to government and corporations.

Additionally, she identifies an important shift in how "the consumer" was understood during the 1930s and 1940s and in the postwar era. During the first period, the idea of the "citizen consumer" prevailed. According to this conception, consumers were expected to demand their rights and participate in government decisions regarding consumption, to contribute to the common good. After World War II, the idea of the "purchaser citizen" predominated. This idea suggests that individuals can promote the common good through their aggregate buying power and thus promote economic growth and greater material rewards for all. The latter idea ultimately won out, undercutting the legitimacy of the earlier view that consumers have political rights they can and should assert in and through government.

During the first wave of consumer citizenship from the 1890s to 1920s, individuals created independent organizations like the National Consumers League that demanded the creation of new federal agencies such as the Food and Drug Administration (FDA) and the Federal Trade Commission (FTC), and pressured government to enact laws such as "the Pure Food and Drug Act and the Meat Inspection Act (1906)" (Cohen 2003: 21). These campaigns sought to insure product safety and to restrict the industrial monopolies' power to engage in price fixing. Additionally, women boycotted retailers to press for lower prices, labor unions staged boycotts against employers who refused to bargain in good faith, and the National Consumers League persuaded many women to only purchase cloth that included a "white label," guaranteeing that it had been produced under ethical conditions, as well as to press government for protective labor laws (Cohen 2003: 22).

The peak of consumer activism lasted from the beginning of the Great Depression in the 1930s until World War II. Much of this activism was sponsored by officials in President Roosevelt's administration, who saw consumers as a "countervailing force" to big business that could help government broaden its regulatory powers to insure citizens' access to safe and affordable goods. The government also enlisted women in efforts to ration goods to support the war effort. White women played a crucial role in mobilizing boycotts and other efforts to limit prices and secure supplies of consumer goods during the war. The government's legitimation of the "consumer" as an important interest group also created opportunities for women to play an advisory role in public agencies such as the Office of Price

Administration and Civilian Supply (OPA) and to play an assertive and public role recruiting other women to support the war effort (Cohen 2003: 65–70).

African Americans also played a key role in consumer activism during the 1930s and 1940s. While they were less involved in government agencies focused on consumer rights, African Americans focused on white retailers' exploitative practices in their segregated communities. They sought access to affordable credit and price controls, and demanded that white merchants hire African Americans when they operated in predominantly black neighborhoods. Before World War II, African Americans engaged in boycotts and riots in order to demand greater access to mainstream consumer goods (Cohen 2003: 83–8).

After World War II, African American veterans sought to redress the injustices they had experienced as soldiers. They were compelled to use segregated facilities and entertainment venues on military bases, and those soldiers stationed in the U.S. were often denied access to public facilities in the North, where Jim Crow laws did not exist but similar practices occurred nonetheless. These wartime experiences catalyzed the wave of well-known boycotts and legal actions that formed the backbone of the Civil Rights movement of the 1950s and 1960s. Cohen argues that a crucial motivation for African Americans to participate in the Civil Rights movement was their desire for equal access to retail and entertainment facilities enjoyed by whites (Cohen 2003: 88–100, 166–91).

After World War II, the political winds shifted in Washington, and government planners developed a different notion of consumers' role in the political realm. Activists' efforts to institutionalize their representation as consumers in government failed. Government policies focused less on price controls than on promoting aggregate consumer demand as the engine that would power the postwar U.S. economy. Hence, the federal government encouraged suburban expansion through credit policies favoring white male veterans, and government officials and companies exhorted individuals to buy more goods to improve their standard of living as well as to insure continued economic growth. Government and business encouraged individuals to support the common good as "purchasers" in the market rather than as "citizens" participating in or pressuring government (Cohen 2003: 112–65; 194–290).

The third wave of consumer citizenship emerged in the 1960s in a renewed partnership between the federal government and citizens. President Kennedy and his successors during the 1960s and 1970s sought to protect consumers in the marketplace and give them a voice in government, ultimately leading to a new wave of regulations securing product quality and environmental safety. However, many of these laws might not have been enacted without pressure from the consumers' movement, most notably through organizations led by Ralph Nader. He first identified serious design flaws that made cars hazardous and continued to champion consumers' rights against corporations. In this movement, women again took the lead, staging boycotts targeting excessive prices at specific grocery chains.

Additionally, the welfare rights movement sought to expand welfare recipients' access to consumer goods. Finally, in riots in Northern cities during the 1960s, African Americans targeted white-owned businesses to gain access to consumer goods they had been denied due to price gouging and the absence of adequate employment in segregated communities.

The third wave of consumer activism was different from its predecessors in that, rather than seeking a voice in government, activists primarily sought inclusion in the ideal lifestyle of mass consumption promoted by government and business after the war. This movement was more focused on providing each individual or family with an opportunity to enjoy a better standard of living than in transforming citizens' relationships with government. Further, beginning in the late 1970s, many of the legislative victories won by consumer activists were reversed as citizens and public officials promoted deregulation of business, which they argued would make businesses more competitive and lead to price savings for consumers (Cohen 2003: 345–96).

Public Citizen, the organization Nader founded in 1971, still exists, and its legacy is evident in periodic consumer demands to ban unsafe products, such as toys with lead paint produced in China and plastic bottles containing the chemical BPA. We might also link the Nader legacy to the successful campaign of parents, teachers, and public-health professionals to get public schools to remove sugary sodas from vending machines, given the well-known links between soda consumption and diseases resulting from childhood obesity. Additionally, groups of consumers have engaged in efforts to gain greater government regulation of dangerous additives, products with unknown health effects (such as genetically modified organisms or GMOs), and food-production techniques with the goal of reducing food-borne illnesses (Reinberg 2006; Public Citizen 2014).

One of the most recent and significant examples of activism in partnership with government, which builds on the third wave Cohen describes, was the creation of the Consumer Financial Protection Bureau (CFPB), brainchild of former Harvard Professor and current Senator Elizabeth Warren. The bureau was created to prevent the abuses of consumers' rights that contributed to the 2007–9 mortgage crisis. Prior to the crisis, mortgage banks misled consumers (particularly members of low-income, minority groups) by offering them mortgages that they could not afford to pay because of hidden fees and interest rates set to increase a few years after the mortgage commenced. Consequently, millions of new homeowners faced foreclosure. The CFPB is designed to protect those consumers with little experience in the mortgage and consumer credit markets when they navigate these complex transactions, and to redress their grievances when they are subject to illegal abuse by banks and credit card companies (Sabatini 2014).

The model of the purchaser citizen is also evident in periodic statements by government officials. It is common for public officeholders to exhort individuals to consume more to bolster economic activity. This was the case in 2001 after the 9/11 attacks on the World Trade Center and Pentagon, when then President George W. Bush and New York Mayor Rudolph Giuliani asked citizens to go shopping so that they could counteract likely investor concern resulting from the attacks (Zukin 2004). More recently, U.S. government officials frequently have made hopeful remarks that consumer confidence might rise again after the 2007–9 mortgage crisis led to home foreclosures, unemployment, and a major recession. Signs that individuals were beginning to increase debts and/or purchase homes again were considered indicators that "normalcy" had returned, notwithstanding the fact that excessive consumer and mortgage debt had been the catalysts for the preceding crisis (Smart 2010).

Cohen's analysis of the "consumers' republic" is significant in several respects. First, it provides substantial evidence that Americans have a long and enduring history of consumer activism. Second, it demonstrates that the two groups in the forefront of consumer activism – women and African Americans – were precisely those who lacked full access to the mass consumption that was offered as a promise to the entire population. Third, it shows the changing meanings of consumer citizenship over time. While this idea emphasized consumers' participation in government in the 1930s and 1940s, it has increasingly shifted since then to focus on participation in American prosperity. This shift could help explain why many observers see consumption and citizenship as antithetical. Nonetheless, her research demonstrates that citizenship can be combined with consumption when governments legitimate consumer citizenship and form partnerships with consumer activists. Hence, she historicizes the less overtly politicized concept of consumption present in U.S. society today.

Consumer Citizenship in Europe and East Asia

The consumer leagues Cohen describes in the early twentieth-century U.S. had counterparts throughout Europe. Reagin (1998) analyzes housewives' associations in Germany between the two world wars. The associations initially imported ideas from the U.S. that encouraged women to become more efficient housewives through the rational management of effort, modeling housecleaning on the changing factory system. Since German women were much poorer than their American counterparts, they could not become more efficient through the use of many electric appliances, but the associations helped women develop recipes that took into account food shortages and encouraged home designs with smaller kitchens so they would be easier for women to clean. The organizations continued to operate under the Nazi regime and many of their programs remained. The author concludes that many of the food promotions and prohibitions dating back to World War I, as well as support for small retailers, influenced women, families, and consumer culture for decades to come.

Chessel (2006) contrasts the French Social League of Buyers to the American Consumers League that Cohen analyzed. Like some of the German organizations discussed above, the French league brought together Catholic women (in contrast to the dominance of Protestant activists in the U.S.) who sought to draw a middle course between traditional charitable activity and more radical feminists by proposing social and political reforms in the sphere of consumption. Because of its links to social Catholicism, the French league encouraged co-operation between labor, business, and the state rather than acting as an independent interest group. While the group was much smaller than the mass-based U.S. organization, the league secured important legal reforms. Chessel's account importantly emphasizes the intensive dialogue between European and American consumers' organizations before World War I. These organizations exchanged ideas, debated policies, and charted their identities in relation to their counterparts elsewhere. Hence, while each group operated within its own national borders, it was part of a transnational dialogue and participated in international congresses, prefiguring the global activism we consider in the next chapter.

The U.S. postwar model of mass consumption did not take the same form in other industrial societies. Garon and Maclachlan (2006) argue that European and Japanese governments developed a different model of consumer citizenship from that of the postwar U.S. Rather than promoting the idea of the purchaser consumer, these governments encouraged citizens to save money and enjoy non-commodified leisure through shorter work hours and longer vacations than their U.S. counterparts. Further, these governments (and later the European Union) have adopted a much more assertive role in regulating GMOs and other food additives than has been the case with the more business-friendly U.S. government. In this sense, consumer rights are far more in the forefront in Europe and Japan than they are in the U.S., while consumer expenditures are much higher in the U.S.

Laura Nelson's (2000) study of consumer nationalism in South Korea provides another interesting counterpoint to the U.S. case. She argues that the notion of *kwasobi*, or excessive consumption, has deep roots in South Korean culture and politics and is a widely shared belief that different groups use to control and limit consumption. This idea of asceticism draws on Confucianism and Christianity. Political activism building on this notion dates back to "Buy Korean" savings clubs founded in 1909. Many Koreans saw frugality and limits on imports as ways to safeguard the country's economic and political independence after the humiliation of Japanese colonial rule. In accord with the Korean government's postwar efforts to promote economic development through exports, both government officials and citizens' groups encouraged South Koreans to limit their consumption, save, and to buy South Korean goods. Several campaigns drew on the notion of *kwasobi* to criticize ostentatious consumption and the purchase of imported goods, which were believed to undermine the country's economic solvency. Hence, in direct contrast to the U.S. case, South Korean activists and government officials discouraged citizens from making purchases in order to promote a distinct road to economic development (based on exports rather than domestic consumption) and rationalized calls for frugality based on a set of valued cultural and political ideals.

In China, modern consumption developed alongside the rise of the nation-state during the first third of the twentieth century. The National Products Movement reflected politicians' concerns that imports would harm the economy and intellectuals' fears that foreign economic influence would limit China's political independence. The movement included government officials, businessmen, and activists, and sought to persuade and coerce Chinese individuals to only purchase Chinese-made goods. Modern consumer culture rejected imports to advance Chinese nationalism (Gerth 2008).

The European, Japanese, South Korean, and Chinese cases offer evidence of diverse and divergent models of consumer citizenship in distinct national contexts. In contrast to the view that the American model of mass consumption has successfully undermined distinct national consumption practices (Ritzer 2003; Smart 2010), these cases demonstrate the importance of nationally based cultural and political histories for understanding specific patterns of consumer citizenship.

Conclusion

In this chapter, we have explored a different dimension of consumption than in preceding chapters. Rather than focusing on consumption as the satisfaction of individual and group wants and desires, we have considered how consumption can be the means to achieve social and political goals for both consumers and governments. In short, we have begun to explore how consumers are simultaneously citizens, and how the identities of "consumer" and "citizen" sometimes intertwine.

Consumers began to organize to achieve collective goals via cooperatives and boycotts beginning in the eighteenth century, and continue to do so until the present day. Using these organizations and techniques, consumers have attempted to satisfy their needs through their own organizations rather than via the market, and have sought to achieve political goals by pressuring companies and governments. These political goals have included supporting workers' demands for better wages and working conditions, securing the civil rights of racial minorities, and guaranteeing product safety. Some of these actions have resulted in the expansion of government regulation of manufacturers to safeguard the needs of consumers.

During the early 1900s, just as consumers organized to achieve collective goals, governments began to assert the connections between consumption and citizenship. During the first period, governments sought to empower consumers so they could receive guarantees of the quality of products and be protected from unscrupulous business practices. During the Great Depression and World War II, the U.S.

government sought to conscript consumers to restrict consumption and collect goods to support the war effort. After the war, the government opted for a market-model of consumer citizenship rather than a notion of consumer empowerment and participation in government. The idea was that increasing wages would lead consumers to spend more, thereby supporting U.S. industry. Hence, today, politicians routinely encourage consumers to shop to support the economy. However, many scholars argue that this is a weak form of citizenship in which consumers have few official channels through which to assert their rights in the political sphere as they relate to consumption.

Nonetheless, the U.S. postwar model of mass consumption was not universally shared, as our discussions on Europe, Japan, South Korea, and China revealed. In these cases, citizens and governments gave greater weight to savings, the value of leisure time over purchasing power, and government regulation of consumption goods than in the U.S. The U.S. model of consumer citizenship is not universal.

As we move into a global world of consumption and media, we also find a new arena of consumer citizenship. Economies have become more intertwined, information travels instantaneously, and, consequently, consumers have become increasingly vocal in their desire to regulate corporate activity on the global stage. In the next chapter, we examine the contours of this new mode of citizenship and its prospects for regulating business.

8

Consumer Citizenship in the Era of Globalization

Introduction

The previous chapter explored consumer citizenship during an era when the scope of consumer action was at the national scale, and, at least during the first portion of this period, national governments sought to involve citizens in the regulation of consumer affairs and industry. With the advance of the most recent phase of globalization, consumer citizenship has changed in focus and scope.

As Soper and Trentmann (2008) note, the increasingly global character of economic life from the 1970s to the present means that consumers have the opportunity (or may feel compelled) to act in relation not only to states but also to markets and other institutions (like global organizations). The rapid advances in communications technologies have also provided activists with information and tools that have allowed them to coordinate across greater distances and to do so more rapidly than in the past. Further, a segment of consumers has begun to call into question the personal and social consequences of their own behavior and to seek more ethical forms of consumption.

In this chapter, we explore this new terrain of consumer citizenship. While these forms of action overlap, we look at each separately. Ethical consumption refers to efforts to make purchases in a manner that reduces harm to other human beings or the environment. Anti-consumption is a more radical effort to reduce one's impact on the environment by minimizing market transactions and energy use through such strategies as "going off the grid" – using renewable energy sources – or growing one's own food. Finally, global consumer activism uses some of the same techniques of boycotts and buycotts that were developed by consumer movements operating inside national borders, but focuses on global problems and increasingly targets global corporations. We consider the origins of these new forms of consumption, as well as their potential effects on producers and the environment. We first consider the primary issue areas that have motivated some individuals to engage in alternative consumption, anti-consumption, or consumer activism – the loss of non-commodified experiences, dissatisfaction with consumption, poor working conditions in consumer product industries, and pollution. We then explore these new forms of consumer citizenship.

Consequences of Consumption

The quantity and range of goods and commodified experiences available to consumers in the Global North and Global South have increased exponentially during the course of the twentieth century and the beginning of this century. Nonetheless, a segment of consumers has expressed dissatisfaction with the "consumer treadmill" due to its effects on their personal lives. Furthermore, consumers have increasingly considered the effects of their consumption on the workers who manufacture consumer goods and on the global environment. Consequently, individuals and groups have sought to minimize the negative effects of their consumer practices on others and the environment.

Dissatisfactions with consumerism result from several factors. As Schor (1998) notes, many individuals in the U.S. have become overwhelmed by the "work-and-spend cycle," the stress and worry associated with the ongoing escalation of consumer competition and "necessary goods," and the feeling that an excessive focus on consumption undermines valued social relationships. Parents have also become concerned that processed foods, media use, and an excessive focus on branded goods have negatively affected their children's physical and mental health, as well as family relationships (Schor 2004). Some consumers have come to feel that consumption undermines their happiness and sense of well-being (Smart 2010). Indeed, Easterlin's (1974, 1995) cross-national survey research shows that while within a given country wealthier people tend to be happier, if all incomes were raised this would not lead to happiness for all because as individuals become more prosperous, their consumption aspirations rise in line with their new peers.

Another group of consumers rejects the standardization of contemporary consumption. These individuals "consume differently," seeking pleasure from non-standardized goods, handmade goods, or unique experiences. This process is linked to the rise of lifestyle-based identities. Rather than pursuing a quantitative increase in consumption as is the case with many contemporary consumers, these individuals seek unique experiences that mark them as different from the crowd due to their focus on low-cost or non-standard goods (Soper 2009).

In addition to many individuals' desire to minimize consumption's negative effects on their quality of life, others have focused on the ethics of consumption. This growing concern follows from the widespread availability of information regarding the global environment and working conditions in consumer-product industries. First, it is now widely known that the global growth of consumption has significantly contributed to the depletion of non-renewable resources (like oil), climate change, and the increase of toxic waste. We routinely receive alarming news reports regarding the dramatic growth of carbon emissions and waste and their effects on weather patterns, sea levels, plant and animal life, and the future of the human species. Increasing carbon emissions and waste can be directly tied to escalating levels of consumption. Fossil fuels are the main energy sources for producing goods and transporting them to market. Increasing auto ownership is adding to carbon emissions (Smart 2010; Miller 2012).

The growing demand for goods and the strategy adopted by businesses of planned obsolescence, used to persuade consumers to periodically replace perfectly functioning goods, draw down mineral resources used to produce these goods (cellular phones, tablet computers, and flat-screen televisions). Additionally, the disposal of these goods creates toxic waste. The growing use of electronic goods like cellphones and computers also utilizes increasing quantities of electricity, and families have developed the expectation that each member should have her or his own computer and cellphone. Much of the packaging for goods is made from plastic, while increased marketing of bottled water creates waste that is not biodegradable and hence takes hundreds or thousands of years to break down. Further, the increasing sale of out-of-season produce and so-called "non-traditional exports" like tropical fruits or fresh-cut flowers reduces the land available for local food production in exporting countries, leads to soil erosion, relies on pesticides that harm agricultural workers' health, and uses fossil fuels as produce is transported ever greater distances to market (Smart 2010).

The declining cost and increasing availability of air travel has also had an important effect on the global environment. A single flight on a commercial jet produces more carbon than driving a car for one year. Hence, increased air travel has led to growing use of oil and release of carbon into the atmosphere (Rosenthal 2013).

Additionally, wood production for industrial use or to clear space for raising livestock, roads and human settlements has an important negative effect on air quality around the world. In particular, forestry in the world's rainforests, most notably the Amazon and Indonesia, has had a notable effect on the oxygen available to all of us. Trees absorb carbon dioxide and add oxygen to the air. Large rainforests serve as "carbon sinks" in that they retain an enormous amount of carbon and also serve as the planet's "lungs" by giving off large quantities of oxygen. When large portions of rainforests are destroyed using "slash-and-burn" logging – a traditional technique of forestry management – the carbon stored in those trees is released into the atmosphere while the oxygen they formerly provided is lost (Gedicks 1999).

These isolated examples need to be understood as part of a package of consumption in the Global North and among upper classes in the Global South. Environmental scientists have developed an indicator to try to capture consumers' total effects on the natural environment known as the ecological footprint. The footprint is calculated by quantifying total resource use plus waste, divided by the earth's capacity to regenerate those resources. Through calculating the ecological footprint, we learn that the standard lifestyle maintained by Americans in particular would be unsustainable if adopted by all of the planet's inhabitants. Aspects of our lives that we take for granted, such as living in a house, owning a car, or eating beef add enormously to our ecological footprint. The U.S. has one of the largest ecological footprints per capita (average per person) in the world, but the total footprint is largest in Asia, due to large populations and fast-growing economies. Consider the impact of a large portion of the citizens of China, the world's most populous nation, switching from bicycles to cars as their main form of transportation. A similar transition, though less rapid, is occurring in India, the country with the second largest population in the world (Global Footprint Network 2010).

Faced with knowledge of the enormous negative effects of consumption on the environment and its implications for global food security, health, and the sustainability of animal and plant life, some individuals have come to question the pace and intensity of their consumption. As we discuss in greater detail in the next section, a segment of consumers has considered a range of alternatives to their current pattern of consumption to limit the negative effects of their everyday actions on the global environment.

A second area of ethical concern for consumers involves the poor conditions endured by the workers who produce many of the goods we consume on a regular basis. Due to the work of activists in labor unions and non-governmental organizations, we have learned a great deal about the "sweat behind the label" in the clothing, computer, and agricultural sectors. As noted in chapter 3, major global companies have become decreasingly involved in manufacturing goods and much more focused on design and marketing, with Nike being the paradigmatic case of this phenomenon. Due to technological changes in transportation and communications, and reduced barriers to international trade (lower taxes on imports in many nations), it became possible for companies in the Global North to contract with other factories or "middlemen" in low-wage countries so that goods could be produced for a fraction of the cost of manufacturing in the U.S., Western Europe, or Japan (Klein 2010; Smart 2010).

Mexico, Central America, and the Caribbean were popular sites for production during the 1980s and 1990s, but China is the most important location today. Companies have sought locations for production where wages are low and government oversight regarding labor rights, workplace safety, or pollution is weak. Because companies like Nike, Gap, Reebok, Adidas, or Walmart may work with thousands of "contractors" around the world, and often begin and end contracts frequently based on how low a company bids for a particular job, it is difficult to know where a specific good is produced. This uncertainty and the long distances between production and consumption locations make it difficult for consumers to know where and under what conditions their T-shirt or cellphone was produced. This is a different situation from the beginning of the twentieth century, when much industrial production was located in the Global North and workers could organize boycotts among their neighbors. The workers could provide neighbors and family with eyewitness accounts of working conditions, and hence the domain of production was much more tangible to consumers. Today, consumers are physically and culturally removed from the people who produce many of the goods they buy and use (Klein 2010; Smart 2010; Bartley and Child 2011; Seidman 2007).

Once activists began to investigate the working conditions in the factories making goods for well-known brands in places like Mexico, El Salvador, Haiti, Singapore, Vietnam, and China, the picture was not pretty. In many settings around the world, local factories prefer young women, who they anticipate will be more compliant than men, and who they believe (based on gender stereotypes) have better fine-motor skills than do men. In many cases, the workers are teens who have migrated from their home towns to find gainful employment. In these factories, wages are low, workers are often required to put in overtime, factories are unsafe, and many women are subjected to sexual abuse and pregnancy tests (Stillerman 2003; Seidman 2007; Klein 2010).

As word got to consumers in the Global North of the working conditions and the massive gap between wages and the retail prices of many of these goods, a segment of consumers began to explore alternatives to purchases from major brands and to consider the contrast between the brand image conveyed through advertisements and the reality of exploitation in the factories where branded goods are produced. As we detail below, these concerns translated into an important wave of activism from the 1990s until the present designed to monitor the conditions under which branded goods are made.

Ethical Consumption

As some consumers have become more aware of the negative effects that products and intensive consumer lifestyles can have on their mental and physical health and the far-reaching consequences of contemporary consumption on working people in the Global South, they have developed a variety of responses that can be summarized under the heading of ethical consumption.

A first response by some consumers is to reduce the quantity of their purchases. As described by Schor (1998), downshifting refers to individuals who seek to escape the stresses and limited satisfactions of the "work-and-spend cycle" by reducing their workforce participation. According to the author, these individuals see a tradeoff between time and money, and choose to maximize the former and sacrifice the latter.

Schor (1998) also identifies a second trend, described as "simple living." These individuals seek to transcend the time–money tradeoff by seeking the pleasures of life without clutter. Simple living may entail a radical reduction in expenses, the use of shared resources (like jointly owned cars), living in cities where car ownership is unnecessary, or seeking to reduce one's impact on the environment by producing one's own food or relying on renewable forms of energy like wind or solar power. Individuals in this category seek to separate their sense of self-worth from their possessions and incomes.

The annual week-long Burning Man Festival held in Nevada is an intriguing example of anti-consumption. Kozinets (2002) highlights festival participants' efforts to reject market exchange and construct community in this intense and unique consumer experience. The festival prohibits sales, encourages gift giving and barter, and promotes community as an antidote to the tendency of contemporary producers and markets to promote individual competition between consumers. Festival participants achieve a temporary escape from the market through the promotion of a "sharing-and-caring" environment that promotes individual self-expression. While this escape from the market is not sustainable, he argues that festival attendance has an important influence on individuals' capacity to imagine emancipated lives for themselves.

Anarchist political activists, in contrast, integrate anti-consumption into their everyday lives by refusing to purchase or consume cars or meat and leather products, throwing away television sets, wearing used clothing, scavenging for used goods, living in housing cooperatives, and rejecting popular musical styles. These decisions are motivated by individuals' personal, moral, and identity choices, as well as their import as symbolic rejections of capitalism (Portwood-Stacer 2012). Similarly, participants in the movement known as "freeganism" engage in exchange of goods and services, recycling and lateral cycling of used and scavenged goods, and sustainable practices like participation in community gardening. The movement is divided between those who pursue an environmentally sustainable lifestyle through purchases, and an "ideological core" that pursue non-market activities to counter capitalist dominance (Pentina and Amos 2011).

Schor and Thompson (2014) examine emerging networks of local, sustainable production and consumption through the lens of the "new economics," which seeks to promote environmentally sustainable and socially equitable economic models. They describe an emerging network of sustainable producer-consumers who act based on the principles of reduced work time, self-provisioning (gardening, sustainable home-energy use), "true materialism" (making goods last, exchanging products), and community-building. They argue that networks of individuals engaged in local, sustainable production and consumption may help build an alternative to contemporary capitalism.

In the long run, a large segment of the population in the Global North and the wealthy in the Global South will need to consume less or reject market-based competitive consumption, but it is unlikely that most consumers will do so voluntarily. A more widespread and economically significant pattern is ethical consumerism. Many middle-class consumers in the Global North have become increasingly devoted to consuming organically grown and locally produced foods and fair trade goods (whereby producers of coffee, chocolate or crafts are paid adequately for their labor). This market segment has grown rapidly in recent years, and some individuals have become more conscious regarding how their consumption decisions affect their health, producers, and the environment (Barnett et al. 2011; Cairns et al. 2013; Micheletti 2003; Sassatelli 2007; Gabriel and Lang 2006; Smart 2010).

Scholars have interpreted these trends in different ways. Sassatelli (2007) argues that ethical consumerism is significant in that it reflects how consumers have challenged the idea that market transactions are merely about the economic cost of goods. In contrast, consumers now consider the "externalities" of goods – that the production and consumption of goods can have negative effects on other human beings and the environment. Consumers demonstrate that their ethical concerns come to bear on their consumption decisions.

Some authors express skepticism about the potential effects of ethical consumerism on the global environment and on labor practices. Both Humphery (2010) and Littler (2009) see these phenomena as potentially positive, but if they are understood and practiced merely as another form of "market choice," without examining the national and global structures that produce threats to the environment and human rights or considering collective responses to these issues, they will have little effect on the problems they seek to address. Cairns et al. (2013) similarly note that organic foods are affordable mainly for middle-class consumers and hence this market solution to health and environmental problems is not available to working-class mothers and families. Further, the idea that purchasing organic foods can solve threats to health and the environment reinforces the neoliberal idea that individuals can resolve collective problems through the market. Further, Smart (2010) and Jaffee (2012) raise the specter of "greenwashing." Large companies have learned that consumers are concerned about the environmental and human effects of their products and hence have used environmental and social responsibility as a new branding strategy that has co-opted social movements while diluting their goals.

Students of "political consumerism" attempt to frame the phenomenon of ethical consumption in a manner that looks beyond the individual consumer. Micheletti (2003) argues that with the intensification of globalization, governments are less capable of managing all of the risks that affect consumers. Consequently, consumers' voluntary efforts to regulate the market through ethical consumerism or activism have created a new and promising form of regulation of corporate behavior that is beyond the scope of individual governments. Furthermore, ethical consumption is often initiated by non-profit organizations rather than individuals. Finally, mothers are crucial protagonists in this field (much as Cohen 2003 argued for the twentieth-century U.S.) because their role in feeding their families leads them to become politicized when they learn that particular products may harm their children or spouses.

Barnett et al. (2011) make a complementary argument. They criticize many scholarly accounts that tend to moralize regarding consumption, viewing consumers as either manipulated by producers or always resisting producers' control. Rather, they argue that ethical consumption emerges when organizations connect with consumers' everyday practices and provide them with new alternatives. Hence, for these authors, "consumption" is a tool fair trade activists use to influence individuals' everyday practices by engaging with consumers in their roles as parents or members of faith communities. They acknowledge that the changes these campaigns make may be limited and locally circumscribed, but they emphasize that the organizations, rather than individual consumers, are the catalysts for ethical consumerism and this phenomenon encompasses changing everyday practices and forms of social regulation of consumption. Hence, the significance of ethical consumerism extends beyond the individual consumer to the realms of everyday routines and politics.

This review of ethical consumption suggests that this cluster of practices represents a significant departure from "consumption as usual" in its goals and its effects on producers. Whether we refer to small farmers supplying local "farm-to-table" restaurants or to massive global corporations like Starbucks regularly stocking fair trade coffee, there is no doubt that ethical consumption has affected producers. Nonetheless, we should consider this outcome with caution. Ethical consumerism is still a niche market that by no means represents the bulk of production in a given product category. Furthermore, numerous scholars warn that market-based responses are unlikely to resolve major global problems like climate change, which can only be fully addressed through concerted governmental and corporate action. Consumption activists have sought to spur on such global changes, as we outline below.

Contemporary Consumer Activism

We have already hinted that ethical consumption is linked to collective action in our discussion of Micheletti's (2003) and Barnett et al.'s (2011) work on organized efforts to transform consumption and its consequences. However, numerous scholars have examined various protest actions directed toward ameliorating the global consequences of consumption.

Culture-jamming is one form of consumer activism, which is most commonly linked to the Canadian magazine *Adbusters*. Culture-jamming refers to efforts to disrupt the cultural power of advertisements and brands by satirizing advertising campaigns or transforming advertising images or texts to point to companies' harmful policies. In addition to the *Adbusters* magazine, culture-jammers often engage in "billboard correction," in which they alter advertisements to challenge individual companies or the culture of consumption as a whole (Klein 2010; Lasn 2000; Drescher 2009).

Over several years, *Adbusters* and their supporters organized symbolic protests designed to heighten consumers' critical consciousness regarding well-known brands. One example of these protests was "Buy Nothing Day," organized on "Black Friday" when U.S. retailers offer customers deep discounts on merchandise in anticipation of the Christmas holiday. The magazine's editors encouraged Americans to boycott the post-Thanksgiving buying frenzy and to attend protests outside Niketowns and other emblematic brand boutiques (Klein 2010).

Adbusters gained considerable notoriety for having "branded" the Occupy Wall Street movement of 2011–present. In July, 2011, Kalle Lasn, the magazine's co-founder, wrote a tweet calling on activists to occupy Wall Street on September 17 of that year. The call activated numerous groups frustrated with the mortgage crisis and related issues, and the protests spread to cities throughout the U.S. and abroad. Today, many observers argue that the Occupy movement's decentralized structure meant that it was unable to influence public policy. Further, Carducci (2006) argues that culture-jamming is unlikely to affect labor practices in the companies that protestors criticize unless culture-jammers ally with grassroots social-movement organizations like labor unions. For our purposes, the significance of culture-jamming lies in its challenge to the symbolic power of advertising, and a culture-jammer's blog post was the spark that ignited a social movement proposing a broader critique of U.S. and global capitalism (Yardley 2011).

While culture-jamming focuses on the hollow promises of the advertising industry and the brands it promotes, another strand of activism is directed at the conditions under which many goods are produced. Anti-sweatshop activists seek to compel global corporations to respect the rights of the workers who manufacture their products. As noted in chapter 3, global companies' decisions to decentralize and subcontract production, which is facilitated by free-market policies and changing communications and transportation technologies, has made working conditions invisible to most consumers in the Global North. The terrible circumstances under which many industrial workers labor were made visible in the 1980s and 1990s as human rights activists identified sweatshops in Mexico, Central America, the Caribbean, and the Far East (Klein 2010; Seidman 2007; Bartley and Child 2011).

While anti-sweatshop activism began with small non-governmental and religious organizations, the movement expanded when students began to examine their universities' sourcing policies for licensed apparel. Activists learned that while global brands like Nike, Reebok, Calvin Klein, and Disney subcontracted clothing production to sweatshops in the Global South where workers are mistreated, underpaid, and labor in unsafe conditions; they sell these goods at an enormous markup to consumers in the Global North (Klein 2010).

Anti-sweatshop activism has involved campaigns designed to publicly shame well-known brands by revealing the unethical conditions under which their products are manufactured. Activists seek to pressure these companies to commit to contract with manufacturers that pay workers a living wage and treat them with dignity, as well as to allow independent monitors to verify that companies fulfill their promises (Klein 2010; Vogel 2010).

After initial optimism that codes of conduct and independent monitoring would press companies to respect workers' rights, subsequent analyses have found that the model of independent monitoring without legally binding authority has influenced the behavior of global companies but is not an effective form of global industrial regulation. Bartley and Child (2011) examined how anti-sweatshop campaigns affected company earnings and reputations. They found that these campaigns affected sales and stock prices for some types of companies and affected specialized company ratings, but had no effect on the companies' reputations among their peers in the business world.

Seidman (2007) examined three campaigns in which independent monitors were utilized in India, South Africa, and Guatemala.

She found that monitoring was most effective when activists secured government enforcement of labor laws in the exporting country. She suggests that framing campaigns in terms of national citizenship rights instead of universal human rights and building alliances with local labor unions increases the likelihood that activists can persuade national governments to legally enforce labor rights. In contrast, when independent monitoring groups are the main source of pressure on companies, these campaigns are less effective. Finally, in an overview of private regulation of corporate behavior with regard to labor rights and the environment, Vogel (2010) echoes Seidman's (2007) argument that global consumer campaigns will only be effective when linked to governments' legal enforcement of labor rights and environmental regulations.

Global environmental activism has used similar strategies to the anti-sweatshop campaigns. Religious and non-governmental organizations in the Global North have supported populations in the Global South who are negatively affected by pollution linked to mining and oil drilling, as well as repressive governments' attacks against environmental and human rights activists. Local activists in the Global South use what Keck and Sikkink (1998) term the "boomerang effect" – they seek influence with activists in the Global North to pressure both the multinational corporations operating in their countries and their own governments. Activists in the Global North have sued companies in U.S. courts, mobilized corporate shareholders to support their cause, and gained support from their governments to block drilling or mining, or to force companies to clean up toxic spills (Klein 2010; Watts 1997; Gedicks 1999).

Kozinets and Handelman (2004) attempted to understand the identities of activist participants in the movements described above, but raise a distinct set of concerns regarding these movements' potential success. Based on interviews with activists in an anti-advertising, anti-Nike, and anti-genetically modified foods organization, and analysis of activist websites, they find that activists' identities and rhetoric may turn off potential recruits. They observe that activists adopt a puritanical language to condemn consumption, and that to some extent they identify consumers as the "enemy" and an obstacle to their goals of holding large corporations accountable. The authors suggest that activists' evangelical zeal ignores the pleasures people gain from consumption and attacks the very individuals they would need to recruit to achieve lasting social change. They propose that anti-consumption activists consider how to build alliances with consumers without sacrificing their principled critiques of large corporations.

Global consumer activism offers an interesting and novel instance of consumer citizenship. Consumers in the Global North choose to boycott or pressure companies on behalf of workers or citizens in the Global South, based on a moral commitment to only purchase goods that are produced by workers who are treated with dignity and under conditions that do not harm the environment. Consumers' activism on behalf of producers echoes some of the early twentieth-century boycotts supporting workers that Cohen (2003) describes in the U.S. context. What is novel in the current setting is that consumers and activists claim a sense of global citizenship that is not linked to their legal rights and responsibilities in a national setting (Soper and Trentmann 2008). While this newer conception of citizenship demonstrates that consumers seek to achieve ethical goals through their consumption practices, scholars also underscore the limitations of global consumer citizenship as a strategy for achieving its lofty goals. The fact that activists are far removed from the workers or native people they seek to support, and their actions in most cases have little legally binding authority over the companies and governments they seek to influence, limits the power of global consumer citizenship.

Conclusion

In this chapter, we have explored the new contours of consumer citizenship in the global age. Consumers have developed two models of citizenship that increasingly reflect the growing ethical concerns of middle-class consumers in the Global North. First, individuals have become increasingly involved in anti-consumption (seeking to consume less in order to reduce stresses related to work and competitive lifestyles, challenge capitalist values, or reduce consumption-related effects on the environment), and ethical consumerism (purchasing goods that do not include ingredients that negatively affect their health and that were produced and distributed in a manner that does not harm workers and the environment). Anti-consumption is a fairly small-scale phenomenon, while ethical consumption is a fast-growing portion of the market. While these phenomena reflect some consumers' broader ethical concerns, scholars caution that market behavior in itself is unlikely to resolve the systemic effects of consumption on working people and the environment.

Global consumer activism attempts to reveal the conditions under which consumer goods are produced and to rectify labor abuses and environmental pollution that are endemic consequences of global production. While global and environmental activists have tarnished the images of multinational corporations, gained greater visibility, and proposed novel conceptions of universal citizenship, campaigns that rely exclusively on culture-jamming or the collective buying power of organized consumers are unlikely to resolve the systemic problems of labor rights and environmental degradation. Scholars note that global citizens are more likely to achieve their goals by influencing the legally binding authority of governments.

This last substantive chapter offers hopeful signs that a segment of consumers in the Global North has begun to consider and act on the negative consequences of ever-escalating consumption. Nonetheless, it offers a sobering view of both the scale and complexity of the global problems that contemporary consumption has generated, as well as the limitations of political strategies that rely on the power of consumers to "change the world" by buying or refusing to buy specific goods. In this context, scholars suggest we need to rethink and transcend neoliberal ideas and practices that lead us to see market responses as the only means to address global problems. In contrast, consumer-citizens need to push governments and corporations to take responsibility for protecting human rights and the environment because only these powerful institutions have the power to systemically address these issues (Klein 2010; Smart 2010; Sassatelli 2007).

9
Conclusion

This book has endeavored to provide the reader with an overview of the historical evolution of modern consumption, taking special note of the rapid changes experienced in recent decades. Further, we have attempted to sketch some of the major theories of modern consumption and to consider the strengths and weaknesses of each perspective. Unlike other valuable texts covering similar terrain, this book promised to highlight three understudied areas of consumption: its distinctive features in the Global North and Global South, the intersection of consumption with different forms of inequality, and different forms of consumer citizenship and consumer politics. In this context, let us consider some of the book's most important conclusions.

Consumption based on market exchange has been a major feature of modern societies across the world. Its characteristics have varied across time and space. In the Global North, modern consumption took shape through the rise of department stores, discount stores, shopping malls, and boutiques. These modern retail forms emerged in nineteenth-century Europe, and by the early twentieth century they had curtailed the influence of traditional retail formats, with important national and regional variations. The development of modern retail was and is much more uneven in the Global South than in the Global North. Higher poverty rates and large informal sectors mean that contemporary retail forms coexist with traditional street markets.

While advertising, branding, and credit were crucial ingredients in the development of modern consumption, scholars initially debated the degree to which advertising influences consumers' identities and choices. Some scholars argued that advertising shapes consumption, while others contended that consumers creatively interpret advertising messages. More recently, scholars have examined the mutual influences of consumer practices and advertising, and others have explored how market research may shape the social reality it seeks to describe.

We have argued that individuals and groups use consumption to shape and transform their social relationships, and to mark out their position in a society divided along the axes of class, race, gender, age, sexuality, and religion. Additionally, we have considered how consumer subcultures and the mass media create source material for advertisers who then reconfigure these ideas to present images that appeal to a broad population.

Our discussions of "multicultural" advertising directed toward Hispanics and Asian Americans illustrate this point. Advertisers engaged in extensive research and trial and error to construct messages that were meaningful to members of these groups, and to frame images of these groups that make sense and are appealing to corporate clients. These messages, in turn, helped create the collective identities of "Hispanic" and "Asian American."

In recent decades, cultural and economic changes have led to a shift in production, design, advertising, and consumption. Countercultural movements of the 1960s era persuaded consumers that they could express their identities via unique forms of consumption. Companies and advertisers followed suit with an increasing focus on product design, branding, experiential products and environments, and tourist infrastructures. Many individuals' consumption is today linked to processes of individualization, through which we seek to shape our life narratives in meaningful ways, and the emergence of subcultures and tribes through which individuals develop consumption-based group identities and rituals. Finally, social media websites and musical software allow individuals to produce and share audiovisual content and music that give them greater power in relation to corporations, but also make those digital platforms ripe for colonization by companies.

These processes are distinct for residents of the Global South. Brazilians visit Disney World to gain status among their countrymen, not to imitate Americans. Belizeans gained a greater appreciation for their national culinary traditions after living in Chicago and Los Angeles. Globalization generates distinct outcomes in different locations as members of specific cultural groups use, interpret, and transform the goods and images produced by global corporations.

Consumption is profoundly shaped by inequalities based on class, status, gender, race, ethnicity, sexuality, religion, and age. An individual's class position can powerfully shape their consumption choices and the ways they use consumption to distinguish themselves from members of other social classes. In contrast to countries of the Global North, in non-European societies like Turkey and Chile, individuals develop class-based consumption patterns in relation to other social classes in their own country, as well as to status images emanating from Europe and the U.S.

As ascribed identities, gender and race function differently from class. While numerous mechanisms keep the class structure intact, upward and downward mobility occurs under some circumstances. In contrast, changing one's gender or race is not possible, barring the exception of sex-change operations. Consequently, our ideas about gender and race powerfully shape and limit the ways men, women and members of different ethnoracial groups see themselves, and these perceptions make their way into consumption.

In this context, women and members of racial minorities are both subjects and objects of consumption. Both groups have developed distinctive patterns of consumption reflecting their own orientations as well as patterns of discrimination they have endured. However, women and members of ethnoracial minorities have been repre-sented through advertising, marketing, music, and film in ways that are appealing to heterosexual white men. Hence, consumption is simultaneously a means of expression for women and members of ethnoracial minorities and a mechanism for reproducing their sub-ordinate positions in society. These patterns and exclusions take distinct forms in the Global South, as evident in the discussions of the fashion for veiling in Turkey and the intensification of indigenous identity through ritualized consumption in Ecuador. We concluded with the idea of intersectionality, which permits an integrated under-standing of how class, gender, race, sexuality, and age work together in shaping consumption.

Consumption has distinct characteristics and takes on different meanings at different stages of the life course. Each of these stages is a field for the construction of meaningful relationships and for strate-gies directed toward the reproduction of individuals' class positions. Processes of individualization increasingly shape emerging and older adults.

Finally, we have explored the different ways in which consumption and citizenship can be intertwined. During much of the twentieth century, consumption became a vehicle through which individuals and groups demanded full membership in national communities, and governments alternately promoted and discouraged individuals to participate as consumers in the political arena. In recent decades, patterns of individualization and globalization have led consumers to develop new forms of citizenship on the global stage via practices of anti-consumption, ethical consumption and global consumer citizenship. While these new forms of citizenship are unlikely to fully achieve the goals these individuals and groups have identified, they point to the important ways in which consumption can be directed toward ethical and political goals in addition to achieving individual satisfaction and identity.

I hope that this book has given you, the reader, a sense of the complexity of contemporary consumption and its dynamic character. Through consumption, we recognize ourselves and the world around us, construct meaningful relationships, reproduce inequalities, and engage with politics. As we learn of the terrible human and environmental costs of contemporary consumption at a planetary scale, citizens, states, and corporations need to find a way to join forces to chart a more sustainable path into the future.

References

Abaza, M. (2001) Shopping malls, consumer culture, and the reshaping of public space in Egypt. *Theory, Culture & Society* 18: 97–122.

Abu-Lughod, J. L. (1991) *Before European Hegemony: The World System A.D. 1250–1350.* Oxford University Press.

Addis, M. and Holbrook, M. (2001) On the conceptual link between mass customization and experiential consumption: an explosion of subjectivity. *Journal of Consumer Behaviour* 1: 50–66.

Adorno, T. and Horkheimer, M. (2000) The culture industry: enlightenment as mass deception. In J. Schor and D. B. Holt (eds.), *The Consumer Society Reader.* The New Press, pp. 3–19.

Allen, D. E. (2002) Toward a theory of consumer choice as sociohistorically shaped practical experience: the fits-like-a-glove (FLAG) framework. *Journal of Consumer Research* 28: 515–32.

Anjaria, J. S. (2008) The mall and the street: practices of public consumption in Mumbai. In D. T. Cook (ed.), *Lived Experiences of Public Consumption: Encounters with Value in Marketplaces on Five Continents.* Palgrave, pp. 203–20.

Appadurai, A. (1996) *Modernity at Large: Cultural Dimensions of Globalization.* University of Minnesota Press.

Applebaum, R. and Lichtenstein, N. (2006) A new world of retail supremacy: supply chains and workers' chains in the age of Wal-Mart. *International Labor and Working-class History* 70: 106–25.

Ariztia, T. (2013) Unpacking insight: how consumers are qualified by advertising agencies. *Journal of Consumer Culture.* DOI: 10.1177/1469540513493204.

Arnould, E. J. and Price, L. (1993) River magic: extraordinary experience and the extended service encounter. *Journal of Consumer Research* 20: 24–45.

Arnould, E. J. and Thompson, C. (2005) Consumer culture theory (CCT): twenty years of research. *Journal of Consumer Research* 31: 868–82.

Babb, F. (2011) *The Tourism Encounter*. Stanford University Press.

Baldauf, A. (2008) "They come and they are happy." A gender topography of consumer space in Dubai. In D. T. Cook (ed.), *Lived Experiences of Public Consumption: Encounters with Value in Marketplaces on Five Continents*. Palgrave, pp. 221–40.

Ball, S. J. and Vincent, C. (1998) "I heard it on the grapevine": "Hot" knowledge and school choice. *British Journal of Sociology of Education* 19: 377–400.

Ball, S. J., Bowe, R. and Gewirtz, S. (1995) Circuits of schooling: a sociological exploration of parental choice of school in social class contexts. *Sociological Review* 43: 52–78.

Barnett, C., Cloke, P., Clarke, N. and Malpasse, A. (2011) *Globalizing Responsibility: The Political Rationalities of Ethical Consumption*. Wiley-Blackwell.

Bartley, T. and Child, C. (2011) Movements, markets and fields: the effects of anti-sweatshop campaigns on U.S. firms, 1993–2000. *Social Forces* 90: 425–51.

Baudrillard, J. (1996) *The System of Objects*. Verso.

Baudrillard, J. (2000) Beyond use value. In M. Lee (ed.), *The Consumer Society Reader*. Blackwell, pp. 19–30.

Bauer, A. (2001) *Goods, Power, History*. Cambridge University Press.

Bauman, Z. (2007) Collateral casualties of consumerism. *Journal of Consumer Culture* 7: 25–56.

Baumann, S. and de Laat, K. (2012) Socially defunct: a comparative analysis of the underrepresentation of older women in advertising. *Poetics* 40: 514–41.

Belk, R. W. and Costa, J. A. (1998) The mountain man myth: a contemporary consuming fantasy. *Journal of Consumer Research* 25: 218–40.

Belk, R. W., Wallendorf, M. and Sherry, Jr., J. F. (1988) A naturalistic inquiry into buyer and seller behavior at a swap meet. *Journal of Consumer Research* 14: 449–70.

Bell, D. (1976) *The Cultural Contradictions of Capitalism*. Basic Books.

Bennett, T., Savage, M., Silva, E., Warde, A. and Gayo-Cal, M. (2009) *Culture, Class, Distinction*. Routledge.

Berfield, S. (2013) On Black Friday, strikes and counterstrikes at Wal-Mart's stores. *Businessweek* November 29. At: <http://www.businessweek.com/articles/2013-11-29/on-black-friday-strikes-and-counter-strikes-at-walmart>.

Bermúdez, E. (2008) Malls: territorios y objetos de consumo simbólico en la construcción de representaciones de identidades juveniles. *Revista Argentina de Sociología* 6: 96–120.

Best, A. L. (2006) *Fast Cars, Cool Rides: The Accelerating World of Youth and Their Cars*. New York University Press.

Bestor, T. C. (2000) How sushi went global. *Foreign Policy* Nov/Dec: 54–63.

Bihagen, E. and Katz-Gerro, T. (2000) Culture consumption in Sweden: the stability of gender differences. *Poetics* 27: 327–49.

Bordo, S. (2000) Hunger as ideology. In J. Schor and D. B. Holt (eds.), *The Consumer Society Reader*. The New Press, pp. 99–116.

Bourdieu, P. (1977) *Outline of a Theory of Practice*. Cambridge University Press.

Bourdieu, P. (1983) The forms of capital. In J. Richardson (ed.), *Handbook of Theory and Research for the Sociology of Education*. Greenwood Press, pp. 241–58.

Bourdieu, P. (1984) *Distinction: A Social Critique of the Judgment of Taste*. Harvard University Press.

Bourdieu, P. (2005) *The Social Structures of the Economy*. Polity.

Bourdieu, P. and Passeron, J. C. (1990) *Inequality in Education, Society and Culture*, 2nd edn. Sage.

Bowlby, R. (2001) *Carried Away: The Invention of Modern Shopping*. Columbia University Press.

Bromley, R. D. F. (1998) Market-place trading and the transformation of retail space in the expanding Latin American city. *Urban Studies* 35: 1311–33.

Brown, E. H. (2011) Black models and the invention of the US "Negro Market," 1945–1960. In D. Zwick and J. Cayla (eds.), *Inside Marketing: Practices, Ideologies, Devices*. Oxford University Press, pp. 185–211.

Cáceres, G. and Sabatini, F. (eds.) (2004) *Barrios cerrados en Santiago de Chile: entre la exclusión y la integración residencial*. Lincoln Institute of Land Policy and Pontificia Universidad Católica de Chile, Santiago, pp. 9–43.

Cairns, K., Johnston, J. and MacKendrick, N. (2013) Feeding the "organic child": mothering through ethical consumption. *Journal of Consumer Culture* 13: 97–118.

Caldeira, T. (2000) *City of Walls*. University of California Press.

Caldwell, M. L. (2002) The taste of nationalism: food politics in postsocialist Moscow. *Ethnos* 67: 295–319.

Campbell, C. (2005) *The Romantic Ethic and the Spirit of Modern Consumerism*, 3rd edn. Alcuin Academics.

Carducci, V. (2006) Culture jamming: a sociological perspective. *Journal of Consumer Culture* 6: 116–38.

Carnoy, M. (1998) National voucher plans in Chile and Sweden: did privatization reforms make for better education? *Comparative Education Review* 42: 309–37.

Carter, P. (2003) "Black" cultural capital, status positioning, and schooling conflicts for low-income African American youth. *Social Problems* 50: 136–55.

Carter, P. (2006) Straddling boundaries: Identity, culture, and school. *Sociology of Education* 79: 304–28.

Cayla, J. and Peñaloza, L. (2011). Mapping the future of consumers. In D. Zwick and J. Cayla (eds.), *Inside Marketing: Practices, Ideologies, Devices*. Oxford University Press, pp. 320–42.

Chace, Z. (2013) The real story of how Macklemore got "Thrift Shop" to No. 1. *NPR*; February 8. At: <http://www.npr.org/blogs/money/2013/02/08/171476473/the-real-story-of-how-macklemore-got-thrift-shop-to-number-one>.

Chan, T. W. and Goldthorpe, J. H. (2007) Class and status: the conceptual distinction and its empirical relevance. *American Sociological Review* 72: 512–32.

Chaney, D. (1995) Creating memories: some images of aging in mass tourism. In M. Featherstone and A. Wernick (eds.), *Images of Aging: Cultural Representations of Later Life*. Routledge, pp. 213–28.

Chessel, M-E. (2006) Women and the ethics of consumption in France at the turn of the twentieth century: the *Ligue Social d'Acheteurs*. In F. Trentmann (ed.), *The Making of the Consumer: Knowledge, Power and Identity in the Modern World*. Berg, pp. 81–98.

Chin, E. (2001) *Purchasing Power: Black Kids and American Consumer Culture*. University of Minnesota Press.

Chirot, D. (1990) What happened in Eastern Europe in 1989? *Praxis International* 10: 278–305.

Clarke, A. (1999) *Tupperware: The Promise of Plastic in 1950s America*. Smithsonian Institution Press.

Clarke, J., Hall, S., Jefferson, T. and Roberts, B. (2006) Subcultures, cultures, and class. In S. Hall and T. Jefferson (eds.), *Resistance Through Rituals: Youth Subcultures in Post-war Britain*, 2nd edn. Routledge, pp. 3–59.

Cochoy, F. (1998) Another discipline for the market economy: marketing as a performative knowledge and know-how for capitalism. In M. Callon (ed.), *The Laws of the Markets*. Blackwell and *Sociological Review*, pp. 194–221.

Cochoy, F. (2011) "Market-things inside": insights from the *Progressive Grocer* (United States, 1929–59). In D. Zwick and J. Cayla (eds.), *Inside Marketing: Practices, Ideologies, Devices*. Oxford University Press, pp. 58–84.

Cohen, E. (2003). *A Consumers' Republic: The Politics of Mass Consumption in Postwar America*. Alfred A. Knopf.

Collins, P. H. (1998) It's all in the family: intersections of gender, race, and nation. *Hypatia* 13: 62–82.

Colloredo-Mansfeld, R. (1999) *The Native Leisure Class*. University of Chicago Press.

Cook, D. T. (2008) The missing child in consumption theory. *Journal of Consumer Culture* 8: 219–43.

Cova, B., Kozinets, R. V. and Shankar, A. (2007) Tribes, Inc.: the new world of tribalism. In B. Cova, R. V. Kozinets and A. Shankar (eds.), *Consumer Tribes*. Elsevier, pp. 3–26.

Cova, B., Maclaran, P. and Bradshaw, A. (2013) Rethinking consumer culture theory from the postmodern to the communist horizon. *Marketing Theory* 13: 213–25.

Crockett, D. (2008) Marketing blackness: how advertisers use race to sell products. *Journal of Consumer Culture* 8: 245–68.

Crockett, D. and Wallendorf, M. (2004) The role of normative political ideology in consumer behavior. *Journal of Consumer Research* 31: 511–28.

D'Andrea, G., Stenger, A. and Goebel-Krstelj, A. (2004) Six truths about emerging market consumers. *Strategy + Business* 34: 2–12.

Dávila, A. (2001) *Latinos, Inc.: The Marketing and Making of a People.* University of California Press.

Davis, M. (1990) *City of Quartz: Excavating the Future in Los Angeles.* Vintage Books.

de Certeau, M. (1984) *The Practice of Everyday Life.* University of California Press.

Dedeoglu, A. O. (2006). Discourses of motherhood and consumption practices of Turkish mothers. *Gender and Consumer Behavior* 8: 296–310.

De Oliveira, O. and Roberts, B. (1996) Urban development and social inequality in Latin America. In J. Gugler (ed.), *The Urban Transformation of the Developing World.* Oxford University Press, pp. 252–314.

De Vries, J. (1975) Peasant demand patterns and economic development: Friesland, 1550–1750. In W. N. Parker and E. I. Jones (eds.), *European Peasants and Their Markets: Essays in Agrarian Economic History.* Princeton University Press, pp. 207–66.

De Vries, J. (1993) Between purchasing and the world of goods. In J. Brewer and R. Porter (eds.), *Consumption and the World of Goods.* Routledge, pp. 85–132.

DiMaggio, P. and Mukhtar, T. (2004) Arts participation as cultural capital in the United States, 1982–2002: signs of decline? *Poetics* 32: 169–94.

Dokmeci, V., Yazgi, V. and Ozus, E. (2006) Informal retailing in a global age: the growth of periodic markets in Istanbul, 1980–2002. *Cities* 23: 44–55.

Douglas, M. and Isherwood, B. (1996) *The World of Goods: Towards an Anthropology of Consumption*, 2nd edn. Routledge.

Dreier, P., Mollenkopf, J. and Swanstrom, T. (2004) *Place Matters: Metropolitics for the Twenty-First Century*, 2nd edn. University Press of Kansas.

Drescher, T. W. (2009) The harsh reality: billboard subversion and graffiti. In A. M. Orum and Z. P. Neal (eds.), *Common Ground? Readings and Reflections on Public Space.* Routledge, pp. 158–64.

Duany, A., Plater-Zyberk, E. and Speck, J. (2010) *Suburban Nation: The Rise of Sprawl and the Decline of Public Space*, 2nd edn. North Point Press.

DuCille, A. (2000) Toy theory: black Barbie and the deep play of difference. In J. Schor and D. B. Holt (eds.), *The Consumer Society Reader.* The New Press, pp. 259–80.

Du Gay, P. (2004) Self-service: retail, shopping, and personhood. *Consumption, Markets & Culture* 7: 149–63.

Dyer, G. (2009) *But Beautiful: A Book about Jazz*. Picador.

Easterlin, R. A. (1974). Does economic growth improve the human lot? Some empirical evidence. In P. A. David and M. W. Reder (eds.), *Nations and Households in Economic Growth: Essays in Honor of Moses Abramovitz*. Academic Press, Inc., pp. 89–125.

Easterlin, R. A. (1995). Will raising the incomes of all increase the happiness of all? *Journal of Economic Behavior & Organization* 27: 35–47.

Feagin, J., Vera, H. and Batur, P. (2001) *White Racism: The Basics*. Routledge.

Featherstone, M. (2000) Lifestyle and consumer culture. In J. Schor and D. B. Holt (eds.), *The Consumer Society Reader*. The New Press, pp. 92–105.

Firat, F. and Venkatesh, A. (1995) Liberatory postmodernism and the reenchantment of consumption. *Journal of Consumer Research* 22: 239–67.

Fiske, J. (2000) Shopping for pleasure: malls, power and resistance. In J. Schor and D. B. Holt (eds.), *The Consumer Society Reader*. The New Press, pp. 306–30.

Florida, R. (2003) Cities and the creative class. *City & Community* 2: 3–19.

Foster, R. (2011) The uses of use value: marketing, value creation, and the exigencies of consumption work. In D. Zwick and J. Cayla (eds.), *Inside Marketing: Practices, Ideologies, Devices*. Oxford University Press, pp. 42–57.

Gabriel, Y. and Lang, T. (2006) *The Unmanageable Consumer*, 2nd edn. Sage.

Galbraith, J. K. (2000) The dependence effect. In J. Schor and D. B. Holt (eds.), *The Consumer Society Reader*. The New Press, pp. 217–22.

García Canclini, N. (1995) *Hybrid Cultures: Strategies for Entering and Leaving Modernity*. University of Minnesota Press.

García Canclini, N. (2001) *Consumers and Citizens: Globalization and Multicultural Conflicts*. University of Minnesota Press.

Gardiner, S. (2013) Judge rules NYPD stop-and-frisk practice violates rights. *Wall Street Journal*; August 12. At <http://online.wsj.com/news/articles/SB10001424127887324085304579008510786797006>.

Garon, S. (2006) Japan's post-war "consumer revolution," or striking a "balance" between consumption and spending. In J. Brewer and F. Trentmann (eds.), *Consuming Cultures, Global Perspectives: Historical Trajectories, Transnational Exchanges*. Berg, pp. 189–218.

Garon, S. and Maclachlan, P. L. (2006) Introduction. In S. Garon and P. L. Maclachlan (eds.), *The Ambivalent Consumer: Questioning Consumption in East Asia and the West*. Cornell University Press, pp. 1–16.

Gayo, M. and Teitelboim, B. (2009) Localismo, cosmopolitismo y gustos musicales. In C. Fuentes (ed.), *Chile 2008: Percepciones y actitudes sociales. 4o. Informe de Encuesta Nacional ICSO-UDP*. Universidad Diego Portales, pp. 111–21.

Gedicks, A. (1999) *Resource Rebels: Native Challenges to Mining and Oil Corporations*. South End Press.

Gerson, K. (2010) *The Unfinished Revolution: Coming of Age in a New Era of Gender, Work, and Family*. Oxford University Press.

Gerth, K. (2008) Consumption and politics in twentieth-century China. In K. Soper and F. Trentmann (eds.), *Citizenship and Consumption*. Palgrave, pp. 34–50.

Gilbert, A. (1998) *The Latin American City*, 2nd edn. Monthly Review Press.

Gill, R. (2009) Beyond the "sexualization of culture" thesis: an intersectional analysis of "sixpacks," "midriffs," and "hot lesbians" in advertising. *Sexualities* 12: 137–60.

Global Footprint Network. (2010) *Ecological Footprint Atlas 2010*. At <http://www.footprintnetwork.org/en/index.php/GFN/page/ecological_footprint_atlas_2010>.

Gökarıksel, B. (2012) The intimate politics of secularism and the headscarf: the mall, the neighborhood, and the public square in Istanbul. *Gender, Place and Culture* 19: 1–21.

Goldman, R. and Papson, S. (2000) Advertising in the age of accelerated meaning. In J. Schor and D. B. Holt (eds.), *The Consumer Society Reader*. The New Press, pp. 81–98.

Gonzalez de la Rocha, M. (1994) *The Resources of Poverty*. Blackwell.

Gordon, A. (2006) From Singer to Shinpan: consumer credit in modern Japan. In S. Garon and P. L. Maclachlan (eds.), *The Ambivalent Consumer: Questioning Consumption in East Asia and the West*. Cornell University Press, pp. 137–62.

Goss, J. (1999) Once upon a time in the commodity world: an unofficial guide to the Mall of America. *Annals of the Association of American Geographers* 89: 45–75.

Gotham, K. F. (2007) *Authentic New Orleans*. New York University Press.

Gottdiener, M. (1997) *The Theming of America*. Westview Press.

Grandclément, C. and Gaglio, G. (2011) Convoking the consumer in person: the focus group effect. In D. Zwick and J. Cayla (eds.), *Inside Marketing: Practices, Ideologies, Devices*. Oxford University Press, pp. 87–114.

Gudelunas, D. (2011) Consumer myths and the gay men and women who believe them: a qualitative look at movements and markets. *Psychology & Marketing* 28: 53–68.

Guy, D. (2012) Purposeful activities: shopping, dining and sociability on Florida Street, 1914–1940 (unpublished manuscript).

Halle, D. (1993) *Inside Culture: Art and Class in the American Home*. University of Chicago Press.

Hamilton, K. and Catterall, M. (2006) Consuming love in poor families: children's influence on consumption decisions. *Journal of Marketing Management* 22: 1031–52.

Hanser, A. (2008) *Service Encounters: Class, Gender, and the Market for Social Distinction in Urban China*. Stanford University Press.

Harvey, D. (1990) *The Condition of Postmodernity*. Blackwell.

Haug, W. F. (1986) *Critique of Commodity Aesthetics: Appearance, Sexuality, and Advertising in Capitalist Society*. University of Minnesota Press.

Hebdige, D. (1979) *Subculture: The Meaning of Style*. Routledge.

Hebdige, D. (2000) Object as image: the Italian scooter cycle. In J. Schor and D. B. Holt (eds.), *The Consumer Society Reader*. The New Press, pp. 214–73.

Holt, D. B. (1998) Does cultural capital structure American consumption? *Journal of Consumer Research* 25: 1–25.

Holt, D. B. (2004) *How Brands Become Icons: The Principles of Cultural Marketing*. Harvard Business School Press.

Holt, D. and Cameron, D. (2010) *Cultural Strategy: Using Innovative Ideologies to Build Breakthrough Brands*. Oxford University Press.

Holt, D. B. and Thompson, C. J. (2004) Man-of-action heroes: the pursuit of heroic masculinity in everyday consumption. *Journal of Consumer Research* 31: 425–40.

Horioka, C. Y. (2006) Are the Japanese unique? An analysis of consumption and saving behavior in Japan. In S. Garon and P. L. Maclachlan (eds.), *The Ambivalent Consumer: Questioning Consumption in East Asia and the West*. Cornell University Press, pp. 113–36.

Hsieh, C.-T. and Urquiola, M. (2006) The effects of generalized school choice on achievement and stratification: evidence from Chile's voucher program. *Journal of Public Economics* 90: 1477–1503.

Humphery, K. (2010) *Excess: Anti-Consumerism in the West*. Polity.

Hussein, S. (2013) Six months after Bangladeshi factory collapse, workers remain in peril. *CNN*; October 24. At <http://www.cnn.com/2013/10/24/opinion/bangladesh-garment-workers/>.

Illouz, E. (1997) *Consuming the Romantic Utopia: Love and the Cultural Contradictions of Capitalism*. University of California Press.

Illouz, E. (2009) Emotions, imagination, and consumption. *Journal of Consumer Culture* 9: 377–413.

Ingram, J., Shove, E. and Watson, M. (2007) Products and practices: selected concepts from science and technology studies and from social theories of consumption and practice. *Design Issues* 23: 3–16.

International Data Corporation (IDC). (2014) Press Release: worldwide smartphone shipments top one billion units for the first time, according to IDC; January 27. At <http://www.idc.com/getdoc.jsp?containerId=prUS24645514>.

Jaffee, D. (2012) Weak coffee: certification and co-optation in the fair trade movement. *Social Problems* 59: 94–116.

Jantzen, C. and Fitchett, J. (2012) Just for fun? The emotional regime of experiential consumption. *Marketing Theory* 12: 137–54.

Jhally, S. (1990) *The Codes of Advertising: Fetishism and the Political Economy of Meaning in Capitalist Society*. Routledge.

Johnson, S. and Kwak, J. (2011) *13 Bankers: The Wall Street Takeover and the Next Financial Meltdown*. Vintage Books.

Jones, L. (1963) *Blues People: Negro Music in White America*. W. Morrow.

Kates, S. (2002) The protean quality of subcultural consumption: an ethnographic account of gay consumers. *Journal of Consumer Research* 29: 383–99.

Katz, S. and Marshall, B. (2003) New sex for old: lifestyle, consumerism, and the ethics of aging well. *Journal of Aging Studies* 17: 3–16.

Keck, M. and Sikkink, K. (1998). *Activists Beyond Borders: Advocacy Networks in International Politics*. Cornell University Press.

Kenner, R. (2008) *Food, Inc.* (documentary film). Magnolia Pictures.

Kılıçbay, B. and Binark, M. (2002) Consumer culture, Islam and the politics of lifestyle: fashion for veiling in contemporary Turkey. *European Journal of Communication* 17: 495–511.

Kjellberg, H. (2007) The death of a salesman? Reconfiguring economic exchange in Swedish post-war food distribution. In M. Callon, Y. Millo and F. Muniesa (eds.), *Market Devices*. Blackwell/*Sociological Review*, pp. 65–91.

Klein, N. (2010) *No Logo*, 3rd edn. Picador Books.

Konrad, A. (2013) Even with record prices, expect a $10 million super bowl ad soon. *Forbes*; February 2. At <http://www.forbes.com/sites/alex konrad/2013/02/02/even-with-record-prices-10-million-spot/>.

Kosetzi, K. and Polyzou, A. (2009) "The perfect man, the proper man": construals of masculinities in *Nitro*, a Greek men's lifestyle magazine – an exploratory study. *Gender and Language* 3: 143–80.

Kozinets, R. V. (2001) Utopian enterprise: articulating the meanings of *Star Trek*'s culture of consumption. *Journal of Consumer Research* 28: 67–88.

Kozinets, R. V. (2002) Can consumers escape the market? Emancipatory illuminations from burning man. *Journal of Consumer Research* 29: 20–38.

Kozinets, R. V. and Handelman, J. M. (2004). Adversaries of consumption: consumer movements, activism, and ideology. *Journal of Consumer Research* 31: 691–704.

Kozinets, R. V., Sherry, Jr., J. F., Storm, D., Duhachek, A., Nuttavuthisit, K. and Seberry-Spence, B. (2004) Ludic agency and retail spectacle. *Journal of Consumer Research* 31: 658–72.

Lacy, K. R. (2007) *Blue-chip Black: Race, Class, and Status in the New Black Middle Class*. University of California Press.

Lahire, B. (2003) From the habitus to an individual heritage of dispositions: towards a sociology at the level of the individual. *Poetics* 31: 329–55.

Lahire, B. (2008) The individual and the mixing of genres: cultural dissonance and self-distinction. *Poetics* 36: 166–88.

Lai, S-C. (2001) Extra-ordinary and ordinary consumption: making sense of acquisition in modern Taiwan. In J. Gronow and A. Warde (eds.), *Ordinary Consumption*. Routledge.

Lamont, M. (1992) *Money, Morals, and Manners*. University of Chicago Press.

Lamont, M. and Lareau, A. (1988) Cultural capital: allusions, gaps and glissandos in recent theoretical developments. *Sociological Theory* 6: 153–68.

Lamont, M. and Molnár, V. (2001). How blacks use consumption to shape their collective identity: evidence from marketing specialists. *Journal of Consumer Culture* 1: 31–45.

Lareau, A. (2003) *Unequal Childhoods*. University of California Press.

Lash, S. and Lury, C. (2007) *Global Culture Industry: The Mediation of Things*. Polity.

Lasn, K. (2000) Culture jamming. In J. Schor and D. B. Holt (eds.), *The Consumer Society Reader*. The New Press, pp. 677–704.

Latour, B. (2005) *Reassembling the Social: An Introduction to Actor-Network Theory*. Oxford University Press.

Leach, W. (1993) *Land of Desire*. Pantheon.

Lee, M. J. (ed.) (2000) *The Consumer Society Reader*. Blackwell.

Lee, S. and Vaught, S. (2003) "You can never be too rich or too thin": popular and consumer culture and the Americanization of Asian American girls and young women. *Journal of Negro Education* 72: 457–66.

Lehtonen, T.-K. and Mäenpää, P. (1997) Shopping in the East Centre Mall. In P. Falk and C. Campbell (eds.), *The Shopping Experience*. Sage, pp. 136–65.

Leiss, W., Klein, S., Jhally, S. and Botterill, J. (2005) *Social Communication in Advertising: Consumption in the Mediated Marketplace*, 3rd edn. Routledge.

Lewis, G. H. (1989) Rats and bunnies: core kids in an American mall. *Adolescence* 24: 881–9.

Lewis, G. H. (1990) Community through exclusion and illusion: the creation of social worlds in an American shopping mall. *Journal of Popular Culture* 24: 121–36.

Lindridge, A. and Hogg, M. K. (2006). Parental gate-keeping in diasporic Indian families: examining the intersection of culture, gender and consumption. *Journal of Marketing Management* 22: 979–1008.

Littler, J. (2009) *Radical Consumption*. Open University Press.

Lizardo, O. (2006) The puzzle of women's "highbrow" culture consumption: integrating gender and work into Bourdieu's class theory of taste. *Poetics* 34: 1–23.

Lizardo, O. and Skiles, S. (2012) Reconceptualizing and theorizing "omnivorousness": genetic and relational mechanisms. *Sociological Theory* 30: 263–82.

Lloyd, R. (2006) *Neo-bohemia: Art and Commerce in the Post-Industrial City*. Routledge.

Lowe, M. (2000) From Victor Gruen to Merry Hill: Reflections on regional shopping centres and urban development in the U.S. and UK. In P. Jackson, M. Lowe, D. Miller and F. Mort (eds.), *Commercial Cultures: Economies, Practices, Spaces*. Berg, pp. 245–60.

Lubar, S. (1998) Men/women/production/consumption. In R. Horowitz and A. Mohum (eds.), *His and Hers: Gender, Consumption and Technology*. University of Virginia Press, pp. 7–37.

Lury, C. (2011) *Consumer Culture*, 2nd edn. Polity.

McAdam, D. (1982) *Political Process and the Development of Black Insurgency, 1930–1970*. University of Chicago Press.

McCracken, G. (1988) *Culture and Consumption: New Approaches to the Symbolic Character of Consumer Goods and Activities*. Indiana University Press.

McCracken, G. (2005) *Culture and Consumption II: Markets, Meaning, and Brand Management*. Indiana University Press.

McFall, L. (2009) Devices and desires: how useful is the "new" new economic sociology for understanding market attachment? *Sociology Compass* 3: 267–82.

McGann, P. J. (2011) Healing (disorderly) desire: medical-therapeutic regulation of sexuality. In S. Seidman, N. Fischer and C. Meeks (eds.), *Introducing the New Sexuality Studies*, 2nd edn. Routledge, pp. 427–37.

McKendrick, N., Brewer, J. and Plumb, J. H. (1982) *The Birth of a Consumer Society: The Commercialization of Eighteenth-Century England*. Indiana University Press.

McRobbie, A. (1997) *More!* New sexualities in girls' and women's magazines. In A. McRobbie (ed.), *Back to Reality: Social Experience and Cultural Studies*. Manchester University Press, pp. 190–209.

McRobbie, A. (2008) *The Aftermath of Feminism*. Sage.

McRobbie, A. and Garber, J. (2006) Girls and subcultures. In S. Hall and T. Jefferson (eds.), *Resistance Through Rituals: Youth Subcultures in Postwar Britain*, 2nd edn. Routledge, pp. 177–88.

Maguire, J. S. and Matthews, J. (2012). Are we all cultural intermediaries now? An introduction to cultural intermediaries in context. *European Journal of Cultural Studies* 15: 551–62.

Manning, R. (2000) *Credit Card Nation: The Consequences of America's Addiction to Credit*. Basic Books.

Marx, K. (1967) *Capital: A Critique of Political Economy*, Vol. I. International Publishers.

Marx, K. (1978a) The German ideology – part I. In R. Tucker (ed.), *The Marx-Engels Reader*, 2nd edn. Norton, pp. 146–200.

Marx, K. (1978b) The Grundrisse. In R. Tucker (ed.), *The Marx-Engels Reader*, 2nd edn. Norton, pp. 221–93.

Marx, K. (1978c) Economic and philosophic manuscripts of 1844. In R. Tucker (ed.), *The Marx-Engels Reader*, 2nd edn. Norton, pp. 66–135.

Martin, D. M., Schouten, J. W. and McAlexander, J. H. (2006) Claiming the throttle: multiple femininities in a hyper-masculine subculture. *Consumption, Markets and Culture*, 9: 171–205.

Matthews, H., Taylor, M., Percy-Smith, B. and Limb, M. (2000) The unacceptable *flâneur*: the shopping mall as a teenage hangout. *Childhood* 7: 279–94.

Mazzarella, W. (2003) *Shoveling Smoke: Advertising and Globalization in Contemporary India*. Duke University Press.

Micheletti, M. (2003) *Political Virtue and Shopping*. Palgrave.

Milestone, K. and Meyer, A. (2012) *Gender and Popular Culture*. Polity.

Miller, D. (1987) *Material Culture and Mass Consumption*. Blackwell.

Miller, D. (1994). *Modernity: An Ethnographic Approach: Dualism and Mass Consumption in Trinidad*. Berg.

Miller, D. (1997) *Capitalism: An Ethnographic Approach*. Berg.

Miller, D. (1998) *A Theory of Shopping*. Polity.

Miller, D. (2005) Materiality: an introduction. In D. Miller (ed.), *Materiality*. Duke University Press, pp. 1–50.

Miller, D. (2012) *Consumption and its Consequences*. Polity.

Miller, D., Jackson, P., Thrift, N., Holbrook, B. and Rowlands, M. (1998) *Shopping, Place and Identity*. Routledge.

Mintz, S. (1985) *Sweetness and Power: The Place of Sugar in Modern History*. Penguin.

Moisio, R., Arnould, E. J. and Gentry, J. W. (2013) Productive consumption in the class-mediated construction of domestic masculinity: do-it-yourself (DIY) home improvement in men's identity work. *Journal of Consumer Research* 40: 298–316.

Moody, N. M. (2013) Beyoncé admits she lip synced at inauguration. *Huffington Post*; January 31. At <http://www.huffingtonpost.com/2013/01/31/beyonce-admits-lip-sync-inauguration_n_2593143.html>.

Morris, A. (1981) Black southern sit-in movement: an analysis of internal organization. *American Sociological Review* 46: 744–67.

Morris, J. (1966) *Elites, Intellectuals, and Consensus*. Cornell University Press.

Mukerji, C. (1983) *From Graven Images: Patterns of Modern Materialism*. Columbia University Press.

Muniesa, F., Millo, Y. and Callon, M. (2007). An introduction to market devices. In M. Callon, Y. Millo and F. Muniesa (eds.), *Market Devices*. Blackwell/*Sociological Review*, pp. 1–12.

Murray, M. J. (2011) *City of Extremes: The Spatial Politics of Johannesburg*. Duke University Press.

Nava, M. (1997) Women, the city, and the department store. In P. Falk and C. Campbell (eds.), *The Shopping Experience*. Sage, pp. 56–92.

Nelson, L. (2000) *Measured Excess: Status, Gender, and Consumer Nationalism in South Korea*. Columbia University Press.

Nguyen, D. (2013) Women claiming gender bias at Walmart denied class action status. *Huffington Post*; August 3. At <http://www.huffingtonpost.com/2013/08/03/walmart-gender-bias-suit_n_3700598.html>.

Nixon, S. (2003) *Advertising Cultures: Gender, Commerce, Creativity.* Sage.

O'Connor, C. (2013) New York AG to Barneys, Macy's: turn over "shop and frisk" racial profiling policies by Friday. *Forbes*; October 29. At <http://www.forbes.com/sites/clareoconnor/2013/10/29/new-york-ag-to-barneys-macys-turn-over-shop-and-frisk-racial-profiling-policies-by-friday/>.

O'Dougherty, M. (2002) *Consumption Intensified: The Politics of Middle-Class Daily Life in Brazil.* Duke University Press.

Omi, M. and Winant, H. (1994) *Racial Formation in the United States: From the 1960s to the 1990s.* Routledge.

Ortiz, S. M. (1994) Shopping for sociability in the mall. *Research in Community Sociology* Supplement 1: 183–99.

Ossandon, J. (2013) Sowing consumers in the garden of mass retailing in Chile. *Consumption, Markets & Culture,* DOI: 10.1080/10253866.2013.849591.

Otnes, C. and Pleck, E. H. (2003) *Cinderella Dreams: The Allure of the Lavish Wedding.* University of California Press.

Öz, Ö. and Eder, M. (2012) Rendering Istanbul's periodic bazaars invisible: reflections on urban transformation and contested space. *International Journal of Urban and Regional Research* 36: 297–314.

Pahl, J. (1989) *Money and Marriage.* St. Martin's Press.

Parker, J. (2009) Burgeoning bourgeoisie. *The Economist*; February 12. At <http://www.economist.com/node/13063298>.

Peñaloza, L. (1994) Atravesando fronteras/border crossings: a critical ethnographic exploration of the consumer acculturation of Mexican immigrants. *Journal of Consumer Research* 21: 32–54.

Pentina, I. and Amos, C. (2011). The Freegan phenomenon: anti-consumption or consumer resistance? *European Journal of Marketing* 45: 1768–78.

Peterson, R. A. and Kern, R. M. (1996) Changing highbrow taste: from snob to omnivore. *American Sociological Review* 61: 900–7.

Phillips, L. (ed.) (1998) *The Third Wave of Modernization in Latin America: Cultural Perspectives on Neoliberalism.* Lynn Rienner.

Piore, M. and Sabel, C. (1984) *The Second Industrial Divide: Possibilities for Prosperity.* Basic Books.

Portes, A. (1994) The informal economy and its paradoxes. In N. Smelser and R. Swedberg (eds.), *The Handbook of Economic Sociology.* Princeton University Press and Russell Sage Foundation, pp. 426–52.

Portwood-Stacer, L. (2012) Anti-consumption as tactical resistance: anarchists, subculture, and activist strategy. *Journal of Consumer Culture* 12: 87–105.

Pridmore, J. and Lyon, D. (2011) Marketing as surveillance: assembling consumers as brands. In D. Zwick and J. Cayla (eds.), *Inside Marketing: Practices, Ideologies, Devices.* Oxford University Press, pp. 115–36.

Public Citizen (2014) Available at <http://www.citizen.org/Page.aspx? pid=183>.

Pugh, A. J. (2009) *Longing and Belonging: Parents, Children, and Consumer Culture*. University of California Press.

Rappaport, E. D. (2001) *Shopping for Pleasure: Women in the Making of London's West End*. Princeton University Press.

Raveauda, M. and van Zanten, A. (2007) Choosing the local school: middle class parents' values and social and ethnic mix in London and Paris. *Journal of Education Policy* 22: 107–24.

Reagin, N. (1998) Comparing apples and oranges: housewives and the politics of consumption in interwar Germany. In S. Strasser, C. McGovern and M. Judt (eds.), *Getting and Spending: European and American Consumer Societies in the Twentieth Century*. German Historical Institute and Cambridge University Press, pp. 241–62.

Reinberg, M. (2006) School soda ban called good first step. *HealthDay*; May 3. At <http://news.healingwell.com/index.php?p=news1&id= 532509>.

Riggs, M. (2004) *Ethnic Notions* (documentary videorecording). California Newsreel.

Ritzer, G. (2003) Rethinking globalization: glocalization/grobalization and something/nothing. *Sociological Theory* 21: 193–209.

Ritzer, G. (2008) *The McDonaldization of Society*, 5th edn. Pine Forge.

Ritzer, G., Dean, P. and Jurgenson, N. (2012) The coming of age of the prosumer. *American Behavioral Scientist* 56: 379–98.

Rojek, C. (2011) *Pop Music, Pop Culture*. Polity.

Rosen, E. I. (2006) How to squeeze more out of a penny. In N. Lichtenstein (ed.), *Wal-Mart: The Face of Twenty-First-Century Capitalism*. New Press, pp. 243–60.

Rosenthal, E. (2013) Your biggest carbon sin may be air travel. *New York Times*; January 26. At <http://www.nytimes.com/2013/01/27/sunday-review/the-biggest-carbon-sin-air-travel.html?_r=0>.

Rushkoff, D. (1999) *Merchants of Cool* (documentary film). PBS.

Rushkoff, D. (2004) *The Persuaders* (documentary film). PBS.

Sabatini, P. (2014) Consumer Financial Protection Bureau empowers credit card consumers. *Pittsburgh Post-Gazette*; January 14. At <http://www.post-gazette.com/business/2014/01/15/Consumer-Financial-Protection-Bureau-empowers-credit-card-consumers/stories/201401150038>.

Sabatini, F. and Cáceres, G. (2004) Los barrios cerrados y la ruptura del patrón tradicional de segregación en las ciudades latinoamericanas: el caso de Santiago de Chile. In G. Cáceres and F. Sabatini (eds.), *Barrios cerrados en Santiago de Chile: entre la exclusión y la integración residencial*. Lincoln Institute of Land Policy and Pontificia Universidad Católica de Chile, Santiago, pp. 9–43.

Salcedo, R. (2003) When the global meets the local at the mall. *American Behavioral Scientist* 46: 1084–1103.

Sandikci, O. and Ger, G. (2007) Constructing and representing the Islamic consumer in Turkey. *Fashion Theory* 11: 189–210.

Sandikci, O. and Omeraki, S. (2007) Globalization and rituals: does Ramadan turn into Christmas? *Advances in Consumer Research* 34: 610–15.

Santora, M. (2014) Barneys agrees to pay $525,000 in racial profiling inquiry. *The New York Times*; August 11. At <http://www.nytimes.com/2014/08/12/nyregion/barneys-agrees-to-pay-25000- to-settle-racial-profiling-suit.html?module=Search&mabReward= relbias%3Ar%2C%7B%222%22%3A%22RI%3A14%22%7D&_r=0>.

Saporito, S. and Lareau, A. (1999) School selection as a process: the multiple dimensions of race in framing educational choice. *Social Problems* 46: 418–39.

Sassatelli, R. (2007) *Consumer Culture: History, Theory, Politics.* Sage.

Satterthwaite, A. (2001) *Going Shopping: Consumer Choices and Community Consequences.* Yale University Press.

Savage, M. and Gayo, M. (2011) Unravelling the omnivore: a field analysis of contemporary musical taste in the United Kingdom. *Poetics* 39: 337–57.

Saxton, A. (2003) *The Rise and Fall of the White Republic: Class Politics and Mass Culture in Nineteenth Century America.* Verso.

Schneider, V., Cockcroft, K. and Hook, D. (2008) The fallible phallus: a discourse analysis of male sexuality in a South African men's interest magazine. *South African Journal of Psychology* 38: 136–51.

Schor, J. (1998) *The Overspent American.* Basic Books.

Schor, J. (2004) *Born to Buy.* Scribner.

Schor, J. and Holt, D. B. (eds.) (2000) *The Consumer Society Reader.* The New Press

Schor, J. and Thompson, C. (2014) Introduction: Practicing plenitude. In J. B. Schor and C. J. Thompson (eds.), *Sustainable Lifestyles and the Quest for Plenitude: Case Studies of the New Economy.* Yale University Press, pp. 1–26.

Schouten, J. W. and McAlexander, J. H. (1995) Subcultures of consumption: an ethnography of the new bikers. *Journal of Consumer Research* 22: 43–61.

Seidman, G. (2007) *Beyond the Boycott: Labor Rights, Human Rights, and Transnational Activism.* Russell Sage Foundation.

Selzer, A. K. and Heller, P. (2010) The spatial dynamics of middle-class formation in post-Apartheid South Africa: enclavization and fragmentation in Johannesburg. *Political Power and Social Theory* 21: 171–208.

Shankar, S. (2012) Creating model consumers: producing ethnicity, race, and class in Asian American advertising. *American Ethnologist* 39: 578–91.

Sheller, M. (2003) *Consuming the Caribbean.* Routledge.

Sherry, Jr., J. F. (1990a) A sociocultural analysis of a Midwestern American flea market. *Journal of Consumer Research* 17: 13–30.

Sherry, Jr., J. F. (1990b) Dealers and dealing in a periodic market: informal retailing in ethnographic perspective. *Journal of Retailing* 66: 174–200.

Shields, R. (1989) Social spatialisation and the built environment: the case of the West Edmonton Mall. *Environment and Planning D: Society and Space* 7: 147–64.

Simmel, G. (1957) Fashion. *American Journal of Sociology* 62: 541–58.

Slater, D. (1997) *Consumer Culture and Modernity*. Polity.

Slater, D. (2011) Marketing as a monstrosity: the impossible place between culture and economy. In D. Zwick and J. Cayla (eds.), *Inside Marketing: Practices, Ideologies, Devices*. Oxford University Press, pp. 23–41.

Smart, B. (2010) *Consumer Society: Critical Issues and Environmental Consequences*. Sage.

Smith, H. (2004) *Is Wal-Mart Good for America?* (documentary film) PBS.

Sombart, W. (1967) *Luxury and Capitalism*. University of Michigan Press.

Song, G. and Lee, T. K. (2010) Consumption, class formation and sexuality: reading men's lifestyle magazines in China. *The China Journal* 64: 159–77.

Soper, K. (2009) Introduction: the mainstreaming of counter-consumerist concern. In K. Soper, M. Ryle and L. Thomas (eds.), *The Politics and Pleasures of Consuming Differently*. Palgrave, pp. 1–24.

Soper, K. and Trentmann, F. (2008) Introduction. In K. Soper and F. Trentmann (eds.), *Citizenship and Consumption*. Palgrave, pp. 1–16.

Stack, C. (1974) *All Our Kin*. Basic Books.

Staeheli, L. A. and Mitchell, D. (2006) USA's destiny? Regulating space and creating community in American shopping malls. *Urban Studies* 43: 977–92.

Stevenson, N., Jackson, P. and Brooks, K. (2003) Reading men's lifestyle magazines: cultural power and the information society. *Sociological Review* 51: 112–31.

Stillerman, J. (2003) Transnational activist networks and the emergence of labor internationalism in the NAFTA countries. *Social Science History* 27: 577–602.

Stillerman, J. (2004) Gender, class, and generational contexts for consumption in contemporary Chile. *Journal of Consumer Culture* 4: 51–78.

Stillerman, J. (2006) Private, parochial and public realms in Santiago, Chile's retail sector. *City & Community* 5: 293–317.

Stillerman, J. (2008) Tradition, adventure and pleasure in Santiago, Chile's informal markets. In D. T. Cook (ed.), *Lived Experiences of Public Consumption: Encounters with Value in Marketplaces on Five Continents*. Palgrave, pp. 31–49.

Stillerman, J. (2010) The contested spaces of Chile's middle classes. *Political Power and Social Theory* 21: 209–38.

Stillerman, J. (2012) Chile's forgotten consumers: poor urban families, consumption strategies, and the moral economy of risk in Santiago. In J. Sinclair and A. Pertierra (eds.), *Consumer Culture in Latin America*. Palgrave, pp. 67–80.

Stillerman, J. and Salcedo, R. (2012) Transposing the urban to the mall: routes, relationships and resistance in two Santiago, Chile shopping centers. *Journal of Contemporary Ethnography* 41: 309–36.

Strangelove, M. (2010) *Watching YouTube: Extraordinary Videos by Ordinary People*. University of Toronto Press.

Strasser, S. (1989) *Satisfaction Guaranteed: The Making of the American Mass Market*. Smithsonian Institution Press.

Strasser, S. (2006) Woolworth to Wal-Mart: mass merchandising and the changing culture of consumption. In N. Lichtenstein (ed.), *Wal-Mart: The Face of Twenty-First-Century Capitalism*. New Press, pp. 31–56.

Straubhaar, J. D. (2007) *World Television: From Global to Local*. Sage.

Sunderland, P. L. and Denny, R. M. (2011) Consumer segmentation in practice: an ethnographic account of slippage. In D. Zwick and J. Cayla (eds.), *Inside Marketing: Practices, Ideologies, Devices*. Oxford University Press, pp. 137–61.

Tanenbaum, S. J. (1995) *Underground Harmonies: Music and Politics in the Subways of New York*. Cornell University Press.

Teppo, A. and Houssay-Holzschuch, M. (2013) Gugulethu™: revolution for neoliberalism in a South African township. *Canadian Journal of African Studies/La Revue canadienne des études africaines* 47: 51–74.

Thompson, C. J. and Holt, D. B. (2004) How do men grab the phallus?: Gender tourism in everyday consumption. *Journal of Consumer Culture* 4: 313–38.

Thornton, S. (1996) *Club Cultures: Music, Media, and Subcultural Capital*. Wesleyan University Press.

Tokatli, N. and Boyaci, Y. (1999) The changing morphology of commercial activity in Istanbul. *Cities* 16: 181–93.

Trentmann, F. (2006a) Knowing consumers – histories, identities, practices: an introduction. In F. Trentmann (ed.), *The Making of the Consumer: Knowledge, Power and Identity in the Modern World*. Berg, pp. 1–27.

Trentmann, F. (2006b) The modern genealogy of the consumer: meanings, identities and political synapses. In J. Brewer and F. Trentmann (eds.), *Consuming Cultures, Global Perspectives: Historical Trajectories, Transnational Exchanges*. Berg, pp. 19–70.

Tuncay, L. (2006) Conceptualizations of masculinity among a "new" breed of male consumers. *Gender and Consumer Behavior* 8: 312–27.

Turow, J. (2010) Segment-making and society-making media: what is a good balance? *Procedia: Social and Behavioral Sciences* 2: 6928–36.

Turow, J. and Draper, N. (2012) Advertising's new surveillance ecosystem. In K. Ball, K. D. Haggerty and D. Lyon (eds.), *Routledge Handbook of Surveillance Studies*. Routledge pp. 133–40.

Um, N-H. (2012) Seeking the holy grail through gay and lesbian consumers: an exploratory content analysis of ads with gay/lesbian-specific content. *Journal of Marketing Communications* 18: 133–49.

U.S. Census Bureau (2014) U.S. and world population clock. At <http:// www.census.gov/popclock/>.

Üstüner, T. and Holt, D. (2007) Dominated consumer acculturation: the social construction of poor migrant women's identity projects in a squatter. *Journal of Consumer Research* 34: 41–56.

Üstüner, T. and Holt, D. (2010) Toward a theory of status consumption in less industrialized countries. *Journal of Consumer Research* 37: 37–56.

Van Bavel, R. and Sell-Trujillo, L. (2003) Understandings of consumerism in Chile. *Journal of Consumer Culture* 3: 343–62.

Vandecasteele, B. and Geuens, M. (2009) Revising the myth of gay consumer innovativeness. *Journal of Business Research* 62: 134–44.

Veblen, T. (1979) *The Theory of the Leisure Class*. Penguin.

Vogel, D. (2010) The private regulation of global corporate conduct: achievements and limitations. *Business and Society* 49: 68–87.

Walters, A. S. and Moore, L. J. (2002) Attention all shoppers, queer customers in aisle two: investigating lesbian and gay discrimination in the marketplace. *Consumption, Markets and Culture* 5: 285–303.

Warde, A. (2005) Consumption and theories of practice. *Journal of Consumer Culture* 5: 131–53.

Warikoo, N. K. (2007) Racial authenticity among second generation youth in multiethnic New York and London. *Poetics* 35: 388–408.

Warren, J. (2008) The handbag dog scandal. *Express*; February 20. At <http://www.express.co.uk/expressyourself/35565/The-handbag-dog-scandal>.

Wassel, J. (2011). Business and aging: the boomer effect on consumers and marketing. In R. A. Settersten, Jr. and J. L. Angel (eds.), *Handbook of Sociology and Aging*. Springer, pp. 351–9.

Watson, J. L. (ed.) (1997) *Golden Arches East: McDonald's in East Asia*. Stanford University Press.

Watts, E. K. and Orbe, M. P. (2002) The spectacular consumption of "true" African American culture: "whassup" with the Budweiser guys? *Critical Studies in Media Communication* 19: 1–20.

Watts, M. (1997) Black gold, white heat: state violence, local resistance, and the national question in Nigeria. In S. Pile and M. Keith (eds.), *Geographies of Resistance*. Routledge, pp. 33–67.

Weber, M. (1946a) Bureaucracy. In H. Gerth and C. W. Mills (eds.), *From Max Weber*. Oxford University Press, pp. 196–244.

Weber, M. (1946b) Class, status, party. In H. Gerth and C. W. Mills (eds.), *From Max Weber*. Oxford University Press, pp. 180–95.

Weber, M. (1958) *The Protestant Ethic and the Spirit of Capitalism*. Charles Scribner's Sons.

Wherry, F. (2008) *Global Markets and Local Crafts*. Johns Hopkins University Press.

Wilk, R. (2006) *Home Cooking in the Global Village: Caribbean Food from Buccaneers to Ecotourists*. Berg.

Williams, R. H. (1982) *Dream Worlds: Mass Consumption in Late Nineteenth Century France*. University of California Press.

Williams, R. G. (2007) *The Cooperative Movement: Globalization from Below*. Ashgate.

Yardley, W. (2011) The branding of the Occupy Movement. *The New York Times*; November 27. At <http://www.nytimes.com/2011/11/28/business/media/the-branding-of-the-occupy-movement.html?pagewanted=all&_r=0>.

Young, L. (1999) Marketing the modern: department stores, consumer culture, and the new middle class in interwar Japan. *International Labor and Working-class History* 55: 52–70.

Zavisca, J. and Weinberger, M. (2013) Exploratory experience: a new model of middle-class consumer lifestyle during the transition to adulthood. Paper presented at the American Sociological Association Annual Meeting, New York; August 2009. At <http://research.allacademic.com/one/asa/asa/index.php?cmd=asa_search&offset=0&limit=5&multi_search_search_mode=publication&multi_search_publication_full-text_mod=fulltext&textfield_submit=true&search_module=multi_search&search=Search&search_field=title_idx&fulltext_search=Exploratory+Experience%3A+A+New+Model+of+Middle-Class+Consumer+wLifestyle+During+the+Transition+to+Adulthood>.

Zelizer, V. (1985) *Pricing the Priceless Child: The Changing Social Value of Children*. Basic Books.

Zelizer, V. (1989) The social meaning of money: "special monies." *American Journal of Sociology* 95: 342–77.

Zelizer, V. (2005a) Culture and consumption. In N. Smelser and R. Swedberg (eds.), *The Handbook of Economic Sociology*. Princeton University Press and Russell Sage Foundation, pp. 331–54.

Zelizer, V. (2005b) *The Purchase of Intimacy*. Princeton University Press.

Zukin, S. (1995) *The Cultures of Cities*. Blackwell.

Zukin, S. (2004) *Point of Purchase*. Routledge.

Zwick, D. and Cayla, J. (2011) Inside marketing: practices, ideologies, devices. In D. Zwick and J. Cayla (eds.), *Inside Marketing: Practices, Ideologies, Devices*. Oxford University Press, pp. 3–19.

Index

brand boutiques 73
brand bureaucracy 11, 69
branding 5, 17, 49, 65–70
    advertising 27–32
    Americanization 79
    average/iconic 68
    children as target 143
    clothing 148
    consumption 152
    cool 131–2
    culture 135
    and distribution 34–5
    emotion 66
    gentrification 105
    goods 175
    identity 73
    intensification 54
    jeans 65
    loyalty to 120–1, 144, 145
    market 49, 52
    social changes 122
Brazil 76, 80, 88, 104, 189
breadwinner role 122–3
breakfast cereals 118
breast cancer research 6
Britain
    Calvinism 9–10
    capitalism 86
    class/consumption 99–100
    consumers 7
    co-operatives 164–5
    Indian immigrants 158–9
    Jamaican immigrants 150
    punk 53
    rave scene 151
    self-service 40–1
    shopping malls 46
    subcultures 56, 150
"bro-ing" 152
Brown, E. H. 130
bubbling up processes
    consumption patterns 52, 89, 101
    cultural practices 153
    style/taste 90, 140
Budweiser 68, 122, 132
bureaucracy 9, 11
Burning Man Festival 180
Bush, G. W. 169
Buy Korean savings clubs 171

Buy Nothing Day 183
buycotts 163, 174–5

cable television 53–4, 62–3
Cáceres, G. 104
Cairns, K. 157–8, 181
Caldeira, T. 104
Caldwell, M. L. 79
Calvin Klein 184
Calvinism 9–10, 26
Cameron, D. 11–12, 32, 57, 68–9,
    121, 122–4
Campbell, C. 9–10, 14, 26, 31, 88–9,
    155
Canada 35, 39, 62, 70, 158, 183
Canclini, N. G. 80–1
capitalism
    alternatives 180
    Britain 86
    consumption 23, 26–7
    credit 10
    exploitation 9
    Marx 23, 86
    Reformation 9
    Sombart 24
    sweatshops 8
    Weber 9
car advertising 118
car culture 151–2, 168
carbon emissions 176, 177
Carducci, V. 183
Caribbean 75–6, 89, 126
carnivals 22
Carter, J. 5, 130
Carter, P. 129
Catholicism 170–1
Catterall, M. 148
Cayla, J. 70, 83
celebrities 3, 19, 66, 67, 88
cellphones 15–16, 153, 176
Centre for Contemporary Cultural
    Studies 149–50
Chan, T. W. 97
charitable causes 6
charter schools 156–7
Chavez, C. 5
Chessel, M. E. 170–1
Child, C. 184
child labor 62, 145